FROM THE MARITIMES
TO MANHATTAN

*My Journey to a Life and
Career in New York City*

by

ROSEMARY SCANLON

Chapbook Press

Schuler Books
2660 28th Street SE
Grand Rapids, MI 49512
(616) 942-7330
www.schulerbooks.com

From the Maritimes to Manhattan: My Journey to a Life and Career in New York City

ISBN 13: 9781957169842

eBook ISBN: 9781966196006

Library of Congress Control Number: 2024908759

Back Cover Photo Credit: Elena Olivo, NYU Photo Bureau

Printed in the United States.

ACKNOWLEDGMENTS

First, to Marion Landew and her class of "Writing Your Memoir," which propelled me to start writing my stories instead of hearing them rattle around in my head over many years. For five semesters I slipped away from my daytime job for these two-hour lunchtime sessions. Marion's teaching style was to keep us writing in every class and to turn in a ten-page ("no more than ten pages") writing segment every week while giving us constant encouragement and providing a safe space in that class where we could read our latest efforts without worry of criticism. We could soon appreciate why Marion had been named Teacher of the Year at NYU's School of Professional Studies.

I am also grateful for the two friends I made in this class — Ruth Seiger Maisel and Carol Sue Barnett, who have heard many of these stories and, in the years since, have read and re-read all these pages, always with encouragement.

Then, heartfelt thanks to Wendie Pecharsky for her keen eye as copy editor, her patience in tackling yet one more set of my notes, and for her courage in learning the formatting required for this publication.

My mother, Agnes MacLellan, with (from right)
Malcolm, Donnie, me, and baby Louise.
Winter 1946.

DEDICATION

To my siblings, Malcolm, Donnie, and Louise,
to share with you my
memories of our young years.

And to my son, Sean, and daughter, Jennifer,
these are some stories
for you, Rebecca, and Bronson,
and for my grandchildren,
Delilah, Brian, Keira, and Ravenna.

And, in Chapter 4, to Michael,
with many good memories.

TABLE OF CONTENTS

CHAPTER 4

INTRODUCTION

Remembrance Day — Then and Now

Tomorrow is November 11, Remembrance Day. That is what we called this day when I was growing up in Canada, not Veterans Day as it is known here in the United States. I will wear a red paper poppy on my fall jacket, one that I brought back years ago from a trip to my hometown, and which I keep in my jewelry box because there do not seem to be any red poppies in evidence these years in New York City.

At 11 a.m. I will stop, wherever I am in the city and set aside whatever I am doing. I will be still and silent for at least one minute, maybe for a few minutes more if the noises and interruptions of daily life in the city can be overcome. There may be a parade up Fifth Avenue on this day, with some marching bands and some surviving veterans from the many wars over these years of our lifetimes. Perhaps this year there will be more veterans from the Vietnam War marching in the parade, as memories of those angry years fade away.

But it will otherwise be a day as usual in the city. The department stores will trumpet Veterans Day sales, traffic will back up on the numbered streets, and the impatient will press on their horns. The sense prevails that the purpose of the day is diffused, diminished in the United States by the more recognized events for Memorial Day, or Flag Day.

In my small hometown in Nova Scotia, the aging veterans from World War II and the Korean War, some now so frail that they will lean on a younger relative or friend, will somehow stand at attention around the Cenotaph, the stone plinth in the center of the small park by the town post office. They will wear their old uniforms with their medals and fading ribbons. Most will wear a beret with a bronze metal pin that has the crest of their regiment and the small red plume of feathers.

When I was growing up, the veterans were younger, of course, the men from World War II were in their prime, strapping men standing tall in still-crisp uniforms, ceding the front ranks of the formation to the men from World War I, many more stooped by then, weary.

The bagpiper has wheezed into silence now, and there is no traffic noise as the cars and trucks have pulled up to the nearest curb and cut their engines. The townspeople gathered in the outer circle are hushed, as the bells from the cathedral begin to peel. It is the eleventh hour of the eleventh day of the eleventh month, the hour of the Armistice of 1918, "The War to End All Wars."

Passchendaele, Ypres, the Marne, the Somme. My mother whispers those names when she teaches us history, for she remembers, as a young girl, the sad roll call of the missing and lost in those battles, read out in their church on Sundays. But the Cenotaph, built to honor those lost in that war, also now stands for the fallen from World War II and Korea — all local boys and perhaps a few women from the nursing corps.

People have been filing up to lay wreaths of red paper poppies. The wreath for my father that I placed there a few minutes ago is closest to us, facing my family. His war was World War II, our war. My brother and my two sisters and I stand very still. We have arranged ourselves on either side of our mother. I hold her arm briefly, but she moves slightly to stand alone and erect, her salute.

The bagpipe growls into a minor chord, then into full bellows: I mourn for the Highlands, whose lands are forsaken... "Lord Lovat's Lament." This is our music, the music of our ancient Highlanders, and this is the saddest of all the laments.

And then the first snowflakes begin to fall. We all stand very still, hushed except for the bagpipe, the large wet snowflakes adding to the silence.

I seem to remember when I was growing up, that the first snowfall of the year came at just the eleventh hour on November 11. And the memory lingers that there was always war, or the trying to recover from war, and then war again in Korea, and then the atom bomb tests and the hydrogen bomb tests, and the terrible fear of that next war.

When my son turned eighteen, here in New York City, the notification came in the mail for him to register for the draft, although the draft had long since been abandoned after the Vietnam War.

"I'm going with you," I said, no doubt fiercely. No government was going to send my son to war. They could take me first.

"Well, okay," he said, sounding doubtful. "But you must promise not to make a scene, Mom. We are just going to the post office window with this form."

In New York City, on November 11, I do not go shopping for the Veterans Day sales. I wear my red paper poppy and have my few minutes of silence for my father and the men of the Royal Canadian Air Force in their Liberator and Lancaster bombers, for the Canadians at Juno Beach, for my friend Larry of the 82nd Airborne and his parachute drop at the bridge of Remagen, for the men and boys on Omaha Beach and at Anzio and Guadalcanal, for the boys of the RAF and those who fought in the Battle of Britain; for the young men who died at Fredericksburg and Antietam more than a century ago, and for those who died in new places in Iraq and Afghanistan — the Ramallahs and the Helmand provinces — names yet to be etched in my mind.

I keep a few minutes of silence for the wars that never seem to end.

CHAPTER 1

Growing Up in Nova Scotia

My Beginnings

I was born on Christmas Day 1939 at about three in the afternoon at Stella Maris Hospital in Inverness on Cape Breton Island in Nova Scotia. My father and mother had moved to Inverness after they were married in September 1938, where my father was the owner and worked as a mechanic in the main automobile garage of the town.

My father, Donald, was from the village of Dunvegan, some eight miles north of Inverness. He was one of nine children born to my grandmother, the former Mary Gillis, and to my grandfather, Angus Donald Neil MacLellan. As children, we always called my grandmother "Little Grandma," although she was tall and sturdy, because my great-grandmother lived with them in those early days of my childhood, and was called "Big Grandma," although my memory was that she was small and always seemed to be dressed in black and knitting furiously as she rocked back and forth on the rocking chair in the kitchen. She knitted socks and sweaters and mittens for the family from the yarn she spun on the spinning wheel that had a pride of place in the kitchen and from the wool of sheep shorn each springtime from the flock that Grandpa kept high on the mountain across the road.

This was not a real mountain, of course, but a large hill that was a beginning part of the much taller Cape Breton Highlands that began some thirty miles farther north. When I was a child, this large hill was mostly bare of trees, so that one could look out from the front yard of the farmhouse and see the cows up on the sides of the hill and the sheep grazing closer to the top.

My people are all Highlanders who immigrated to Nova Scotia from Scotland. My father's forebears came mostly from the Western Highlands, around the village of Morar. They had family names of MacLellan, Gillis, McFarlane, Coady. The first wave of immigrants in my father's family came about 1820, bringing their kilts, their bagpipes and fiddles, their Gaelic language, and their strong attachment to the Catholic Church.

We learned more about those early immigrants from my grandfather's first cousin, Dr. Malcolm MacLellan, who was a Catholic priest and schooled in Gaelic as well as Canadian English, and who later became president of our local university, St. Francis Xavier in Antigonish, on the Nova Scotia mainland. Dr. MacLellan once visited the Scottish Highlands and pored over baptism records in the local parishes, written in Gaelic, seeking to establish our MacLellan ancestor. He discovered that there were three men called "Red John" MacLellan on those early registers. He could distinguish our ancestor because he was called, in the Gaelic, "Red John the Carpenter." Those skills had been handed down through the generations, and my grandfather was a carpenter as well as a farmer.

Although my great-grandmother, Big Grandma, was a product of several generations born in Nova Scotia, she spoke only Gaelic, and that was the language of the kitchen on the family farm. Both my grandparents spoke Gaelic as well as English, and my father, who was reportedly fluent in spoken Gaelic, engaged often in warm conversations with his grandmother.

When I was about three or maybe four years old, on one of his rare visits home with us, my father taught me my basic prayers in Gaelic.

The Scottish habit of naming people by their parentage as well as by their skills was carried down through to the decades of my childhood. My grandfather MacLellan was known to all in the surrounding villages of Dunvegan as Angus Donald Neil, where Neil was the name of his father. My father was called Donald Angus Donald Neil, and once, when I was twelve and visiting my grandaunt in a village some thirty miles south of Dunvegan, I was introduced to her neighbor as Rosemary Donald Angus Donald Neil. No last names were necessary, as the woman smiled and said, "Oh yes, of course, I know who she is."

My mother's people were MacDonalds from the clan Ranald MacDonalds of the Isle of Lewis in the Outer Hebrides. Our forefather, Ronald MacDonald, arrived in the 1790s as a young lad of twelve on one of the later voyages of the ship Hector, which brought the first Highland settlers to the mainland of Nova Scotia, arriving in what is now the small seaport of Pictou. He is buried in the churchyard of St. Mary's Church in Maryvale, Nova Scotia, which was our family church as we were growing up in nearby Pleasant Valley. His headstone has long since fallen and is barely visible in the overgrowth of the old part of the graveyard. My grandfather MacDonald was also named Ronald, from the village of Egerton in Pictou County. My grandmother, Mary, came from another MacDonald family. She grew up in Maryvale, which is in Antigonish County, down the coast some twenty miles from Egerton. My mother,

Agnes, was born in 1909 and grew up on the family farm in Egerton with her seven brothers and sisters.

Many years later I was to learn how my mother met my father and how that initial meeting was postponed long enough so that they had the opportunity to get beyond the initial introduction.

I was invited from my job in New York City to Sydney, Nova Scotia, as a guest speaker for its annual Port Days event and brought my mother from her home in Antigonish to accompany me. We had just checked into our hotel room when a call came in from the front desk to tell me that a Mr. Basil Skinner was in the lobby to see me. "Do you know this person?" I asked my mother, who said she remembered someone by that name working in the garage in Inverness the day that she met my father.

That day, in 1937, my mother had driven her mother from Egerton, some 80 miles away, to Inverness, crossing the Canso Strait by ferry in those days. The deep, fjord-like Canso Strait separates Cape Breton Island from the mainland of Nova Scotia, and since the early 1950s, is crossed by a mile-long causeway.

Grandmother MacDonald was visiting her sister who lived in Inverness and upon arrival, my mother said she had to take the car to the garage because something was wrong with the tire or the wheel. Donald Angus MacLellan was the owner and mechanic in that garage, working alongside Basil Skinner. Basil continued the story: "I could tell that your father liked this young woman right away, and when he said that we could probably fix the problem by late afternoon, I interrupted and said to her, 'We can have this fixed by tomorrow morning.'

"After your mother thanked us and left, Donald turned to me and said, 'Why did you say that? You know we can do the work this afternoon.' I replied, 'But Donald, there is a dance at Glenville tonight.'" Glenville was a village about five miles south of Inverness. "'I know you like this young lady, so go and ask her to the dance.'" Which Donald did, and my mother, Agnes, agreed.

My mother was amazed, and I think amused, listening to this story, as this was the first time, she knew the full circumstances of meeting my father. He had never admitted the small ruse of delaying repairs on the wheel and the tire so they could go to the dance and have the chance to get acquainted.

The stories of that Christmas Day when I was born were told to me years later by my mother. She spoke about lying in the hospital bed, uncomfortable and groaning "a little bit, sometimes," while my father and the doctor, Dr. Ratchford, sat cheerily by the bed talking to each other about events in and around the town. The nurse came in carrying my mother's dinner tray, a full Christmas dinner of turkey and all the usual trimmings of mashed potatoes and turnips, carrots and canned peas, cranberry sauce, and plum pudding with hard sauce. Mother said she "took one look at that tray" and groaned again. My father looked over to inspect the tray, said he would be happy to eat the dinner if she couldn't, and so Dr. Ratchford told the nurse to bring in another tray and he would eat his Christmas dinner along with my father.

And they did, happily talking to each other "and not paying any attention to me," my mother always said each time she told the story. Then, just before three in the afternoon, she groaned more loudly than before. Dr. Ratchford looked over at her, set down his teacup, and said, "Well, Donald, I think the time has come," and went quickly to the door to call the nurses and orderly, who rushed mother's bed down the hall to the delivery room. I was born a few minutes later.

Mother said that after my father had seen me wrapped in the newborn's blanket and was assured that my mother — and I — were in good health and that she needed to rest, said he would drive back to his village, Dunvegan, so he could bring his mother in to see the new baby. My mother did rest, even slept for a few hours, she remembered.

When I was a little girl and she would tell me this story, I would ask her, "But Mommy, did you ever have your Christmas dinner?"

"Yes," she would say. "I had dinner after I woke up; it was delicious. And I could have it all to myself."

Christmas Day, which is such a special day in the Christian world, is not a great day to have a birthday when you are a child. Every family in our valley was together with their own celebrations and gift openings and special dinners and desserts. This was not a time for birthday parties or birthday cakes. For many years when I was growing up, my mother always made sure that there were two gifts under the Christmas tree for me, one that was labeled, HAPPY BIRTHDAY.

In the days before Christmas, my mother would pause amid her marathon holiday baking of breads, cookies, pies, and brownies, turn to me with her arms still covered in flour and her face flushed from working around the coal-fired stove, and say: "Dear, if you really want a birthday cake, I will make one for you."

I could not have her work any harder, so I said something like, "The brownies will be just fine; they are my favorite."

I had my first birthday party and first birthday cake and first-ever set of special birthday presents the year that I was in graduate school when my fellow grad students learned that I was a "Christmas Baby" and had never had this traditional celebration. They brought a birthday cake with candles and gave me a book, *Alice's Adventures in Wonderland and Through the Looking Glass,* with reproductions of the original sketches, a gift I treasured for many years. I did not mention this birthday party to my family when I arrived home for our traditional holiday, lest all would feel guilty for my many years without a birthday celebration.

In my years as a mother and now a grandmother, I have discovered that Christmas is a great time to have a birthday. The chances are good that all or most of my own family will be together for this holiday. When they were children, my young son and little daughter would go into the kitchen on Christmas morning, and with a great clatter of pots and pans and mixing bowls and jostling over who would get to lick the spoon or the bowl and who was to make the frosting, would turn a Betty Crocker packaged cake and frosting mix into a birthday cake for me, splattering the frosting with red and green sprinkles. These years, my little grandchildren gather close to help me blow out the candles on the Buche de Noel French-style chocolate Yule log, which is now our favorite holiday cake, and sing "Happy Birthday" in their sweet soprano voices.

That first year after I was born, we lived in Inverness and for several months I was cared for by my Aunt Isobel, who returned home to Nova Scotia from her nursing position in New York to take care of my mother, who had contracted rheumatic fever shortly after I was born, and me. Aunt Isobel was to meet her future husband during this time, a man named Bernie, who came from my father's village of Dunvegan.

Then, in the early months of 1940, when the war was spreading throughout Europe, my father decided to join the Royal Canadian Air Force. All of the Canadian services were at that time voluntary and many of my father's friends and young men from the neighboring villages were volunteering for service. We moved for some months to St. Thomas, Ontario, where my father was in basic training, then came back to Egerton, Nova Scotia, for Christmas of 1940. I was turning one year old, and my mother later told me that once we were settled into Grandmother MacDonald's kitchen, I turned to my mother and said, "Could I please have a ghee of water," where "ghee" meant glass. My grandmother was startled to hear this complete sentence from one so young and always reminded me of this when I was growing up.

We moved then to a bungalow house in the center of the village of Egerton, near the main road of the village and across from the railway tracks just beyond the road. From our kitchen window, we could see several more houses clustered together, and the railway station with its post office and general store was visible at the head of the road.

My brother Malcolm was born in April 1941 in the nearby town of New Glasgow. My MacDonald grandparents, whose farm was a mile away from our bungalow, took care of me while Mother was in the hospital.

My own memories begin in the summer months of 1942 when I was two and a half. These are shards, dimly remembered, scattered over those early years. Fragments, no doubt imperfect, but mostly, as best as I can tell, these are my memories and not events that were later recounted to me:

It is summer and we were visiting my MacLellan grandparents on the farm in Dunvegan. One day I ventured out of the enclosed flower garden, where my mother had sent me to play, to follow the parade of geese walking toward the barn only to be chased by an angry gander. My grandfather, who was in the barn, heard my wails and came running out to pick me up and shoo the gander back to his flock.

My next memory also took place in that flower garden that summer. My mother had dressed me in my pretty new dress with its pinafore and let me out into the garden with strict orders not to go beyond the picket fence. Little Grandma's peonies had just come into full, plump buds. I went from stalk to stalk pulling off the buds and putting them in the pockets of my pinafore, then came to the front door and announced to my grandmother — and my mother's horror — "I have a present for Little Grandma!"

Dear Grandma, even knowing she just lost most of her glorious summer blooms, said to my mother, "Don't scold her; she was giving me a present."

Another day, I wandered out of the back door and started up the hill to the pasture; perhaps some of the sheep and lambs were there that day, and I was going to visit. But I tripped and fell on a tin can that had been discarded in that field. Its jagged top, from the type of can opener used in those years, sliced into my left hand. My mother, terrified by the amount of blood that was running down my arm as I came howling back down the hill, said to Grandpa, "This is serious. We must get her to the doctor." There was no car at the farm that day, so my grandfather hitched his fastest horse to the small carriage, settled me on the floor next to my mother's knees, and drove us the eight miles to Inverness and the doctor.

My mother had wrapped a dishtowel around my hand, and that dishtowel was red with blood when we arrived at the doctor's office. But I was afraid when I saw the doctor and crawled under a table in his office. Mother told me later that the doctor lured me out with a lollipop, which kept me distracted while he stitched up the wound.

I grew up with that scar on my left hand. Many years later, a doctor examining my hand remarked on the straight-line scar, asked how I'd gotten it, and then said that I was very lucky, that a gash even a millimeter longer could have severed critical nerves in the hand, perhaps incapacitating the thumb. The scar is on my left hand; I am left-handed and have been since I could first hold a spoon, according to my mother.

It is the next summer when I was three and a half, and we are back again visiting my grandparents on their farm in Dunvegan. I had taken my little brother, Malcolm, by the hand and walked him down the hill, past the cherry tree where our grandfather was up on a ladder picking the ripe cherries and yelling at the crows to go away. My brother was a little over two years old, and he was my project in life. I would take him around to peer through the fence at the pigpen and yell at the pigs or help him run out of the way if the cranky gander got loose from his pen and headed toward us. As our grandfather told us, "You must run to the house or inside the picket fence because that gander doesn't like children."

But today, I was taking my brother down to see the polly-wogs in the little brook at the foot of the hill. Perky, Grandpa's big friendly collie dog was with us, padding along the path to the brook. I tugged my little brother along and got him to kneel on the grassy bank so we could watch the pollywogs, which were swimming around in zigzag patterns in the clear water of the little pond formed by the brook.

The next thing I knew I was sprawled on the grass, wet all over and gasping for breath and my grandfather was running and yelling to us. Perky, the dog, had my brother by the collar and was shaking him, and Malcolm was gasping for air. My grandfather reached us, helped me to stand up, yelling up the hill for my mother and my grandmother. He picked up my little brother who was crying now, frightened and wet, his face, hair, and shirt soaked. Perky, the dog, stood very still beside our grandfather, and we could hear our mother calling to us as she started to run down the hill. Grandpa reached down to pat the dog's head. In later years, my mother said that we must have become mesmerized watching the pollywogs and fell into the brook headfirst and that Perky pulled us out, me first, by the back of my pinafore dress, then my little brother, "by the scruff of his neck," as my mother said.

I have clear memories of that dog, Perky. He was a large brown-and-white collie with long silky hair and large brown eyes, patient and careful with us, "always watching out for us" my grandfather told me years later.

Even in those early years, as young as I was, I would stand in the front yard in the early-summer evening watching Grandpa and Perky go down the hill, cross the little bridge over the brook, then climb up the hill to the main roadway. There were few cars since those were the war years and few people in Dunvegan had a car, or if they did, hadn't the gasoline, which was rationed, to drive it around except in emergencies. Our grandfather had an old Model T Ford, which sat in the yard with an empty gas tank. We used the horse and buggy to go to church on Sundays or for food shopping in the town of Inverness.

Once across the road, Grandpa would open the gate to the pasture on the high hill and call out to Perky, who would race up the hill to where the cows were grazing. We would watch Perky go from cow to cow until he nudged them into a single line waddling slowly down the hill, coming home to be milked. Grandpa said that Perky nipped at their heels, always gently, but the cows understood and got in line, with Perky keeping watch from the rear. This was our early-evening entertainment each evening on those long summer days of vacation.

Perky was killed by a car a few years later, as most people bought cars in the years just after the war and often drove them fast down that stretch of road. Perky was not used to expecting cars and was hit just as he had shooed the cows safely across the roadway.

That summer on our visit to my grandparents' farm we were joined by my Uncle Jim's wife, Marian, and her two chil-dren, a girl my age and a little boy about the same age as my brother. The men of the family were either away at war — my father was in the Canadian Air Force and his brother, John was overseas with the Canadian Army — or like my uncle Jim, working in a steel mill in Ontario for the wartime production.

My Aunt Marian dressed her daughter, Darlene, in starched pink dresses with small white lace aprons and white shoes with lacy white socks. Darlene also wore a large white ribbon and bow in her curly hair. I remember my mother saying, "This is a farm. The children get quite dirty running around the yard and visiting the barn." I too thought that Darlene was too fancy, especially in those shoes and socks.

One day while Darlene was wearing her crisply starched outfit, we four — both little brothers were tugged along by our hands — decided to visit Grandpa at the barn, passing the pigsty on the way. Darlene said she wanted to see the pigs and climbed up the rungs of the fence, leaning over the top. I think I told her to be careful, the rungs were slippery (I wasn't allowed to get that close to the pigs or to climb that fence), when suddenly Darlene toppled off the top rung and landed in the muck on the inside of the pigsty, the pigs squealing loudly and me shrieking for our grandfather. By this time Darlene was screaming also, standing there in pigsty muck, her face and clothes covered with the watery dirt, her fancy hair bow lying in another puddle. Grandpa came running from the barn, calling for the women and climbed over the fence quickly to pick up the howling bespattered little girl. I wanted to laugh but thought that wouldn't be right, as my mother and aunt came running out of the house, one of them yelling, "Holy Mother of God!"

Darlene was unhurt, but her clothes were beyond salvaging. The next day she borrowed one of my pairs of brown ribbed socks and my rain boots. But we did get dressed up to go to church on Sunday.

There was another incident that summer, a frightening incident that has stayed with me all of my life. For many years when I was in my preteens or teens, I wondered if it was something I'd dreamt about. I would not ask my mother — was I afraid that to bring it up she would be upset? — and it wasn't until I was well into my forties and home for a visit while we were sitting with a cup of tea and her homemade biscuits and raspberry jam that I thought to ask her. "Did it really happen? What was going on that night?"

"No," she said rather too quickly and firmly. "You must have had a bad dream."

Yet this is what I remember. The four children — Darlene, me, and our two little brothers — were all put to bed, and we were asleep. Then my mother was shaking me awake, saying, "Be very quiet. Do not say anything," as she picked up my sleeping brother and laid his head on her shoulder. My aunt Marian was waking Darlene and saying, "*Shhh, shhh,* be quiet. Come downstairs with us."

These were the war years, World War II, and most of the men were away. Only my young Uncle Peter was there at home with his parents; he was then about seventeen, finishing school and working daily beside Grandpa on the farm.

"We'll go down the back stairs," said Aunt Betty, my father's younger sister, who was also home that summer, and she held my hand tightly as we went down the stairs, my mother behind me, and then Aunt Marian and her two children. We walked quietly through the kitchen and there was our grandmother, looking worried and reaching for Darlene's hand.

Aunt Betty asked her mother, "Where is Peter? Is he all right?" Grandma opened the back door and said, "We must go quickly," and we were running up the small hill in the back pasture.

There were some large rocks there, and my mother said, "Let's hide here; everyone get down on the ground, and *shhh*! Don't make a sound."

The ground was damp, probably from dew on that summer evening, and I felt cold. We children were wearing white nightgowns. My mother said, "We must lie flat and stay below the rocks." I was suddenly frightened because I knew my mother was worried. Aunt Betty, who was holding me close, was shivering. She was frightened also.

Then there were shouts and doors slamming and my grandfather's voice: "Leave now!" He was shouting. "And don't come back. There is no one here that you are looking for!"

I heard car doors slam and then car lights came on and the motor started. The car moved fast over the gravel driveway and then Aunt Betty peeked around the largest rock and said, "They are going. The car is going down the hill." She was quiet for a few minutes, then said, "The car has turned onto the highway. It is going down the road."

Grandpa started to walk up the hill in the back pasture and called out to us, "You can come back now; they are gone." And then he called, "Peter, you can come out now."

Grandma asked, "Where was he?"

Grandpa said, "In the hayloft in the barn."

Many years later, I saw my cousin Darlene at her father's funeral. It was the first time we had seen each other since that summer long ago, as she grew up in Ontario and I left Nova Scotia for the U.S. after I finished my university years. I decided to ask if she remembered the summer we spent together at our grandparents' farm when we were little girls.

"Oh yes," she said. "I remember the gander and how scared I was of him when he would chase us through the yard." She didn't mention her tumble into the pigsty and I thought better of bringing it up, when she suddenly said, "Do you remember the night we had to hide in the pasture, when the drunken men came to the house and they were looking for someone, and we were all so scared?"

I said, "So it really happened? My mother said I had a bad dream."

"Oh, it happened all right," Darlene said. "I remembered something also and pestered my mother until she told me the story of how the women were so frightened that they woke us up and took us up to the pasture."

I asked, "Were they worried about Peter?"

"Oh yes. Grandpa thought they were looking for someone, not for Peter and they were so drunk and angry that they would think Peter was the person they were looking for. But Grandpa hid Peter in the barn and then he took the pitchfork, waved it at the men, and told them to leave, and at once."

Did my mother repress that incident? Or was she so determined that it should not be in my memory that she opted for the "bad dream" explanation? I find it a relief to know that the incident actually happened but think also that this must have been terrifying for my beautiful Aunt Betty, who was especially young and vulnerable, but also for my mother and Darlene's mother, Aunt Marian, both of them still young, needing to protect their children but also themselves from drunken, angry men, and with little protection except for Grandpa and his pitchfork and his courage to order them away.

My sister, Donalda, was born on August 23 of that summer, in the same hospital in Inverness and with the same kindly doctor as for my birth. As we were growing up, Donnie, as she always wanted to be called, and I would always say to our first cousins in Cape Breton Island when there for a visit, "We are Cape Bretoners, too!"

Starting School and the One-Room Schoolhouse

My elementary and secondary school education took place in a one-room schoolhouse through the 9th grade. Just after Christmas 1945, when I turned five years old, my mother decided to send me to school. An empty seat had become available in the primary section of the one-room schoolhouse in Egerton, where we lived, and since this was a small village, the usual school rules of starting age could be easily overlooked. Besides, my mother knew the teacher, whose name was Goldie. Goldie probably had a full first and last name, but I never knew that and in later years forgot to ask. She was just Goldie. I didn't call her that, of course, and now cannot imagine what I would have called her. Perhaps "Please, Miss," assuming I could utter any word since I sat there in terrified silence, totally tongue-tied during those first few months.

I do vividly remember my mother's stern words to the teacher as she left me at the schoolhouse door that first morning. "She is left-handed, but don't touch her. She already knows how to write and she can read also." It was many years later before I could understand what my mother meant by "don't touch her." At that time, in that last winter of World War II, being left-handed was still considered to be a form of disability, some mistake of nature, and teachers, if not parents, were apt to "correct the child," to force writing to the "proper" hand.

Whether Goldie was surprised to learn that I could read and write at five years of age is not something that seemed important to me at the time. It just was. My mother had been a teacher for ten years before she married my father, and since she was home alone with us — me, and my younger brother and sister — during the war years while my father served in the Royal Canadian Air Force, she taught us all to read, to tell the time on the large kitchen clock, to print our capital and small letters, and to read our picture books. Before I turned five, she told me later, I could read to my younger siblings. My first book began with, "Here I am. My name is Nan. I have a dog. I have a cat, too."

There would be little chance that I would have to read aloud in this classroom, where the demands of the middle and high school students would absorb most of the teacher's attention. There we sat, the few of us in the small desks in the front row that formed the primary section.

Luckily, in those early weeks, the teacher did not concern herself with me, never sent me to the blackboard to write my alphabet letters, which was an excruciating assignment for the little ones, since the older students might giggle aloud at our efforts. The teacher just looked over my scribbler to see that I kept up printing and writing words or to see that I joined in with the primary and first grades if we were asked to recite in unison. This left me free to listen to the lessons of the upper grades and practice drawing circles for our penmanship drill.

One-room schoolhouses are an amazing place to learn, perhaps not for five- or six-year-olds, but certainly for third to sixth graders, before the more demanding work of middle school begins. But even in that first year, I did listen to the lessons being taught to the upper grades, to the history and the English grammar, and the poetry recitals, and especially to the geography lessons, when the teacher would point out different countries with her long wooden pointer and talk about the different customs and what kind of clothing the children of those countries wore.

After these few memories of my first weeks of school, everything disappears from my memory for the next year and a half, except for one incident. I am quite sure that this memory loss was not just because I was so young, but because I lost my father some six weeks after I first began school. I don't know how many days or weeks I was kept home from school after his plane was lost, and it has never seemed useful or appropriate to ask.

The one incident that stands out in those next months was when Johnny Perry and another boy pushed me into a ditch on a miserable rainy day when the ditch held about a foot of furiously running muddy water. This must have been when I was six because I was walking to school alone. Maybe my mother was busy with the new baby as well as with my brother and other sister. I was wearing a new raincoat, which we called a "slicker" in those days, with matching rain boots and maybe even a mini version of a "sou'wester" rain hat. I left that morning feeling very satisfied with my new yellow coat, like that of a real fisherman. Even though I was a tall, strong six-year-old, I was no match for the two eight-year-old boys who taunted me about my fancy clothes and then pushed me into the ditch full of muddy water. I was devastated and came home crying, wet and miserable. My mother consoled me, got me into dry clothes, and kept me home for the rest of that day. But the incident was traumatic. I was frightened and humiliated, and in later days, just plain angry. For years after, I thought that if I ever saw Johnny Perry again, I would sock him in the jaw.

I completed primary school those months between January and June 1945, and in September, went back to that one-room schoolhouse where I completed both the first and second grades. Perhaps this was not such an astonishing feat since all lessons for both grades were taught together and only the exam was different. I took the test for first grade and then the test for second. The credit for this must go to my mother for her early and constant teaching when we were little.

My memories start again with the next major change in our lives. In the summer of 1946, when I was six and a half, my mother was asked to take over the one-room school in a hamlet called Pleasant Valley, located some thirty miles away in the

county of Antigonish. My mother moved her small family —
me, my brother Malcolm, who was fourteen months younger,
my sister, Donalda "call me Donnie," fourteen months younger
than my brother, and the baby, Louise, who was born three
months after our father's plane was lost and was now fifteen
months old — to a new house that the men of the village had
built for us that summer. The house was near the school and
had a small plot of land with enough room for a vegetable garden in the summer. There was a great old pine tree that towered
over the house and whistled during November wind and rain-
storms and a scraggly old apple tree beyond the garden patch
that boasted beautiful blossoms in early June but produced apples so inedible that our mother declared they were not even
good enough for jelly, much less a pie. That old apple tree did
have one sturdy branch that held a swing, a place of wonderful
respite for me on long summer evenings.

My mother was "The Teacher" — my teacher — and we
were known all of our lives in that valley as "The Teacher's
kids."

When I finished high school in the two-room school in a
nearby village and passed my eleventh-grade provincial exams,
I was the first person from the village to finish high school and
to go on to college.

In those early years, my mother taught all of the grades in
that one-room school, from primary through tenth grade, and
all subjects: algebra and geometry, English grammar and literature, history and French, geography, and social science. She
even taught us choral singing, and each Christmas season she
staged concerts for the parents and our neighbors in the village

with carols and tableaux with arrays of angels (the primary and first-grade students), wearing costumes that she made.

In a one-room schoolhouse, the lesson segments are brief but concise: the fourth-grade students learned their math in a fifteen-minute session while the seventh graders were expected to parse sentences in preparation for writing their results on the blackboard. The 9th- and 10th-grade students were expected to do their algebra and geometry assignments while Mother taught history to the eighth and ninth graders. She had to double up on some subjects, so she needed to remember the following year just who had already been taught what level of each subject.

Of course, there were no labs, and thus no chemistry or physics throughout my entire secondary education, but my mother made sure that we had wonderful lessons in botany, teaching us mostly about plants and trees. Over the years, she led us on excursions to the woods or the farmers' fields to collect and identify samples of leaves or stems, seeds and flowers, branches and pinecones and taught us to construct displays on large poster boards for our science assignments.

The schoolroom was square, with the primary grades in smaller desks in the first row, middle school grades in the middle rows, and the more senior grades in the back row. Since the desks for the primary through third grades were set lower, I remember that year in the third grade hearing an eraser or rubber band being snapped our way by someone from the upper grades, but as a rule, the younger grades were generally protected, as the small missiles were usually directed by the boys in the eighth or ninth grade to the boys in middle school, especially to the peskier ones. But order prevailed in this schoolroom; mother was strict about our behavior, and she expected everyone to get along.

The centerpiece of the room was a wood-burning stove with an elbow-shaped stove pipe that went through the ceiling. It was a rotating responsibility for the farmers in the valley to supply the school with cords of wood. Since my mother started the fire in the old wood stove when she arrived in the morning, it was important that the wood that had been delivered was dry and could be easily ignited, especially on winter mornings when the winds howled, the temperature dropped below freezing, and the windows were covered with frost.

One winter, the family in charge of supplying the wood failed in their duty and we literally ran out of wood. My mother was furious and had no choice but to cancel school for two days. On the afternoon of the second day, when the wood shipment still had not arrived, she strapped on her old skis and went to the offending farmhouse, letting them know in her stern, no-nonsense way that the children were suffering and that they simply must deliver the needed wood immediately and that it must be dry so it would ignite, not wet or green so it wouldn't catch a flame. Bundles of dry wood were delivered overnight, and school resumed the next day.

In the coldest of winter days, my mother would use the wood stove to heat the contents of giant-sized cans of soup that she had bought at the beginning of the fall term, so that all of the students had something warm and nourishing at lunchtime to supplement the cold sandwiches that everyone brought to school. I can't imagine and have never discovered where she found those restaurant-sized cans of Campbell's tomato or chicken noodle soup or where she found the money to pay for them. She was adept at organizing card parties and raffles for the adults of the village and perhaps used those activities to raise any funds needed for our lunch supplements as well as for the poster boards, colored chalk, and other supplies that would otherwise be unavailable.

My mother, "The Teacher," was also skilled at enlisting the older students to help out. She considered it part of their education and skills training to ladle out the soup, stoke the fire, help the little ones bundle up for the walk home, and make sure that everyone had a walking companion, no matter how brief the trip or benign the weather, but especially so in a blizzard or rainstorm. Since electricity had not yet reached the valley, the older students took turns filling the kerosene lamps and cleaning the glass lampshades, important during the winter months, when the mornings, as well as the afternoons, were nearly dark. The older students also carried in the buckets of water we needed each day from the well at the edge of the schoolyard.

In addition to the Christmas concerts my mother staged for the pupils and families, every winter she would put on a one-act play featuring adults from the village that she cajoled or intimidated into participating, if not to act in the production, then at least to build a set or make a curtain (usually made from old bedsheets). I do not know where she found the plays since there was no local library in those days, but her productions were memorable, with lines quoted for years among the villagers. ("Me Olga from da Volga, me vash dish" was one favorite snippet.) I am sure that before her, no one in that village had ever seen a play or even heard one on the radio. To these farmers and loggers, my mother, "The Teacher," became a cultural force, bringing music, plays, and any books she could find for the children as well as for the adults, the latter passed from house to house during those long winter months.

Aunt Isobel, Uncle Bernie, and Shirley

All three moved in with us to the newly built house in Pleasant Valley in late August of 1946. My aunt Isobel was our mother's sister; weeks after I was born, she had come home from New York to take care of me while my mother was recuperating from rheumatic fever. It was during those months in Inverness that Isobel was to meet the man she was to marry, and who became our Uncle Bernie.

Now, Aunt Isobel was ill with cancer; she needed care when not in Halifax for treatment, and someone had to take care of their daughter, Shirley, adopted when she was five, and now eight, two years older than me.

So there we all were, suddenly in a new village and a new house, strangers in a household that had grown enough to fill every room available. Uncle Bernie worked at an administrative job in the nearby town, although I did not know then what kind of work he did, just that he dressed in a suit and white shirt and tie every morning to go to work. We had a housekeeper, Rita, who lived about a mile down the road, a wonderful young woman, big and capable, moving around the kitchen with Louise, the baby, now just over a year old, on her hip and making yet another large pan of baking powder biscuits for dinner or oatmeal raisin cookies and brownies for our treats and school lunches. Over the years Rita also learned to make bread just like our mother's, wonderfully flavorful white or wheat bread, and pans of rolls that would glisten with melted butter after coming out of the oven.

Shirley arrived at our household in the middle of a temper tantrum, angry at either her adopted mother or father or maybe both. She yelled, stamped her feet, wailed even louder when Uncle Bernie slapped her on her bum, telling her in a stern voice to be quiet and to behave. Shirley was to explode into that temper tantrum at least once each day for the next three years that she lived with us.

By the end of that first week, I detested Shirley. Our new household arrangements were shocking enough: we were in a new village, in a new house that did not have electricity or in-door plumbing, and in a new schoolhouse with all new class-mates. Shirley dominated the household before and after school. In addition to her mean temper, she was greedy, always the first to reach for a cookie and take more than one when Rita set the plate of cookies on the table for our after-school snack. When we were getting dressed for school and Shirley, Donnie, and I would line up by Aunt Isobel's bed to have our hair braided, Shirley howled with protest each morning, yelling that Aunt Isobel was hurting her by the struggle to pull the brush through her mop of tangled hair. Shirley would dance from foot to foot despite the order to stay still, complaining about the tight elastic bands used to hold her braids in place. Then she would demand to see herself in the mirror, which led to another set of howls of "How ugly I look!" or sometimes, "You made me not pretty!" I never liked my braids either, they were always too tight, but Donnie and I knew not to protest or complain. Each morning as we walked up the road to school, Shirley would grab the ends of the pigtails, pull off the rubber bands and yank at the braids until her hair was loose.

Our mother would have gone ahead to the schoolhouse to get the room ready, help the smaller children out of their boots and jackets, and light the fire in the pot-bellied stove on the colder autumn or winter days. She would spot Shirley arriving with her wild mop of hair and then make her sit still while mother went through the braiding exercise again. Shirley wasn't any happier but would not make the same scene in front of our mother as she would in Aunt Isobel's bedroom. Also, Mother insisted that all of the girls in the school who had long hair must wear braids, or pigtails as we called them, to help keep the frequent plagues of head lice under some measure of control.

As a teacher, Mother was kindly but also a strong disciplinarian, and she would not allow outbursts of temper or backtalk from any of the pupils. But Shirley would whisper conspiratorially to her seatmate and she would frequently burst into tears when asked to recite her assignments because often enough those had never been completed.

But it was during the after-school hours that I was tormented by Shirley and tormented daily. We all had little chores to do to help Mother out in the evenings, but Shirley usually refused to do hers, then would argue loudly, "But Rosemary was supposed to do it," or "That was Malcolm's job." Poor five- then six-year-old Malcolm was all too often caught in a situation where Shirley was goading him into a stand-off with her, then Shirley would lie to our mother or her father. "I didn't do that," she'd say, or "It wasn't my fault; it was Malcolm's, or Rosemary's."

Mother would take me aside and caution me. "You must keep the peace, Rosemary. You are the oldest." Of course, I was the oldest of my siblings, but Shirley was two years older than me.

Sometimes, when Mother could see that I was miserable with this girl, she would pull me aside and whisper, "Remember that Shirley is an adopted child. She was in an orphanage until she was five and she hasn't had an easy life." She certainly wasn't making my life easy, and this was going on every day.

How did Malcolm react to those tempestuous days? I think he learned early to keep away from the ongoing meanness, playing alone in the yard with his slingshot or when he was old enough, digging for worms in the garden and taking his homemade fishing pole down to the brook to find some rainbow trout.

And how did I manage to survive each day and evening? I stayed close to my mother, helping her with the chores, cleaning the table, washing the dishes, helping to get little Louise ready for bed. I would bring the tray of dinner up to Aunt Isobel on the weeks when she was still with us, tell her about my day and what I was studying, and which subjects I liked best. I burrowed into my homework, always enjoying the assignments and happy to lose myself in learning the fractions or long division for arithmetic or writing the essays in my composition book. I would practice the piano, grateful that everyone left me alone then. If there was time left before bedtime, I would read and reread a favorite book.

These were also still lonely years, despite that noisy household, full of worry for my mother because she had so much work to do, and I could tell that she was worried because her sister looked sicklier with each passing day and week. The adults were careful to say little when we were around, but I somehow knew the days when Aunt Isobel was in pain and knew that she would have to go to Halifax again.

"They are giving her cobalt treatments," I overhead Mother telling Rita, our housekeeper, one day. I didn't know what cobalt treatments were and thought better to ask, but I also figured that these must cause even more pain because the few times Aunt Isobel did return to the house, she would come home pale and weakened, no longer able to braid our hair. But I would tiptoe into her room before leaving for school to whisper goodbye and tell her I was leaving for school.

In 1947 my grandfather MacDonald died before I was aware that he, too, had been very ill for the past year. My mother must have traveled by herself on several occasions to visit him, but I only remember seeing him in his casket during the wake. Dear Granddaddy, as we always called him, he was always so kind to us when we were little children and especially the year after our father's plane was lost, when he and Grandma would come down to spend time with us at our bungalow in the village of Egerton or bring us all up to their farm for several days. There, we followed him around as he fed the horses and the cows and toss slops, as he called the food for the pigs, into the trough in the pigpen.

He was even forgiving the summer day that Ronnie, my first cousin who was my age, Malcolm, and I took the little package of tissue papers he used to roll his cigarettes and his matches from the pocket of his overalls, ground up the yellow center of some daisies and rolled three cigarettes, one for each of us, and then, sitting at the back of the barn, lit them, trying to produce a puff of smoke.

Suddenly Granddaddy was coming around the corner of the barn, clearly looking for us, running to get the cigarettes from us and stamp them out on the ground.

"Don't you know you could have burned the barn down?" he asked. He was upset but not terribly angry.

Our normally gentle grandmother was sterner, saying, "Ronald, you must discipline those children. After all, they took your papers and matches as well."

But Granddaddy said to her, "I think they've learned their lesson. They know how serious this could have been." And we did. We sat glumly in the front yard, thoroughly ashamed of ourselves and worrying what our mother would say to us when she came back from the store.

Then the week came when Aunt Isobel no longer returned to our house after her treatments in Halifax but was taken to her mother's new home in New Glasgow, where Grandma had moved with her son, my uncle Malcolm, and young daughter, Norma after Granddaddy died. Our mother dressed us all, including Shirley, in our best clothes and shoes and drove us the thirty miles to New Glasgow. "You are going to see your Aunt Isobel," she said. "And say goodbye to her because she is very sick."

We stood outside the bedroom door and mother said, "Shirley, you go in first, and then come out so Rosemary can go in. Just say a nice goodbye and don't make a fuss. She wants to see each of you."

So one by one we went into the bedroom and approached the bed. Aunt Isobel was too weak to hold my hand, but she smiled at me and she was still pretty even though she was so thin and pale. I think she whispered to me, "Be a good strong girl for your mother." I don't know what she said to Shirley, but Shirley was in tears when she came out of the room. That was the only time in three years that I had any sympathy for Shirley.

Aunt Isobel died a few days later. "It was cancer of the cervix," I overheard my mother tell her other sister, Tillie, around the time of the funeral. I don't remember the church service, but I still remember standing beside my mother at the gravesite when the coffin was being blessed by our parish priest.

Did Uncle Bernie cry at the funeral? I have a memory that he wept at the graveside as the coffin was being lowered, but maybe I have imagined that over the years, as I thought that was something he should do, and it would show us that he had some kindness in his heart, for rarely did we ever see any kindness from him when he was around the house. He was not at all like my two grandfathers, who were always warm and kind to us, or like my Uncle Malcolm, who was playful and teased us into giggles or sheer mortification when he was visiting, asking, "How are Weezy the Witch and Donnie the Bitch?" generating peals of laughter from us because he used a swear word until Mother would come along and say, "Malcolm, stop it.

You mustn't use that language with the children." We were never allowed to even say damn. "Darn will do," Mother would say. Louise must have called her little self "Weezy" as she was learning to talk.

But Uncle Bernie was stern and would order us to stay quiet at meals, although sometimes he would order us to give an account of what we did during the day. We all replied with shaky voices. He would order us to bed and say threateningly, "And no giggling!" even though our mother was standing there, and I always considered it was her place to send us to bed.

There was always one of his commands that sent Shirley into another temper tantrum. She would refuse to do as he asked and he would bellow back at her as the rest of us sat in frightened misery until the storm passed, usually when Mother would step in to soothe and quiet everyone.

Sometimes at night, when we were in bed and supposedly asleep, I would hear raised voices from the kitchen and know Mother was arguing with Bernie. I never knew what the arguments were about. Maybe she was defending us.

Uncle Bernie did have a few lighter moments with us, taking time to teach us a Gaelic song, then telling me, "Now, Rosemary, you have to learn to play that song on the piano."

Before Halloween, he would gather us around the living room stove, turn down the glow from the Aladdin lamp, leaving only the hiss of its burning kerosene on the wick as background noise while he told us ghost stories. We would sit there, paralyzed with fear as he got to the part where the ghost reached out from the wall to grab the woman (or the man) in the story or where the devil appeared on the road in front of the horse carrying the priest on his back, who was taking communion to a dying person in the village. Afterward, we would huddle together in bed, fighting sleep because we knew there would be nightmares that night and for nights to come.

Then there was the winter of the three pigs. One evening in spring, Uncle Bernie came home from work with three little piglets on a mat in the back seat of his car. "We're going to raise these so we will have our own bacon and pork roasts in the winter," he said, and then named then Molotov, Gromyko, and Gryzanko.

He not only insisted we learn how to spell the pigs' names but also to learn that these were Russian names and that we needed to be able to find Russia on the map. Of course, we could. Our mother had taught us geography, pointing out the continents and the countries on the wall map in the schoolhouse. Russia was the large red splash on the map, larger even than Canada.

Uncle Bernie made an agreement with our neighbor Dan MacEachern to rent a small plot of land near the frog pond, and he and Dan built a pigpen and a wooden trough for the pigs' food. Each morning and evening that summer, we carried pails of food scraps down to the pigpen, tossing the grubby food into the troughs and saying hello to the three pigs, calling them by their Russian names. I remember leaning over the fence to watch the pigs eat their slops and marvel at the muddy mess they made of this small patch of land. We kept watch on how much they grew and reported back to our uncle.

Then the cooler days of October arrived, signaling the onset of winter. Was that a year later? Perhaps, because by this time, the three little pigs had grown huge, particularly Molotov. We used to joke about getting a saddle for him and learning to ride around the pigpen.

On that next Saturday morning, our uncle announced that we children were to stay in the house all morning, not venture out, and certainly not go near the pigpen by the frog pond. Nothing more was said that day, and on Sunday morning, after we came back from church and had our breakfast, we slipped out of the house and headed down the road to the frog pond. There was no longer a fence and there were no longer three large pigs grunting around. Only their messy, muddy patch of ground was left.

Weeks later that winter, when smoked ham was being served or a Sunday roast of salt pork, we four children silently ate our vegetables and mashed potatoes, politely passing on the platters of ham or pork. It was years before any of us would bring up the subject of Gromyko, Gryzanko, or Molotov.

One evening at dinner, as the bowl of cottage cheese — we called it curds —was being passed around the table. Uncle Bernie helped himself, then passed the bowl to me. "No thank you," I said, as I began to pass the bowl along.

"What do you mean, no thank you?" he bellowed. "You will eat these curds; they are good for you."

"Thank you," I replied, getting scared of him now, "but I don't like curds."

"You will eat these curds; pass me back that bowl," he said as he scooped out three or so large spoonful's and put them on my plate.

"Eat!" he thundered at me. "Everyone else, finish up your dinner and leave the table, except for you," he said to me. My mother looked worried, perhaps she even said, "But Rosemary doesn't like curds, so she shouldn't have to eat them."

Bernie thundered at her as much as at me. "She will eat them, and I will sit right here until she does."

I struggled to swallow each mouthful, gagging as it went down. The mound before me seemed to grow in size, not diminish. How long did this take? Perhaps a half-hour. He sat there, glowering at me, watching me struggle with every spoonful. Finally, there was just the last small mound left. I somehow swallowed it down, then ran from the table, out the back door to a corner of the yard, where I threw up the entire mess, trembling in fear and anger. To this day, I have never been able to stand the look or the smell of cottage cheese.

Then there was the Sunday when we four children and Shirley all got the giggles during Mass. We were lined up together in a pew, Uncle Bernie on the aisle, Mother next to him. None of us later could remember what we were giggling about or who started it, but the giggles passed through the five of us, through me, my three younger siblings, and Shirley. Our bodies were shaking with the fit of laughter, all of us straining to keep from laughing out loud.

"Shhh," whispered our mother. "Stop that now." Bernie leaned over her, glowered at us, his face turning red with anger. That alone frightened us, and the giggling fit finally passed.

When we got back to our house and mother began preparing breakfast, Uncle Bernie came into the kitchen and said,

"Where is the leather strap?" This usually hung in the back porch and was used to sharpen knives.

"What is this for, the dog?" my mother asked. Our silly little spaniel, never properly trained, still ran after the car when we left the house, barking loudly until his little legs could no longer keep pace with the car.

"No, for the kids," he said. He then ordered us all to the backyard, ordered us to line up by age, so Shirley was first. He said, "Pull up your skirt and drop your underpants," as he put her over his knees and gave three or four strong lashes with the leather strap on her bare bottom. I was next and then Malcolm, shrinking as much from having to take down his underwear as dreading the punishment that was to come. Then came Donnie, who got only two lashes. Only Louise was spared. She stood there, her brown eyes wide with terror.

"You're too little to be spanked," he said to her. "But you mustn't ever laugh again in church — ever." Louise ran back to the house to stay by our mother's side for the rest of the day and evening.

How did we four manage through the rest of that Sunday? Humiliated, embarrassed, for there we were, witnesses to one another's bare bottoms. And we were all hurting, perhaps there was no bleeding from the lashes, but I had large red welts on my bottom for a week. Sometime that afternoon or evening, I found some ointment to rub on my welts, and Donnie's. I passed the tube to Malcolm. Did he take it? I only remember his silence and the grim look on his young face. Perhaps the three girls were able to cry, but not Malcolm. Over the years, I have thought that he was more affected by this outburst of cruelty from Bernie than even the rest of us.

The day finally came when Bernie and Shirley left our house. He had met a woman named Gert and was to marry her and move to a village in Cape Breton, at least 60 miles away and across the Strait of Canso. You needed a ferry in those days to get to Cape Breton, so we could feel safe that they wouldn't be visiting us very often.

Occasionally Mother would say, "We should go visit Bernie and Gert." But each of us had a ready excuse: a softball or hockey game, a piano concert to practice for, anything that would hold off us being included in such a visit.

We did learn that Shirley continued to be a difficult child and teenager, yelling back at Gert, storming out of their door when her father scolded her. Years later, Mother told us that before finishing high school, Shirley ran away with a boy from that village, going to some town in Ontario, where they got married and had three sons.

Decades later, on one of my frequent trips to Nova Scotia to visit my mother, I arrived from the Halifax Airport, pulling my rental car in the yard behind an unfamiliar station wagon, rather than my mother's car. I walked up the steps to the back door, leaving my suitcase on the back seat but carrying my purse, to be greeted by my mother, who said, "Come in, dear, we have visitors. They are in the living room having a cup of tea."

"Who is it?" I asked.

"Why, it's Shirley. She is here with her husband and one of her sons. I think this is her second husband."

Shirley stood up as I came into the room. She was smaller than I imagined, shorter than me. Her gray hair was cut short but still curly. We just looked at each other. I stood still, struggling to be polite. We were strangers. There was no handshake, certainly no hugs. She introduced her husband and her son. "How do you do?" I managed.

"Excuse me," I said. "I will move my car out of the yard; it's blocking yours." To my mother I added, "I will bring in my suitcase."

Shirley got my message, and by the time I had backed out onto the street, they were coming down the front steps and getting into their car. I watched them reverse their station wagon and head slowly down the street, old painful memories rushing back.

"Hi Mom, how are you?" I said, coming through the back door to the safety of her kitchen, saying, "You look so well and such a welcome sight. Could I have a cup of tea? And do you have any of your biscuits and jam?"

This little feast is what my son Sean calls "Nova Scotia penicillin." It could always dispel all fears.

Preparing for Winter in the Valley

In the late 1940s and early 1950s, my small hamlet of Pleasant Valley had yet to be wired for either electricity or telephones. We were seven miles from the county town of Antigonish, but in those days, we may as well have been seventy miles away, since the trip along the winding gravel roads was done by old pickup trucks or even older jalopies, or by horse and sleigh for many trips during the winter months when heavy snows, or even thaws and floods, could make the roads impassable for cars or trucks.

Preparing for winter in the cold realities of the Canadian north involves the very basics of life: shelter, fuel for warmth in that shelter, warm clothes and boots to brave the outdoors, and food — stored and stored-up: canned and pickled meats and fish, hundred-pound bags of flour for bread and tea biscuits, root vegetables and jams and jellies to be stored in the cellar, and whatever canned juices and fruits we could find and then afford to buy, stored in the pantry. Our family needed to buy wood from our neighbors who had farms and large woodlots and to buy coal for the winter furnace from the nearby town.

We began to actively prepare for winter during the summer, picking wild strawberries, raspberries, and blueberries for jam. By September, the crab apples would be ready for harvest. These made poor eating but wonderful jelly. We also made jelly from the sour and acidic red berries from the chokecherry bushes that thrived throughout the valley. You could not eat these raw; they were too bitter and filled with acid. We used to tease our mother that the birds wouldn't eat them either. However, Mother knew how to take these questionable offerings and turn them into tangy, delicious jelly.

In mid-October, when the pumpkin crop turned the vegetable patch bright orange, we set aside one or two well-shaped pumpkins to use as jack-o'-lanterns for Halloween, but we used most of the pumpkin crop to make jam. With our mother's recipe and technique, this was a surprisingly delicious concoction of diced pumpkin soaked for two days in sugar, lemon juice, orange slices, and whole cloves, resulting in a jam that was perfect on a cold day in winter on whole-wheat toast or as a topping for vanilla ice cream, when that rare commodity came home in the Saturday shopping.

After the gathering of fruits and berries and jam-making was the preparation for making pickles: chow (relish) made from diced pickled green tomatoes, onions, and spices; mustard pickles made from cucumbers that were soaked in vinegar, sugar, mustard, and spices; or pickled beets soaked in vinegar, sugar, and cloves.

Once we decided that the root cellar was filled with enough jars of jam, jellies, and pickles to get us through the winter and also aromatic with piled-up beets, carrots, parsnips, potatoes, and yellow turnips (rutabagas, they are called here in New York City supermarkets), we turned to knitting socks, mittens, scarves, and, when we grew older and more accomplished, cable-knit sweaters. "Turning a sock," the phrase for making the heel part, usually brought out tears of frustration in those early years, with Mother or the housekeeper needing to step in to offer guidance as well as to urge patience.

These activities kept us busy while the adults put up storm windows, which were a strong outside layer of thick glass and sturdy frames that would shield us from the rainy and windy nights of late November and early March, and above all, from the roaring winds that would bring in the blizzards of January and February, with snow hitting those windows like needles. Some of the men from the valley would travel around to build wooden cribs in front of the stone foundations of the houses, which they then filled with saw-dust from the sawmills. This rudimentary form of insulation did help to keep the floors warm.

Our indoor warmth in those years came from the kitchen stove, which in summer used kindling and cut wood, but in winter was started with kindling but fueled by coal, and by the large cylindrical furnace in the living room, which was also started with kindling wood and stoked by coal. An old, two-ton truck, dusty with black soot, would arrive before Halloween with a ton or so of coal, which was kept in a small shed in our backyard. We would stand back, cautioned repeatedly by our mother to stay out of the way, but fascinated by the gleaming lumps of black coal that came thundering down from the jacked-up container of the truck. The coal was piled high in pyramids in the shed to make it easier to break apart on an icy day. This was our main source of heat throughout the winter.

By early November, our mother would go to the grocery store in the nearby town with her long list of provisions for the winter. She bought flour and sugar in hundred-pound bags, sacks of rolled oats for oatmeal, boxes of shortening, baking powder and spices, and cans of condensed milk. We used the condensed milk for cooking since we bought our milk for drinking from the Purcell's farm up on the hill.

In the days before refrigerators and freezers, and far removed from any grocery store except for the Saturday visits, the question of what we would eat for dinner must have been a constant challenge for our mother. Fresh meat was a rarity, except for chickens, which were raised on most of the farms in the valley and which could be slaughtered for Sunday dinner, with any leftovers available for sandwiches early in the week. On special occasions, particularly if our Uncle Malcolm would be visiting on Sunday, Mother would buy a large cut of beef to be roasted with root vegetables for Sunday dinner.

Every autumn, our neighbors, the MacEacherns, slaughtered their adult pigs, and they would make smoked hams in the small shed behind their barn, or salted pork roasts in large clay pots. We would buy one ham and one of those clay pots at the beginning of winter. The ham would be delicious but needed to be eaten in a few days. We groaned over dinner when the salted pork roast was brought to the table since no amount of soaking in cold water and roasting with root vegetables could make it palatable for us.

Fresh fish was never to be had once the summer months passed, so Mother bought salt cod at the grocery store, which would be our staple on Fridays, as eating fish on Fridays was mandatory for Catholics in those days. Her technique was to soak the large wooden-like slabs for two days in cold water that she would change frequently. Then, as she was getting the vegetables ready, she would poach the codfish, and in a separate pan, make a white sauce of flour, milk, and butter and add a chopped hard-boiled egg. This made for a delicious Friday meal. For variety on Fridays, we would make a noodle casserole with either canned salmon or canned tuna, served with canned peas.

Years later when my mother was visiting us in New York, I took her to Dean & Deluca, the gourmet food store, not just to marvel at the displays of exotic fruits and tempting chocolates, but to steer her towards the fish counter so she would see the slivers of salt cod wrapped in thick plastic, imported from Lunenburg, Nova Scotia. I pointed to the price tag: $9.75 for a small package. "See, Mom," I said. "Salt cod is no longer fish for poor people; it even has a fancy name, bacalao."

Saturday evenings we frequently had a special dinner of homemade baked beans and Mother's whole wheat rolls. She would begin soaking the beans on Thursday night, and the rolls were part of her regular batch of bread that she started early every Saturday morning. Mother's bread was legendary in the valley, even heralded by all the other women who regularly made their own bread. So, too, were her baking powder biscuits, which she would also make on Saturday while the oven was heating for the bread. We liked to eat the biscuits right out of the oven, with butter dripping on each half and then topped by one of our homemade jams. Mother also made cookies: molasses or sugar cookies for our school lunches the following week and either date squares or date-filled cookies for a special treat on Saturday evenings. Then there were her pies: apple or lemon meringue, a raisin pie in the winter, or blueberry pies in the summer. One of those pies would be our dessert for Sunday dinner.

Surviving the Winter in Pleasant Valley

My memories of winter are shaped as much by the length of the season, which began in mid-November and lasted until mid-April, as by the severity, which varied from year to year because of the influence of the Gulf Stream. This could sometimes leave our maritime province basking in 52-degree temperatures in mid-February, setting off major flooding along the brooks and in the intervales, as we called the lowlands on either side of the brooks.

But in other weeks or years, the Gulf Stream could move far south of the coast and leave us subject to the major storms that came in from central Canada or up from the northeast U.S. and which could sometimes leave us immobilized under several feet of snow. Those storms usually arrived in a full blizzard, with howling winds, plunging temperatures, windows coated with drifting snow, and roads that were often impassable for days. Only the farmers who had horses and sleighs or the few of us who had skis of some rudimentary style could travel about until the snowplows arrived from the nearby town to clear a path on the roads.

We heated our houses with coal during the winter, supplemented with chopped wood in the kitchen stove. The coal was necessary to use in the large cylindrical furnace in the living room, which was our only source of heat for the entire house in the days before central heating. This stove gave off waves of welcome heat on a cold winter evening when we gathered around to read books or do our knitting, once our homework was finished. On a cold night, the heat would not penetrate far beyond the dining room next door and certainly not to the second-floor bedrooms, so we warmed the irons that we used to do our ironing with on a Saturday afternoon in the oven of the kitchen stove, then wrapped them in towels and put one in each bed, tucking our flannelette pajamas and socks near the towel covers to warm them before we climbed into bed. The irons were a better idea than a hot water bottle, which, more often than not, would begin to leak water into the bed — pleasant enough when hot, but miserably cold later, especially if the stopper came loose and the bed got soaked. But with the swaddled irons and layers of heavy wool Hudson Bay blankets on each bed, we were usually able to stay warm through the night.

As we youngsters each turned ten, we were allowed to wield the small axe on the chopping block in the backyard to cut kindling from the stacks of wood. The kindling was stacked to dry on the porch. Since my brother and I were the oldest of the four children, we had the responsibility to bring in the kindling and the buckets of coal to heat both the kitchen and living room stoves, an easy enough task on a mild November day, but a challenge in the worst days of January, when we had to be careful not to touch the coal bucket with our bare hands in case our skin would be torn away by the icy handle.

Lighting in the house in those evenings before electricity came to the valley was by kerosene lamps: two on the kitchen table where we did our homework, two on the end tables in the living room, and one large lamp we called an "Aladdin lamp" on the main table in the living room. This lamp hissed and burped but gave off the brightest light for reading or craftwork.

The lighting source for the lamps, kerosene, was a dangerous fuel. We were taught from our earliest years that kerosene needed to be handled with great care each time we refilled the lamps or carried the kerosene can back and forth from the tank in the outdoor shed. Mother always made us stand a good distance back from the fuel truck that would come every few weeks to refill the tank and taught us how to carefully fill the spouted can and never to leave any drops of fuel in the kitchen when we were refilling the lamps. We knew from listening to stories from our classmates of houses that had gone up in flames because someone was careless or smoking a cigarette and dropped live ash near a puddle of kerosene.

Our first job when we got home from school each afternoon was to go back to the well in the schoolyard and bring in the buckets of water we needed for the evening and for washing in the morning. But our second and equally important job was to wash and dry the glass lampshades, trim the wicks, and then refill the base of the kerosene lamps. This had to be done every day in the winter, when night fell early, just after four in the afternoon. We would use up almost the entire lamp base of fuel by the time we finished our homework and went to bed. Since I was the oldest, most of this detailed work was mine, until later, when my brother was old enough to help. He was particularly precise at trimming the wicks and pouring in the kerosene but then expected me to take care of the lampshades.

This was our daily job, except for the large "Aladdin lamp" in the living room, which was at least three times the size of the kitchen and other table lamps and was considered too big and too complex and important to be trusted to anyone but our mother. Mother always refilled this lamp herself and cleaned the lampshade. She was the one to light the wick and reset the large glass shade.

We did have one near catastrophe involving those kerosene lamps, caused by Malcolm and me tussling with each other and ramming into the kitchen cupboard that held our flour, sugar, and other staples, including Mother's supply of tea and precious allotment of coffee. The cleaned and filled kerosene lamps were lined up on top of this cupboard, safely away from small hands, but the kerosene lamps were not safe from our rambunctious play that afternoon. The cabinet came away from its fasteners to the wall and went crashing down on the kitchen floor, splattering the glass of the lampshades and spewing their volatile oil over the spilled flour and sugar and broken glass, but miraculously missing the hot kitchen stove that was just to the right of the toppled cabinet. We all stood there, transfixed in horror, even the two younger sisters, who were aware of how dangerous this situation was. We all knew that if the kerosene had hit the stove, the house would have exploded.

"Jesus, Mary, and Joseph!" our mother yelled. That was her strongest epithet. She was furious with Malcolm and me and stayed furious for the several hours it took us to mop up the mess, carefully pick up the shards and small pieces of glass, and then sweep everything again, just to be sure. The younger girls were confined to the living room and given apples from our porch to eat until everything was cleaned enough to permit us to prepare dinner.

Malcolm and I were in disgrace, and we stayed in a shameful cocoon for many days. We were truly horrified by what had happened and painfully aware of what worse could have happened. We hardly spoke to each other, did our after-school chores together but silently, and slunk to respective corners of the living room to work intensely on our homework, all the while in misery. We were saved from total approbation by our mother, because her tea bags and her coffee had been in covered tin cans, and thus had survived the calamity.

Without electricity, we washed our clothes with water we carried from the pump in the schoolyard up the road, two pails each, but some always spilled, and then we had to return to the schoolyard for more water, which was then heated on the kitchen stove. Most of the clothes were woolen, so they were heavy to pick up and wring out by hand, like the denim pants in the summer, and the sheets, when we hung them out on the line in winter would freeze "solid as a board," as our mother would say, before the last of the clothespins were attached. I was never convinced that we should have hung them outside at all since when we went to reel in the clothesline, the stiff-as-a-board sheets were frozen solid, so had to be brought into the kitchen to be draped over the chairs to thaw, which would mean they would be dripping wet and so had to be left to dry by the kitchen and living room stoves during the night while we slept.

Not having a refrigerator or icebox was no problem for us in the wintertime when the bottles of milk could be left on the covered porch. Our vegetables were stored in the dry cellar under the kitchen floorboard — the hundred-pound bags of potatoes, the stacks of carrots, turnips, beets, and onions and maybe parsnips, still with their feathery or leafy tops, all snuggled together next to the racks of homemade jam and the crock of homemade butter.

Our old kitchen range on those winter days wrought miracles at our mother's hands. She knew just how many lengths of wood were needed to warm up the oven to just the right temperature for baking her wonderful homemade bread, which she needed to do twice a week with our family of four children plus a housekeeper, during those early years before my youngest sister was ready to begin school. I remember that the temperature gauge on the oven door was never accurate: Mother would open the oven door, put her bare elbow in halfway in to judge the temperature, then say in triumph, "It's just right." The bread was always perfect, as were the many pans of cookies or brownies or baking powder biscuits she made for us each week.

One of our memorable winter storms arrived on Easter when I was home for a week from my freshman year at university. Easter was early that year, in late March or early April, and when that storm hit with high winds and drifting snow, it left drifts of five to six feet throughout the valley. It took the snowplows almost a week to cut through those drifts, and when the snowblower finally arrived to take over from the failed attempts of even giant-sized trucks with plows, there were walls of snow that ranged anywhere from ten to fifteen feet high along the narrow path that once was a two-lane road. My brother and I took our longest yardstick to measure these "snow walls," and I took pictures with my Brownie Hawkeye camera.

In February of my freshman year at university, we experienced a dramatic swing in weather. One Tuesday it was minus 18 degrees. A temperature that low was most unusual as was any temperature even close to zero. That morning as we went to our classes on campus, we were warned to double up on sweaters, put socks inside our boots, wrap scarves around our faces to cover the nose and mouth and dash between the buildings. We were even allowed to wear snow pants at a time when pleated skirts were a must for girls' campus wardrobes. I can still hear the dry crunch of that snow underfoot, the electric hum in the air from the low humidity.

Then, the following Tuesday, the temperature climbed up to fifty-two, a full seventy-degree swing. By that afternoon, the two large brooks in the town had overflowed their banks and icy water flooded the intervales and nearby streets. The large blocks of ice carried by the rapid flow of water washed away the bridge on Lower Main Street, which led up to the regional hospital. We did not go out that evening or to classes the next day.

But two other storms of my childhood still dominate my memory of those winters. One February night when I was about twelve, our neighbors across the intervale, the MacEacherns, called on our newly installed telephone line to say that one of the children was quite ill and feverish with a high temperature and asked if our mother could come over with whatever medicines she had to help the child. We lived seven miles away from the town where all of the doctors were located.

There had been a large snowfall two or three days earlier and the roads were still not plowed. The temperature had warmed up during the day, so the snow had started to melt and could stick to the skis, although the wind was coming up again and the night would be cold. I put another coat of wax on the bottom of Mother's skis and helped her find some aspirin and whatever other medicines we had before she set out.

My mother was not a nurse, but in those days in the valley, when we were so isolated, women who had a winter's stock of over-the-counter medicines or who knew the old-fashioned medical remedies were always in demand.

My mother pulled on snow pants, boots, her jacket, wool hat, and gloves. I opened the back door while she strapped on the skis. Our front door, which faced the road and the strongest winds, was completely blocked by snowdrifts, but the back door was still accessible, sheltered somewhat from the wind and drifting snow. The fence along the field leading to the MacEachern farm was almost covered with snow; she would be able to ski over the fence and directly across the field. My young Aunt Norma was with us that year, helping out with the housekeeping while finishing her final year in high school.

After Mother left on her skis, Norma and I prepared dinner for the younger children, then she tucked them into bed and I settled in the living room by the Aladdin lamp to do my homework. By that time, the wind had come up, growing in intensity, howling through the pine tree next to our house and flinging wet snow against the windows. This would make Mother's return trip difficult. I peered through the front window to see if I could make out any shapes, but the blowing snow was too thick, and the windows were already crusted with the drifting snow. If Mother was on her skis coming back across the intervale, could she find the bridge over the swollen brook? What if she veered too far and missed the bridge? Then she would be skiing directly over the brook. Could she see the lights of our house? I went out to the kitchen to tell Norma that I was worried. She called the MacEacherns to learn that Mother had already left. I went back to the window in the living room. Then, through the howling wind, I thought I heard her calling, "Rosemary!" and then, "Norma!"

I yelled to Norma: "It is Mom. I know it. She is out there somewhere," and ran for my jacket and boots, rushing out the back door, and around to the front of the house, the direction she would be heading if she could see our lights.

"Help!" I heard her call, and I yelled back, "I'm coming, Mom," as I struggled through the snow to cross the road and over the top of the fence.

"Call to me, Mom, so I can hear your voice," I yelled. By this time, I could hear Norma behind me, also calling to Mom, as she too struggled through the snow. Then I could see Mom. She was sinking into the snow with every step, almost up to her hips. Where were her skis? Norma and I finally reached her and took each of her arms to help her through the snow, across the top of the fence, and then across the road. Mother was close to sobbing.

"My snow pants are frozen," she said, "and I lost the skis in the river." We three staggered around the house, through the back door and into the kitchen. I ran upstairs for blankets and Mom's pajamas while Norma stood her in front of the large stove in the living room and pulled off her frozen clothes. We helped her into the pajamas, wrapping her tightly in the blankets and settling her as close to the stove as safety would permit. I dashed to the kitchen to put the kettle on for tea.

Through chattering teeth and shivers, my mother told us what happened. While she was at MacEacherns, she gave aspirin to the sick child and together with the child's mother sponged her with cool washcloths to help break the fever. Mother had brought a lemon, a precious item to have in the winter in those days, to make a hot drink for the child.

"But you better go now, Agnes," Mr. MacEachern had said as he looked out their window. "This storm is getting stronger, and it's dark now."

By that time, the snow and ice on the river had broken through, flooding the intervale with blocks of ice and melted snow. In the dark, Mother could barely see the small bridge over the river, but as she began to cross, her skis were pulled off in the thick, wet snow. She reached down through the frigid water to try to find her skis, which soaked the sleeves of her jacket and her gloves as well as her snow pants. Then the icy wind began to freeze her clothes and block out most of the visibility. She said at that point she was truly frightened and wondered if she could wade through the icy muck and up the slight hill toward the fence before the full flood caught her. She made it over the little bridge but by then, she was sinking into the snowdrifts, fearful of falling and her feet and hands were beginning to freeze. The wind was howling as she called to us, hoping that, somehow, we could hear her. She thought that the fence would guide her to our house, which it did. We did hear her, but it was a close call, more so for our mother than for the child who needed medicine, who recovered in a few days.

The second major incident also involved my mother. It was a Friday in late February or early March and the roads and fields were bare of snow from a recent warm spell. That year my mother was teaching in the school in the village across the high hills that we called "a mountain." She drove the nine miles each day, down the road to one of our two exits from the valley, then around the edge of this high hill and the few miles to her one-room schoolhouse in the village of North Grant. Shortly after lunch period that Friday, she looked out the window to see snow arriving suddenly, moving fast and almost horizontal. The snow had not been in the forecast in those early days of weather prediction.

From her years of experiencing winters, she knew that this would be a blizzard and decided to close the school at once. This would give the children enough time to get home safely, even if they were fighting against the blizzard. She enlisted the older children to help the smaller ones get bundled up and made sure that each child had a walking companion or that groups of children would be walking together. This was the last winter before the telephones were installed, so it was not possible to call any of the families.

By the time she shut down the wood stove, found her jacket and gloves, and locked the school, the roads were impassable, and her car was already submerged in snowdrifts. My mother was wearing a skirt and sweater that day and did not have snow pants or any other winter clothes in her car to wear in a snowstorm. So with the wind howling and the snow blinding her face, she struggled to the nearest farmhouse and asked to borrow some winter clothes and boots and a set of skis. She announced she was going to ski over the mountain.

"You can't ski that mountain, not in this blizzard," the man and woman of the farm told her.

"But I must," she said. "My children are alone in the valley, and it is Friday. If I don't get there this afternoon, they will be alone for most of the weekend. Isn't there a woodcutter's trail that goes up to the top of the mountain? Just point me to where the trail begins, then I can find my way up through the woods and down to one of the farmhouses in our valley. They'll help me then."

The farmer and his wife found snow pants and boots, a heavy jacket and hat, and a set of skis for Mother. The farmer put on his winter clothes and skis and accompanied Mother through the fields and up to the tree line, where he found the woodcutter's path for her. He tried to convince her not to do this alone, but she was insistent, and said to him, "The wind is not so bad here inside the tree line. I will be all right."

But once she reached the top of the mountain and began her descent into our valley, the winds and snow were blowing strongly, and the snowdrifts were already several feet deep. She lost her skis in the drifts and could not find them in the deep snow. She was sinking to her hips in the soft snow, so she lay down on top of the snow and rolled down the side of the mountain, telling herself that if she rolled quickly, she would not sink into the snow.

Meanwhile, I was at home with my younger brother and two little sisters. I was eleven that winter, and while we still had a housekeeper that year, once I arrived home from school, she left for the weekend, knowing that our mother would be home within the hour.

"The chicken is in the oven. You will know when it is finished, and you know how to prepare the vegetables," the housekeeper told me as she was putting on her jacket. As I was peeling the potatoes and carrots from our cellar and looking out the kitchen window, I could see that a storm was coming up suddenly. The snow began to pile up by our fence, and little of the road was still visible. I peered down the road through the snow, trying to see the lights of Mother's car.

What if she was driving blinded by the blizzard? Or maybe her car had slid into a snowbank, and she could not move at all? I decided that we four children had to stay busy and that I must not appear worried. I asked my brother to make fudge and suggested to my two little sisters that we three make brownies for dinner.

My mother first reached the Delaney farmhouse on our valley side of the mountain and banged on the door. The family, who were gathered around the kitchen stove were startled to see her, got her a chair and some blankets while Mrs. Delaney put on a pot of tea and got a plate of biscuits.

"I have to get home," my mother told them. "My children are alone. Can you help me get to the MacDonalds? They have a horse and sleigh." The older Delaney son agreed to help her down the rest of the mountain.

At the MacDonald farmhouse, Mr. MacDonald and his two sons got into their snow gear and went out to the barn to harness their two horses and hitch them to the sleigh, while Mrs. Mac-Donald made a pot of tea and insisted that mother have a cup and a slice of bread. Once outside, the men wrapped Mother in a bearskin rug and heavy blankets and drove her the two miles or so through the valley to our house.

The brownies had just come out of the oven when over the howl of the wind I heard sleigh bells and voices outside, then my mother's voice calling from the back door. She was safe at home and with us. We found out the next week that all of the children from her school had reached home safely, too.

Our mother became a legend in her time, known in all of the communities near our valley as "The teacher who skied over the mountain in the blizzard of 1951."

Winter's Illnesses

As youngsters in those last years of the 1940s and into the early 1950s, we had just about every sickness common to children. We had the measles and the German measles. I never did learn the difference, but the doctors of those days insisted that measles were of a different origin and had a different effect. We had the mumps, chickenpox, annual versions of the flu, and one winter, I got whooping cough and coughed for three months.

Another winter one of us brought home "The Itch" from school, and it quickly spread through the whole family. Maybe it has a medical name, but we called it "The Itch." It was some strange parasite that nested underneath the skin and formed milk-colored bubbles that drove us nutty, and which required our mother, in the depth of winter, to wash every piece of clothing for we four youngsters plus herself and every item of bedding from five beds, including heavy woolen blankets, in some type of bleach or chemical detergent. She then put everything out to dry on the clothesline to blow in the wind, hoping that the process would take care of every parasite. But somehow this treatment worked, and Mother had conquered the parasitic "Itch."

The next winter, one of us brought head lice home from school, so the scrubbing and chemical shampoos and hours of having our hair raked with a fine-tooth comb began again, as it seemed to each winter, with each of us looking at the other's pigtails or crew cuts with suspicion for the weeks after Mother thought she had quelled those particular pests. We four were always ready to blame someone sitting near us in school as the source, but Mother would not permit such talk. Being the schoolteacher, she could also demand that all of the families put their schoolchildren through the same regimen so the small critters would not just leap from one head to the other throughout the winter months.

The illness we feared the most, the dreaded polio, seemed to happen in summer. In those years before the first vaccines became available, there was little knowledge of the disease or its prevention, just fear and terror that one of us, or one of our schoolmates, would be stricken. All swimming except in the ocean was forbidden in those summers, so there was no more damming up our favorite pool in the nearby river. We were lucky. None of us in the valley ever caught polio, but we all had seen the vivid photographs in *Life* or *Look* magazine of children encased by an iron lung, struggling for every breath, and reading stories that said even if they survived, they would never walk again.

So in winter, we coughed our way through the long dreary months with colds, bronchitis, and the worst of the coughing ills, whooping cough — there was no pertussis vaccine then. For chickenpox, we endured baths of baking soda in the galvanized tub in the dining room, wearing cotton gloves to bed so that we would not scratch the ugly itchy pustules and "have scars on our faces for the rest of our lives," as our mother would warn. We had the flu every winter. One year was particularly severe, and all of us four children were abed at once, muscles and joints aching, feverish, too miserable to read or play cards or Chinese checkers.

When the day came that the fevers broke and we had an appetite for something other than toast and jam and weak tea, our mother roasted a chicken, made mashed potatoes and cooked carrots from our root cellar, and brought dinner up to each of us on four separate trays. On each tray, she had put a small glass of apple juice and a dish of crabapple jelly to have with the sliced chicken. I can still smell the aroma of that chicken and gravy and see the attractive color mix on the trays. We were on the road to recovery and back to school within days.

Of the many illnesses we endured in those winters, the worst and most frightening were measles of whichever type. It seemed that we got measles more than one winter, and like whooping cough, there was no vaccine available and few antidotes. We were feverish, covered with red dots, sick all over. We were told to stay in darkened rooms in case our eyesight would be affected by too much light.

The most severe strain, perhaps the German measles, affected my brother Malcolm the most. He was about eleven that year, a year younger than me, and on a stormy winter's night his fever kept rising and the doses of aspirin and sponging with cool cloths from the snow that we scooped off the back doorstep with a pan were not having any effect. My mother was worried; usually she would be careful not to show her concern to us, but this was different, more alarming. My young Aunt Norma was with us that winter. I remember my mother saying, "Malcolm's fever is not going down. It will take stronger medicine. We need the doctor. Norma and Rosemary, you must keep sponging him down and try to get him to swallow an aspirin."

That was the first year we had the telephone system, a party line that connected all of the families in the valley, all of whom, it seemed in those first months, listened in on every phone call because it was such a novelty.

I don't remember the arrangements. We did have a car that year but this night with a new storm, the roads were filling up with snow. Mother must have called the doctor, who said he would come, but with the new snow, he knew that his car would not get through the roads beyond the Clydesdale turnoff. She then telephoned the nearest farmhouse, the MacEacherns where there was a horse and sleigh, and traveled with the farmer and his sons about five miles to the intersection with the larger road, which was more frequently plowed. They met the doctor and bundled him up in the sleigh with the heavy rugs and began the long trip back to our house.

This I know from my mother's side of the story, which she told me many years later. But my own memories are vivid. I stayed by my brother's bed, talking to him and putting the cool clothes on his forehead, alternating with my Aunt Norma to take his temperature. At one point the thermometer read 105.5 degrees, a dangerous level.

Norma, frightened as I was by now, said she would run back downstairs for more snow to cool off the washcloth to put on his forehead. I kept talking to him, hoping he would not lapse into a coma. What did I know of medicine? Words or whispers overheard from the wise elderly women in the valley who raised large families with rarely a doctor, using the old remedies. I didn't know those old remedies but decided he needed another aspirin, anything that might help, so urged him to sit up just long enough to swallow the Bayer with a glass of water. Malcolm then promptly vomited up everything, aspirin and water, just as Norma was coming back in the room with the pan full of snow. We sponged his forehead frantically.

I think that is when I began praying, silently.

Please, please let the doctor and Mother get here soon.

I knelt by his bed, holding his hand, saying to myself that when I go fishing with him next summer, I will never chatter on, never. He had threatened not to take me along again because I talked too much and scared the fish from biting. I enjoyed those fishing trips with him, as we would follow the river up toward the mountain. I loved all of the river's magical twists and turns, the surprising flowers along the banks, and the quiet forests. I didn't want to be cut out of those adventures.

Dear God, I thought, *I would gut and scale every darn trout he had on his alder "gad," as he called it, and I would not complain, and I would fry them for him without scorching the skin. I would make the extra trips to the well for water so he could go fishing, anything. Please, God, don't let him die.*

"Malcolm, you must stay awake," I said. "Please have some more water, even if you throw up, please." I think I wanted to say, "Please stay with us; don't leave us," but he was frightened, too. He knew how ill he was. Then, we heard the sleigh bells and the horses' whinnies and the crunch of the sleigh runners on the snow and the hurried voices. The doctor came up the stairs quickly, carrying his black bag, taking off his coat and gloves, looking at us, and saying to my mother, "These children must leave. They shouldn't be here," as he bent over to touch my brother's forehead and pulled out his stethoscope.

Norma and I were too relieved to be insulted; she was in her late teens, no longer a child, and while I was twelve, I felt old, so old. But above all, I was grateful. By some miracle, the doctor had arrived while my brother was still conscious and could answer some questions. The doctor had brought medicines, more than we had or even knew about.

What types of pharmaceuticals were used then, in the early 1950s? I think sulfa drugs, as I heard the adults say later. Whatever it was that the doctor administered to Malcolm, his fever broke quickly and stayed near normal for the next few days. My mother slept in a chair by his bed that night while the farmer and his sons drove the doctor the five miles back to his car. I was sent to bed and cried with relief into the pillow, thanking God and the universe and our neighbors with the horses and sleigh and my mother with her courage and this dedicated doctor who would travel the ten miles round trip in an open sleigh during a winter storm for an ill little boy.

Fun and Frolic on Snow and Ice

In between bouts of childhood sickness, winter beckoned with its delights of skating or skiing, or one winter before an accident occurred, flying down the mountain slope on a newly built toboggan.

The ideal conditions for skating would appear with sudden frosts, "a cold snap," that came before the snows, when the nearby frog pond would freeze solid enough for us to safely skate on its smooth surface. We were well warned by the adults to check the ice carefully, so we would find some heavy rocks and first throw them, then slide them over the surface to see if the ice held. Most times, Mother came down to the pond with us to check the ice herself before letting us begin to skate. We all knew the stories of the children who wandered onto a pond or crossed over a frozen river or brook only to fall through too-thin ice and drown.

On occasions when the Big Pond at Ranley MacDonald's farm, about a mile down the road, would solidly freeze, some of the adults would gather with a larger group of us schoolchildren for an evening skating party. This was made festive by the bonfires at the side of the pond, lit from old tires, and by the treat of hot cocoa that our mother would bring in several thermos bottles. The best skating, of course, was when the temperature was the coldest, but that also meant our toes and fingers would begin to go numb and we would have to get near the fire to "thaw out," as we said.

For the girls of the valley, each skating excursion always had its irksome side because the boys arrived with hockey sticks and pucks ready to start a game of hockey. It was not for them to swirl around the ice, holding hands with the girls.

They say all Canadian boys are born with hockey sticks in their hands, and our valley boys certainly fit the image as they darted, feigned, and tried to body check each other, chasing some semblance of a puck, while the girls were pretending to be figure skaters, trying to carve out a figure eight on the ice or practice a spin. There was no instruction on any of this: how to play hockey or how to figure skate. I don't remember how we acquired the images in our minds of what to do in those days before television. We did get to see a movie in the town on a Saturday afternoon of our shopping and my piano lesson day, so perhaps there were newsreels that showed excerpts from a hockey game or of the Canadian figure skating champion Barbara Ann Scott.

No one taught us to ski, either, but when the snows came and piled up on the slopes at Purcell's farm, where I skied for the milk or the even steeper run down John Joe Smith's hill, we set off with our basic skis, freshly waxed and with whatever poles or old broomsticks we had for ski poles. We never had proper ski boots in those early years, just our regular winter boots. Yet, without any instructions from adults, since none in the valley knew how to ski, we somehow learned to leave the spring clamp of the skis ajar at right angles on each boot, so that if we fell going down the hill, the skis would instantly come off. None of us ever had so much as a sprained ankle in all of those years, although we grumbled plenty as we trudged down the hill to the bottom of the slope to find our missing ski or skis.

The year that the teachers in the province went on strike was also the winter that featured one of the heaviest snowfalls of our childhood. Of course, with our mother as teacher, there was no real holiday from school during the five weeks the strike lasted, as our mother woke us on schedule every morning, fixed our breakfast as always while we dressed as if for school, and then settled the four of us around the kitchen table with our schoolbooks and scribblers and taught us arithmetic and history and had us write our English compositions and read our geography texts. We would finish by lunchtime, and after lunch and finishing our chores for the day, bringing the buckets of water from the well at the schoolyard just up the road, restocking the firewood and coal for the evening, and, in my case, skiing to Purcell's farm for the milk, we were then free to go skiing for the afternoon.

"Now watch Louise carefully; she doesn't really know how to ski," our mother would say as we headed out the back door with Louise, the "baby," who was now six years old or so, lagging behind us, bundled in her snowsuit and scarves, needing help to strap on her skis and begging us to wait for her and not go so fast. But she learned quickly, and once she learned to climb the ski slope with the crow's feet pattern we had somehow learned, or better still, be tugged along by me or her brother (we would have her hold onto one of our ski poles and pull her up the hill behind us), she was fearless in heading down the slopes, shouting, "Whee!" to the wind and the flying snow and laughing if she tumbled into a snowbank.

After one of the many overnight blizzards that winter, the snow built up a bluff of some eight feet on the side of John Joe Smith's hill, so we older ones decided we would try ski jumping over that bluff. Perhaps we saw films of ski jumping on the movie newsreels or maybe in one of the picture magazines we had but try it we did. Malcolm and I and our schoolmates Edmund and Joe Gaudet and Wayne Dunn would take turns, daring each other, as we climbed the hill far enough above the bluff to pick up extra speed and then fly over the eight-foot bluff, landing in a heap in a large snowbank. None of us ever made it down the hill, but we were unhurt, although our mother was furious with us when she found out what we had been doing that afternoon. The younger children had tattled on us, describing our jumps, and with much embellishment, our "crashes on the hill."

We were not as fortunate with our one attempt at tobogganing. Mr. Purcell, who was a skilled carpenter as well as a farmer, built a toboggan out of hard maple wood, and with his son Edmund's help, varnished and polished the wood to a high, slick sheen. We set off one cold, crisp night with a full moon giving us almost daylight visibility, climbing the long slope at John Joe Smith's farm and discussing which would be the best of the runs for trying out the new toboggan. Only the older ones of our crowd were there: Malcolm, Joe Gaudet, Wayne, me, and Donnie, my next sister, who begged our mother to let her go along, and Edmund, proud of his role in helping to build and polish the toboggan and anxious to see how it would work.

There had been a fresh snowfall the day before, blown around by the wind, so we knew that our old ski tracks would be covered and not catch us in a rut if we were traveling fast, or so we hoped. We arranged ourselves on the toboggan, Edmund in front holding the rope for steering, then my brother and me, with Donnie settled safely between us, followed by Joe and Wayne to give extra weight at the back of the toboggan. We set off and quickly were flying over the snow, much faster than we ever achieved with our skis, even under the best snow conditions. Suddenly, we hit an icy patch swept to the surface by yesterday's wind, which made us go even faster, but then the toboggan hit the fresh, new snow, which changed the speed abruptly, and we flipped over at top speed. We had been holding onto a small groove near the bottom of the toboggan since side rails had not yet been added on, which meant that when the sled capsized, my right hand scraped heavily on the edge of the icy snow and even through my gloves, I could feel the scrape and sense that blood was already flowing. Two of the boys hit the snow so heavily that they had instant nosebleeds. Donnie was crying, and we were all shaken and frightened. Was my hand broken? Were their noses broken? We helped each other up and limped home, pulling the offending toboggan behind us, to face the alarm and then the wrath of our mother as we appeared at the door.

"Mother of God, what happened?" she yelled at us as she saw the bloody faces and my limp hand and Donnie still crying. (Mother of God was the closest she came to a curse; we knew any situation was serious when we heard her burst out with this phrase. It was only topped by "Jesus, Mary, and Joseph!" which she kept for truly alarming situations.)

Mother brought us all into the kitchen, helped us take off our jackets and boots, and, since part of the wool was already fused into the bleeding scrapes, gingerly edged the glove off my right hand. She examined the boys' noses, decided they were not broken and gave each boy a cold washcloth to hold over his forehead, showing them how to pinch their nostrils together and rest their elbows on their knees to help the blood coagulate. She then inspected our ankles and hands to be sure that none were broken and began dabbing mercurochrome on my fingers and hand, saying, "Mother of God, what were you thinking? You have your piano lesson on Saturday. How are you going to play with those fingers?" But I could tell she was relieved that the hand was not broken. The sores and the scrapes healed enough so that I was able to have the piano lesson.

The toboggan was never seen again. We became convinced that Mr. Purcell burned it, probably because our mother had scolded him for making such a dangerous item. We were never sure, since Edmund, his son, was at school when it might have happened and reported to us later that when he got home there was no sign of the toboggan, but there were some ashes at the corner of the barn and an odd smell that stayed around for days.

"Ah, that must have been the smell of the burnt varnish," we told each other.

Winter's Entertainment for the Adults

Through those long winter weeks and months, the adults in the valley had their entertainment, too. People listened to their old crystal radio sets at night for the hockey games from Montreal and Toronto. The games were brought vividly to life in those days before television by the audio descriptions of great radio announcers. My generation grew up listening to the famous voice of Danny Gallivan — "He shoots, he scores!"—calling all the plays in a hockey game.

On Saturday night, there was the "Lux Radio Hour" featuring current Hollywood actors presenting plays or dramatization of books. Mother let me stay up to listen with her, which was a real treat. Gregory Peck and Dana Andrews were favorites of ours, but the episode that still brings chills to me decades later was the dramatization of *Sorry, Wrong Number,* featuring Barbara Stanwyck. Both mother and I were terrified by the time that episode finished. We wouldn't admit the effect the broadcast had on either of us, but I sure had difficulty sleeping for many nights afterward.

Books, or any reading material, were scarce in those early years. The mailman brought the Halifax Herald newspaper from Monday to Saturday, which I eagerly awaited for its news and features, but by all of us for the comic strips. "L'il Abner" was the favorite of we four children, while our mother liked *Dagwood and Blondie*. We had a subscription to *Reader's Digest* book series, so a new set of condensed books arrived every two months or so, and we also subscribed to the Saturday Evening Post, which was eagerly awaited each week for its featured short stories and the Norman Rockwell covers.

Sometimes, on the Saturdays when we went to the town for our weekly shopping, we would pool our allowance money on the latest *Photoplay* magazine, with its profiles and beautiful photographs of Hollywood stars. Doris Day was a favorite of my sister Donnie, while I looked forward to stories and full-page color photographs of Susan Hayward.

The few real books our mother could find in those days before there was a bookstore in the town or any form of traveling library were read eagerly by her and our housekeeper and then were passed from house to house to the farm women in the valley. I do not recall that any man in the village admitted to reading a book.

One favorite book the year I was nine years old was Ernest Hemingway's *For Whom the Bell Tolls,* the full-sized book, not the abridged version that might be featured in *Reader's Digest.* I overheard the women talking about this book when they got together, and months later, when the book was finally returned to our house, well-thumbed and with many dog-eared pages, I decided to see what this book was about. So on Saturday mornings, when it was my task to change all of the bedding on each of the five beds upstairs, I carried that book from bed to bed, stopping to read between putting on the sheets and the blankets. Hours went by and then my mother, clearly annoyed, called from downstairs, "Rosemary, what are you doing? Haven't you finished yet?"

I shoved the book under the mattress and hurried to finish whichever bed was in front of me. This way, it took me many Saturdays to reach the end. I liked that book and I liked the main character, the laconic American, and that wonderful opening sentence, He lay on the pine-needle floor of the forest. I was intrigued by the war scenes, knowing nothing at that time of the Spanish Civil War. I was further intrigued with Maria and wondered why her head had been shaved, and I couldn't understand why she would get into his sleeping bag with him, but I decided it would be better to not ask any of the adults.

There was little access to culture in our valley unless one counted the hockey games and dramas on the radio or the quilting bees the women held each winter, or my piano. Everyone listened to the radio, and most of the villagers liked country and western music. There was some affinity for Scottish fiddle music, but nothing like the passion of my Cape Breton Island relatives, where the fiddle and the bagpipe ruled the airwaves. But above all, there were card games. These were the glue and the fiber that kept the adults functioning and relatively sane in those long weeks of winter. Perhaps my mother was the prime organizer because every Friday evening there was a "card party," where eight to twelve adults would gather at someone's house to play Auction 45, with prizes of some type for the winner of each of the rounds.

Our mother was a genius at cards; later in life, she became a winning bridge player and she regularly trumped me at cribbage when I visited her from New York. I can no longer remember how to play Auction 45, although we youngsters played it regularly as well. Like bridge, it did involve remembering who played what suit, so there was definite skill involved, not just the luck of the draw. Mother regularly came home from these Friday-night card parties with a chocolate cake or a smoked ham or jars of mustard pickles, whatever the prize of the night. Then one Saturday morning, as we sleepily appeared for breakfast, she said, "Rosemary and Malcolm, you have to go over to MacEacherns this morning and pick up my prize from last night's card games. I won two chickens."

Malcolm and I set off on our skis across the intervale, knocked on the back door, and told Mrs. MacEachern that we were there to collect our mother's prize from last night's card game.

"Well, you will have to go out to the barn. Danny [her husband] is out there. He will get it for you."

So we went, as told, and found Mr. MacEachern, who said, "Follow me. They're in the hen house." And there, inside the smelly hen house, he took a burlap bag and cornered two squawking hens, not chickens as my mother had said, and stuffed them inside the bag.

Somehow, we got home, taking turns holding on to the bag with two furious hens inside. "What happens now? Mother didn't say that her prize was live chickens," I said to Malcolm as we made our way over the snowy fields on the way home.

Mother met us at the back door. She looked at the burlap bag with the noisy hens and said: "Well, they didn't say the chickens were alive, so you two will just have to kill them. Get out the axe and cut off their heads on the chopping block. Then you can help me pluck the feathers. I know how to dress a chicken."

Mother had been brought up on a farm, although she never claimed to be a farmer of animals. Her father and brothers took care of that part of the farm, while her mother's task was to milk the cows and collect the eggs from the hen house. Our mother and her sisters tended to the large vegetable gardens and the berry fields and drove the horses and wagon during haymaking season. Malcolm and my little sisters and I lived in a farming community, but we just had our small plot of land and we planted vegetables and some flowers each year or helped out the neighbors by driving the horse and wagon or tractor in hay season, or, one summer, picking the cultivated strawberries at the farm next door, for which we would be paid a few cents per box. We were completely sheltered from the more brutal aspects of farm life, whether it was the "preparation" of chickens or pigs or the mating of bulls and cows.

"You mean we have to cut off their heads?" we asked our mother. We were incredulous.

"Just do it swiftly, so they don't suffer," said Mother as she closed the back door firmly.

Malcolm got the axe from the coal shed and then we both just stood there, the noisy fluttering burlap bag between us and the chopping block, which suddenly looked fearsome, like a guillotine. Neither of us moved. Finally, I said: "If I hold the first hen, will you chop its head off? Then if you hold the next hen, I will take the axe to it." And that is what we did, amid the furious noise and the frantic squawking. At least both of us were proficient with the axe, since one of our daily chores was to chop wood blocks into kindling to be used both for the kitchen stove and the living room furnace. For that task, we kept the axe well sharpened.

I pulled one hen by its neck out of the burlap bag, struggling to get hold of its cold rubbery legs. The hen was furious and frantic, almost as if she knew what was to happen. I slammed the poor creature down on the chopping block, closed my eyes tight, and yelled to Malcolm, "Now!"

I guess Malcolm swung hard and accurately, for when I opened my eyes, the head was off. I let go of the legs and to our horror, the hen began to fly around us. I was taller than my brother, so I leaped up to catch the body of the hen, just as it thankfully fell toward the ground.

By the time we finished with the second hen, there was blood spattered all over the stacked wood and the kindling and on our faces and clothes. We knocked on the back door, told our mother that we were finished and that the chickens were there by the chopping block, but said we didn't want to pluck them. In the cold air of the late morning, we both silently walked down the road to the brook, found a section that had not frozen, and splashed the icy water on our faces and over the front of our jackets. We said nothing to each other, went back home and to our rooms and the sudden safety of our schoolbooks and our homework.

Sunday, after coming back from Mass at the Maryvale Church, we all were sent to our rooms to do our homework while Mother prepared dinner. I could smell the pleasant aroma of roast chicken, so I knew there would be mashed potatoes and maybe turnips to go with it and certainly gravy.

When mother called us to dinner, we all eagerly gathered around the table. "It's a special dinner today," our mother said. "I have made an apple pie for dessert. And a big surprise! We have the roast chickens that I won at the card game on Friday night." Malcolm and I looked at the roast chickens on the platter, then at each other. He put his head down; my heart fell. I loved roast chicken and was hungry, but not for these chickens. I noticed that my brother did what I was doing, quietly passing on the plates of sliced chicken and the gravy boat to the next person, while we ate our mashed potatoes and turnips and later the apple pie. We were both quiet throughout the meal. I am not sure if our mother noticed that we didn't eat the chicken or take any gravy, although she must have noticed how unaccustomedly quiet, we both were. She never again referred to that Sunday's chicken dinner. But we also noticed that she never again came home with live chickens as her winning prize from the Friday-night card games.

Skiing for the Milk

Where I grew up, milk came from the cows on the nearby farms. The cows were milked mostly by the women of the household. The milk was carried in pails to the little dairy building next to the barn, called the creamery, to be "separated" — that is, the raw milk was poured through a steel machine that somehow separated the rich cream from the whole milk. No one ever made milk with 1 percent or 2 percent fat in those days, much less skim milk. And no one, to the best of my knowledge, pasteurized the milk that was to be used for household consumption, in that little dairy shed. Instead, most of the milk was poured into large steel cans, perhaps three feet high and covered tightly. Every two or three days, one or two of the farmers would gather up these cans from the village and bring them into the commercial creamery in the nearby town, some seven miles away, where it was then pasteurized and bottled as whole milk, with the rich cream sold separately in pint or half-pint bottles at the town's grocery stores.

Since our half-acre or so was large enough to grow vegetables but much too small to hold any farm animals, we bought our milk and cream from the Purcell's farm. On summer mornings, my two younger sisters and I would leisurely walk hand-in-hand down the road, cross over the small wooden bridge that spanned our village brook, then take a right turn at Joseph Purcell's road and climb the long hill up to the Purcell's house and barn. If the daisies or clover were in bloom, we would pick a bouquet for Mrs. Purcell, holding them up to see her smile and thank us sweetly and maybe offer us some freshly baked cookies when we knocked at the kitchen door of the house. She would then send us to the creamery shed, where Mr. Purcell had finished the separation process, to wait shyly while he packed the three quarts of milk and a pint of cream in my knapsack and wished us a good day.

On the return trip, we picked a bouquet of white daisies and purple clover for our mother. My younger sister, Donnie, would lean over the bridge to check on how the tadpoles were growing and whether there were any rainbow trout to be seen so she could tell our brother.

In the warm days of spring and early fall, we made the trip after school, hurrying along so that we could get home to help our mother prepare dinner and then do our homework ("The Teacher's kids" always did their homework). But often we hurried the trip because those were the seasons that the farmers spread manure over the fields for fertilizer and "it didn't smell like daisies," as my little sister, Louise, would say.

Late fall, winter, and early spring presented different challenges. Since I was the eldest, it became my job to go for the milk alone, fighting my way up the hill during the blustery rains of November or March and then on skis once the snow fell. In those winter months, my mother would strap the old army knapsack on my back and cinch the clasps at my waist, putting in the three or four empty glass bottles that she wrapped in newspaper to protect me. "In case you fall," Mother would say with a tone of voice that said, "Of course you must not fall."

After a big snowfall, I had to be extra careful during the first part of the trip on the level stretch of road leading to the wooden bridge to be sure that I was in fact on the bridge and not on a snowbank that was directly over the brook. In winter, the brook, unlike the lazy stream of summer, was filled to the banks with snow but not always iced over. When I turned right to begin the stretch up the long hill, I would make "herringbone" tracks with the skis to navigate the climb. Where did I learn that? I was surprised, many years later, to see footage of accomplished skiers and learn that this was the way they climbed a hill. None of the adults in the valley were skiers, and in these pre-television days, such video views did not exist.

Once up the hill and in front of the house, I would wave to Mrs. Purcell, whom I could see through her kitchen window. On a crisp morning, I would go directly to the creamery shed, although there were some bitterly cold days when Mrs. Purcell would signal me to ski to the back door where she would pass me a mug of hot chocolate. Mr. Purcell would pack the filled bottles into the knapsack on my back and warn me kindly, "Now best not to fall, Rosemary."

There are many kinds of snow. We read in our schoolbooks that the Eskimos had many different words for snow. Skiing along on a frosty morning on fresh snowfall that had fallen over a good, built-up base was always the most pleasant and the most fun. But there were winter days in that valley in Nova Scotia when the temperature suddenly moved up to the mid-forties and I had to lift each ski and rub off three to four inches of wet snow that were stuck to the bottoms. In those conditions, no amount of fresh wax would enable the skis to glide along; I simply clomped from foot to foot or in frustration took off the skis, put them on my shoulder, and stumbled along in the wet snow. The next day could be the opposite. A sudden freeze overnight would turn the snow on Purcell's hill into a sheet of icy glass, so that it was necessary to tack up the hillside, much as a sloop must do in a short wind and go back down the hill in a long *S* curve, horizontal for few yards, then do a careful turn and, using the ski poles as leverage, step down a foot or two before reversing the horizontal path. It took at least three times as long to get home on snow like that.

Setting out during a real blizzard was more a test of character than a test of skiing ability. In a blizzard, the wind is whipping the snow around, wiping out visibility, stinging the face, and blocking the breath. Where is the bridge? I needed to be sure I was on the wooden bridge and not directly over the swollen brook. If the snow was already deep, I could no longer see the alder branches that we had put in the snow to mark the low railings of the bridge. With the wind howling and the snow swirling in front of my face and already piling in drifts, Purcell's hill looked twice as long and twice as high. There were times when it was tempting to just sit down in one of the snowbanks and wait until the storm passed. But we'd heard stories about that, of people found frozen to death in some outer pasture or wood trail just because they stopped for a rest. I knew my mother would be worried about me and we needed the milk, so I clutched the ski poles and kept skiing up the hill.

"How was it, Sis?" my younger brother would sometimes ask.

"No big deal," I'd say, but then once thought to say, "Perhaps next time you could come with me? It would be easier if I had company."

I don't know if the Eskimo vocabulary on snow covers the following circumstance, but in all those years, the worst I ever encountered was one afternoon, the day after a blizzard, when the sun had come out around noontime, melting some of the top snow, but then was followed by a cold wind that came whipping up to blow some of the fallen snow in small drifts. That wind swept through other sections, leaving a smooth, icy top. I had just begun the descent, full milk bottles in the knapsack on my back, thinking that this was good skiing. I had freshly waxed skis and the snow at the top of the hill was cold and powdery, just fine for the downhill part. Suddenly I was on ice crust and flying over this patch at almost double the speed. Then my skis hit a patch of dry-packed snow and I came to a stop so suddenly that I was thrown sideways into a drift of snow, luckily, and not on the ice crust. Lucky also that I fell sideways. I quickly moved over on my face to keep the milk bottles from breaking. Getting up was difficult because the skis were crossed under and behind me. I struggled to open the clamps to my boots, took off the skis, hoisted them on my shoulder, picked up the knapsack, and struggled home through the banks of snow.

My mother's face was pressed to the kitchen window, watching my progress up the road from the bridge, and my brother and two sisters were standing anxiously by the kitchen door as I came through the porch. They helped me take the milk bottles out from the knapsack and set them on the shelf. Not one of the bottles had broken or showed even a crack or chip.

"Are you okay, Sis? Was it bad skiing? You were carrying the skis," my brother said.

"Guess what," I said, out of breath and longing to sit by the stove to get warm. "This time next year I'll be away at college and you kids will get to ski for the milk."

Years later when I was living in Virginia, my roommate announced she was going cross-country skiing in the western part of the state. "What is cross-country skiing?" I asked. She was a teacher of tennis, golf, and synchronized swimming. This must be another sport.

"Oh, it's just skiing across fields and up and down little hills. It's not at all like downhill skiing."

I thought about this for a few minutes, then said, "Oh. Where I grew up, it was called 'skiing for the milk.'"

Music Lessons

I began music lessons the fall I was seven and entering the fourth grade. Somewhere, somehow, my mother had found a piano, an old upright with real ivory keys and beautiful mahogany wood. I have no memory of when or under what circumstances the piano was delivered to our house and brought into the living room, where it occupied the wall across from the kitchen. I do remember some scratches on that wood casing and every so often I would assist my mother in rubbing those scratches with an oil-based furniture polish, which had a strong odor that permeated the entire length of our rectangular-shaped living room. Those odors would fade once we began burning coal in the great cylindrical stove that served as our central heating system during the cold months of November and the very cold months of winter. But that lingering scent of oil always spoke of the piano and I would be drawn to play even before my homework, or my assigned chores were finished.

Nor do I remember when I first learned to play any piece of music. Did I start picking out some basic song lines, even before the music lessons began? I just remember always playing some song or other.

But starting those music lessons, and my travels to those lessons, are vivid memories. The only place to take music lessons was in the nearby town, Antigonish, our hometown, which was seven miles away from our valley.

The year I was seven, our mother did not yet have a car. She taught at the school that was almost next door to our house, so she was able to walk to work. My music lessons were on Saturday mornings at the women's college, Mount St. Bernard, which was part of St. Francis Xavier University in Antigonish. Mount St. Bernard was operated by the Sisters of Notre Dame, a French order based out of Montreal. Several years later, this women's college would be my residence, with its music halls and chapels and winding stairs and mysterious corridors, when I went to the university.

My mother must have taken me for my first lesson, for how else would I know which entrance to use and how to find my way up the various stairways and through the corridors of Immaculata Hall to the music room and my teacher? But my memories are mostly of being alone once I arrived at "the Mount," as it was called, and of navigating those long halls and staircases by myself, hoping that I had remembered the route properly and would not make a mistake by opening the wrong door.

That first year, when the weather in October and November was still mild enough, I traveled to my music lessons with Ranley Mac Donald, who had a two-ton truck and on Saturdays delivered cans of milk for several of the farmers in the valley to the creamery in Antigonish. Sometimes I was able to ride in the cab with Ranley and one of his sons, but if his wife was going along for a shopping trip to the town, I rode on the back of the truck with his sons amid the steel cylinders of milk.

When the snow arrived, either in December or January, I went into town with Mr. Baxter, who lived down the road from our house and who was the mailman for the valley. In the spring to fall months when the roads were clear, Mr. Baxter drove a carriage with his team of horses, and some Saturdays, when Ranley did not have any milk to deliver, I rode in the carriage with Mr. Baxter. But come winter, and with snow covering the roads, Mr. Baxter hitched his team of sturdy horses to a sleigh. I would walk down the road through the snow to meet him at his gate and climb up into the sleigh. He had an old black bearskin rug, and he would say, kindly, "Now just tuck yourself in there and stay warm," and off we would go, around the curves and the small rises and dips that marked the seven-mile trip to the town.

I remember those days with fondness. Mr. Baxter was a friendly old gentleman, with white hair and a white mustache. He was kind to me and kind to his horses, talking them through the dark patches of spruce and pine trees that would loom up at us from the sides of the road, especially on days when we were traveling through a snowstorm, or worse still, through a blizzard of driving snow. The horses would be spooked by the dark trees that swayed and rustled in the winter winds or maybe it was the stress from the snowdrifts that made their footing difficult. I would snuggle under the blanket, trying to keep my hands and fingers warm, watching the horses' tails move back and forth. I think I was always anticipating the piano lessons, worrying that maybe I had not practiced enough to be good at those basic Bach or Mozart pieces and that the music teacher would be cross at me again.

Were the nuns mostly unkind to me in those years? I always felt uncomfortable. I felt that they considered me of a lower class or certainly an odd creature from the country who was far removed from their accustomed urban territory. The nun who was my music teacher was stern and enforced discipline. I was expected to play all of the assigned exercises precisely and crisply, with no wrong notes, and to have prepared my written assignments with perfectly drawn music clefs and rest stops. If my fingers strayed onto the black keys when I was supposed to be in the key of *C*, she would strike my knuckles with the steel edge of a ruler, scolding me for not having practiced more.

Yet, there were also glimmers of kindness. One day when I arrived in a blizzard, a young, sweet-natured nun met me at the back door that I used as my entrance to Immaculata Hall. She seemed astonished by my snow-covered clothes and no doubt red nose and cheeks, especially when she discovered that I had traveled seven miles from the country in a horse and sleigh. She stopped to help me take off the jacket and boots and had me sit down near the radiator while she went to the kitchen area, bringing back a bowl of hot soup and some crackers, saying, "Here dear. You must have something warm. And you can wrap your hands around that soup bowl so that your fingers will be warm for your piano lesson."

Another week, on a bitterly cold morning, when she also answered the door, she brought me a cup of steaming cocoa with a froth of real cream on top. It smelled delicious, and again, provided a warm enclosure for my cold fingers. It must have also eased the dread of the stern music teacher's criticisms and that painful crack across my knuckles when my piano exercises were less than perfect.

I grew to hate Bach, and then Mozart. I did practice those pieces at home on the upright piano, but probably never enough to fully master the fingering and the precise staccato needed for the Bach or the intricate movements needed for the Mozart. And I did learn to sight-read, although I think I was always slow to recognize quickly enough the more complex chords and arpeggios until I could get the music into my memory. It was many years later, living in New York City and having the opportunity to go to Lincoln Center or Carnegie Hall or some of the great organ concerts at one of the many churches in the city, that I could listen to Bach fugues or Mozart concertos without shuddering at the memories of that steel-tipped ruler.

But in those early days, I never heard a symphony or an etude played by a professional or on a record or anywhere on our local radio station, which played mostly jigs and reels and country and western music. But the biggest pitfall for my mastery of fugues and sonatinas was the joy I found playing contemporary music: pop songs, country ballads, old-fashioned standards, and Celtic jigs that I played at home every evening and every weekend. My fingers picked out the melodies and the chords without any written music, all based on songs that I heard on the radio.

I was thirteen before we had a record player and early 78 platters, as by then, the valley was finally wired for electricity, so most of the music I learned was coming from the radio station CJFX in Antigonish.

The radio was always on as we were having breakfast and then getting ready for school, and later, when I was in high school and we had a car with a radio, we listened during the eight-mile drive to the high school in the next village. The radio station played pop music, and ethnic music around any special holiday such as St. Patrick's Day or St. Andrews Day, and in the month before Christmas, we heard the latest seasonal songs such as "Rudolf the Red-Nosed Reindeer" or "Frosty the Snowman," offered along with the familiar carols.

On Saturday afternoons, CJFX had a two- or three-hour show of the top 40 hits. I volunteered to do all of the family ironing then so that I could listen to the radio. Eartha Kitt, Connie Francis, Frankie Laine, the young Tony Bennett, Gogi Grant, Kay Starr, Doris Day, Patti Page — these were the singers of our early teen years, and we learned every word of their songs while I worked out the chord structures on the piano.

There was a special category of World War II and World War I songs, and the big band songs of the 1930s and 1940s, which were played during an early-evening program on CJFX. These were not considered "old" music, but rather were treated as contemporary, as if those decades were existing alongside the pop songs of the 1950s. But my special source of music over the radio came after nine at night. By then, the airwaves became exceptionally clear, and I could pick up WNEW in New York City and the William B. Williams Show. This came through as a direct line, as the signal traveled up the Atlantic from the city to Nova Scotia. When it arrived, that signal was as clear as if it were coming from a nearby town. Between nine and at least ten in the evening, the outer limits of my bedtime, there would be a cornucopia of music — early jazz and the great bands of the 1930s through 1950s; and the great vocalists from the previous three decades, ranging from Crosby to Sinatra to Dick Haymes, Billie Holliday to Dinah Shore, and the music from what is today known as The Great American Song Book: Irving Berlin, Hoagy Carmichael, Johnny Mercer, Sammy Kahn, or Harold Arlen. I would lean toward the old crystal radio set, keeping the volume fairly low since my younger brother and sisters were already in bed. My fingers explored the chords on the piano, as silently as possible, trying to sort out the open seventh chords and the diminished ninths.

I learned those terms many years later, but in those early years, I worked out the chord structures and learned hundreds of songs, trying out several each weekend. I always had encouragement from my mother, whose favorites were all from the war years or the 1930s.

And then there was church music. This emerged without the benefit of music lessons from the nuns (they continued with the Mozart and Bach), when the local parish priest decided he wanted music and a proper High Mass, sung in Latin, with an organist and a choir. My mother said to him, "Well, Rosemary could learn that music on the organ, and I could help her put together a choir."

So there I was, on the Christmas Eve when I was turning thirteen, frightened beyond words at the prospect of the grumpy old priest turning around from the altar to glare at me and the choir as I was pumping the pedals on the old moth-eaten organ where, we were convinced, the neighborhood mice camped out for the winter, and hoping beyond bearing that old Mike McGuire, who insisted on singing in our choir of eleven- and twelve-year-old's, would stay on key, and above all, hit the high notes of "O Holy Night," which he considered his specialty. Somehow, we got through it all that Christmas Eve, and with my mother's help, we learned the Latin words for the High Mass and the carol "Adeste Fidelis." I was to remain the church organist until I went to university two years later.

Yet, I did practice for my music lessons: the scales and arpeggios, the Bach and the Mozart, and, more happily, the Shubert and Mendelssohn pieces when those were finally introduced. Each spring my mother entered me in the county-wide music festival, which featured a piano competition as well as singing and poetry reading. The year I was a junior in high school, I came in second in the piano solos, losing to a young man from the town. I was stung by losing as well as by his smug confidence in winning as he accepted the first-prize certificate. I resolved to do better, to win the competition the next year. If the music teacher said I must practice more, then that is what I would do. Scales, arpeggios, even the Bach.

But meanwhile, another opportunity arrived: I was asked to accompany fiddlers at country dances. Again, that music was not part of my music lessons at "the Mount," but jigs and reels were part of our culture, and in between Bach and Hoagy Carmichael, I would limber up with the piano version of some local violinists' repertoire, reproducing the melodies as well as the chord structures. The summers that I was thirteen and fourteen, I earned all of my pocket money playing country dances, accompanying the fiddlers on the piano, with my mother keeping a careful eye on the proceedings from the sidelines.

The summer that I was fourteen and a half was the beginning of my career as a party pianist. I was at home with the younger siblings one Saturday evening in July, in charge of the family while my mother attended a wedding party in the next village. I was just putting down my book to go to bed when a car pulled into the driveway and a young couple, whom I knew, knocked on the door.

"Your mother says that you are to come to the wedding reception; they do not have a pianist and they need you to play for the party."

I went upstairs and shook my thirteen-year-old brother awake and said, "Malcolm. You are now in charge. I have to go to the wedding; don't light any candles or the stove while I am away."

I put on a summer dress and sandals, brushed my hair, locked the front door behind me, and drove with the young couple to the next village to be greeted by cheery partygoers. That was a long night of playing with the fiddler, and then, as soloist leading a round of popular songs to end the festivities.

The first year I was in college, my mother asked if I could come home for a weekend to play at a party for her teachers' group. They were having a dinner and card game but would then appreciate a sing-along to end the evening. I sought permission to go home for the weekend and spent the evening playing my own version of pop tunes and the great World War II-era songs. Then, one of the male teachers, my mother's colleague and a veteran of that war, asked: "Do you know 'The North Atlantic Squadron?'" I knew lots of WWII songs, but this one was new.

"I will sing it for you, then you can play it and we will all sing it," he said as he swung into the verse and melody.

Make way, make way, for fife and drum. Here we come, full of rum, looking for ladies...

I was picking out the melody line and the chord structure and those assembled around the piano with me were launching into a rousing rendition when suddenly, there was my mother, who had been out in the kitchen helping the other women prepare a late-evening lunch. "Jack, whatever are you doing teaching that girl those songs?" she asked. I was graduated from college before I learned the rest of those forbidden lyrics.

During my final year of high school, I furiously practiced scales and arpeggios in preparation for the Music Festival competition. I was determined to win this year, to best that arrogant young man from the junior-year competition.

My selection was a fairly modern Scottish classical piece, a lament whose Gaelic title I no longer remember. This was an intricate and haunting piece that demanded excellent finger work and the capacity to modulate chords as well as tempo to understand the emotion behind the lament.

I won that competition. I can still remember the hushed silence in the music hall when I finished that last, sad chord. I remember the sight of my usually stoic mother with unaccustomed tears in her eyes. Above all, there was my stern music teacher, she of the ever-ready ruler across the cold knuckles, first lowering her head, and then lifting up to look at me directly, and starting to clap along with the rest of the audience.

Middle School in the One-Room Schoolhouse

When I was in the 7th through 9th grades, my mother left our hamlet school to teach in the village over the mountain range, a daily drive of almost nine miles in often difficult weather. During those three years, she closely monitored my homework and that of my brother and sisters to be sure we were being properly and thoroughly taught. She would supplement homework and math exercises if she found that the replacement teachers were remiss in any area, particularly when I was in the 8th and 9th grades.

The teacher for my 7th-grade year asked to board at our house, which meant that I gave up my bedroom for her and shared a bed in the open loft area with my youngest sister, Louise. That was the least of our problems that year, since this teacher, Miss MacDonald, was a grouchy, middle-aged spinster who dictated the same strict rules of behavior when she was at home with us in the evening as she did during school hours. While we always did our homework for our mother, during this year we were ordered, nightly, to sit at the kitchen table after dinner and not leave until she, the teacher, and not our mother, was satisfied that the work was finished. We were all quietly miserable, softened only by weekend time with our mother when "The Grouchy Miss" as we called her, went to stay with friends she claimed she had in the nearby town.

As grouchy as she was, and a strict disciplinarian, she was also a superb teacher. The 7th-grade grammar and spelling lessons she gave were so thorough that they carried me through the rest of middle school, into high school, and through my college placement tests to be assigned to an advanced sophomore literature course. Spelling drills may have terrified us, but we became adept at a sweeping range of vocabulary. In those days in our pragmatic Canadian education, we learned all of our spelling in both English and American versions: labour, labor; arbour, arbor, aluminium, aluminum. The English spelling was always to come first, but in most cases, our pronunciation was closer to the American. This got me in severe trouble with Miss Grouch on one of my days up in front of the class:

"L-i-e-u-t-e-n-a-n-t," I spelled, "pronounced LOO-ten-ant."

"It most certainly is not!" said Miss Grouch so loudly that all of the children in all of the grades looked up from their assignments, startled. "It is pronounced LEFT-ten-ant."

"Miss," I said with confidence, "in the U.S., it is pronounced LOO- ten-ant."

She stormed over to me and struck me over my left ear. I was so shocked that I can still feel the sting of that physical rebuke decades later. But I did forgive her, finally, when visiting my mother many years later, I learned that Miss MacDonald, long since retired, was planning to move back to the province where she was born and where she still had some distant relatives. I called her right away and invited her to join

Mother and me for lunch the next day and said I would drive down to pick her up and bring her to the house. I prepared a plate of fresh-cooked lobster and homemade potato salad, with stewed rhubarb and cookies for dessert. She was touched and left me that day with sadness in her eyes as well as gratitude in her voice.

"You were always one of my best pupils," she said, "and I am so proud of you." We were stunned to learn that two days after moving to her ancestral home, she died suddenly.

During the eighth and ninth grades, we had two different teachers, young and inexperienced, each just out of teacher's college. We suddenly had the opposite problem of not having enough discipline in the class. The boys became unruly, the girls would whisper back and forth to each other during lessons. At night, my mother found it necessary to double up on our homework assignments.

"You must do these extra exercises," she would say to us, clearly worried. "You cannot fall behind in your work."

The lack of discipline soon carried over to problems in the schoolyard during our recess and lunch periods. The young teachers would stay inside, not providing any supervision to our play or trying to resolve little spats. One of the 8th-grade boys became a particular problem.

I was thirteen that spring; he was older than me by two years. I was just as tall, and we both were much taller than the boys in the 7th and 8th grades. I was over in another area of the playground organizing hopscotch with the younger girls, when this boy, Danny, was arm wrestling the boys and hurting them. I heard them plead with him to stop. I went over to the writhing mix of boys and said to Danny, "Stop it. You're hurting them. They're smaller than you."

"Mind your own business," he snarled back to me as he twisted young Frankie McAllister's arm behind his back. I leaped at Danny, pulled Frankie away, and I guess I punched Danny in the nose, since it began to bleed, then punched him in the stomach and kicked his shins. He began to howl in pain. I ordered him to leave the schoolyard and go home and watched him slink up the hill, looking back at us furtively. The young boys looked at me in amazement, quietly picked up their jackets, and headed back inside. I said nothing, but when Mother came home from her school, my younger sisters told her what had happened.

"Rosemary beat up Danny, the bully," they said. Mother was furious with me.

"Whatever were you thinking? You are the older one. You are supposed to be taking care of everyone in the school. Girls don't get into fights."

She was not going to remember that I was two years younger than the school bully. I was in disfavor with her for days, as were my younger sisters with me for tattling, but Danny the bully never came near those boys for the rest of the spring term. He dropped out of school that summer and left the village to find work in Ontario.

Summer in the Valley

If the sun was shining the day after school finished for the year, June 25 or so, depending on how many snow days we had to make up each year, we would lace up our tennis shoes and put on our oldest pair of jeans, find some sort of hat and plastic cups, and one or two pails, and head off to the pasture at Ranley MacDonald's to pick wild strawberries. The best berry fields in the valley were here, a trek down the gravel road of just under a mile. Mother would make sure we had a container of water and maybe some sandwiches since she hoped we would keep picking long enough to have our lunch there and try to fill at least one pail with the small, sweet berries. She would caution us not to start eating them as we were picking, "or you'll never put any in that pail," she would say. I eventually learned that she was right about this and found that if I resisted the temptation to have even one, or at least until I was finished picking for the day and just about ready to start for home, I could fill a small pail.

One great part of picking the wild strawberries was finding a large patch of ripe berries and sitting in the middle of it, picking everything around us before moving on to the next patch, but not before Donnie and I would gingerly walk around the patch to be sure there were no garter snakes nearby.

"They won't hurt you," our mother constantly reminded us, but no matter, we could not have been more terrified than if the pastures or the hayfields were populated by cobras. Neither Donnie nor I would ever again go near one quadrant of the Baxter's hayfield, where one day a grass snake slithered away just as we walked by.

That first day when we arrived home with our pail, triumphant, Mother would make her special baking powder biscuits for a strawberry shortcake topped with whipped cream from

Mr. Purcell's thick, rich cream. But that was the only time we would have these berries fresh since all the rest that we could pick in the coming days were to be used for strawberry jam, one of Mother's specialties and a treat for Sunday breakfasts during the cold winter months. We came home, perhaps in triumph, but always covered in bites from the little black flies that were the torment of June and with sunburned noses, arms, and ankles. Louise, the youngest, would be whimpering in misery from the fly bites, which seemed to affect her more than the rest of us.

"They're getting up my nose and, in my eyes, and ears," she would wail, while Donnie or I would sponge her bites with some of our precious drinking water.

And so began our golden summers, when we four children were growing up in Pleasant Valley: summers of picking berries, playing softball or going to the softball league games on Sunday afternoons, fishing for trout along the brook that ran through the valley, and on days when Mother was available and not cooking bread and the weather was hot, packing a picnic lunch and heading for a swim in the Northumberland Strait at Doctor's Cove, favored over the beach at Arisaig, which sometimes was left strewn with pebbles after the spring ice pack had receded.

Doctor's Brook offered us the choice of swimming in the freshwater pool that formed before the brook entered the ocean and preferred if the ocean water was still too cold for comfort. Most visitors considered the waters of the Northumberland Strait to always be too cold for comfort, but by August, we would find the temperature bearable.

Picking raspberries, the next crop of the summer berry season, offered a different set of challenges. The best and largest of the wild raspberries grew in the old wood cuttings up on the mountain above Purcell's farm, so first, we would have a long climb before even reaching the area. Next, we needed to stand on fallen logs to reach up to the ripe berries on the canes, get scratched from the thorns, and every so often, sink into the ground when an old rotten log gave out from under us. "More scratches when we fall," we would cry out to one another.

Then there were the wasps, who also liked the raspberries and would surround us in fury. More than once during the day, one of us would be stung, forcing us to drop our cup of precious berries on the ground and howl in pain. Our mother taught us to get a handful of soil, spit on it to form a paste, and plaster this over the wasp sting. It usually worked, easing the worst of the sting and allowing us to go back to filling the pail. The goal was also the jam that Mother would make and the knowledge of how great that raspberry jam would taste on toasted home-made bread on a winter's morning.

By August, the wild blueberries would have ripened, so we headed up a different mountain to the large pasture behind the Connolly's farm, where blueberry bushes grew wild with the small, tasty berries. These were easier to pick, even though it meant getting down on our knees to gather the small berries into our plastic cups and then pour them into the larger pail, but only after Donnie and I did our serpent reconnaissance.

Wasps seemed to be less of a problem in the blueberry fields; instead, our mother warned us of another possible predator: the black bear. Rumors were that a family of bears, including cubs, lived in the woods around that pasture and, as Mother said, "Bears like blueberries, too."

But, in all of our years picking on that mountain, we never saw a bear or bear cubs. And, at any rate, we were so determined to have at least one pailful of berries so that Mother would make us a blueberry pie and Donnie and I could make blueberry muffins that we staked our position amid those low bushes without fear.

Sunny summer mornings would find Mother and me weeding and hoeing in our vegetable garden, where in early June, once we were sure that the frosty nights were past, we had planted seeds for leaf lettuce, peas in the pod, string beans, carrots, beets, radishes, potatoes, tomatoes, pumpkins, and corn. Each July we watched the corn seedlings sprout and with eager anticipation followed the corn stalks as they grew tall and began to produce small corn cobs. But never once did those corn stalks on the cornrow produce a full-sized edible ear of corn, only these small stubbles that soon withered with worms. We had to buy our summer corn at the grocery store on our Saturday shopping trips.

Oh, how we hated weeding the smelly lamb's-quarters that were the first to flourish in the garden. There were mornings when Donnie, three years younger than me, might join us to pull up some young radishes or check on the tomatoes, but the lamb's-quarters would soon send her away to play with Louise. Malcolm would already be long gone to the brook with his homemade fishing pole made from an alder branch and the can of worms he had dug out in the garden.

"We grow vegetables in our garden," we would tease Malcolm, "you grow worms." He was not about to be cajoled into pulling out lamb's-quarters. But the early crop of leaf lettuce and radishes made for a delicious summer salad — our mother would make a dressing of white vinegar with sugar — and gave us confidence that this labor in the garden would pay off with the tomatoes as they fleshed out and ripened in August along with the beets and carrots, ready by late summer, that would help carry us through the winter.

Summertime also brought the promise of fresh fish, not just the brook trout that Malcolm brought home most days and expected me to gut and clean so that he could pan-fry it for his dinner. The lobster season on our coast began in early May. In those early years of the 1950s, almost all of the lobster was immediately shipped out to Halifax and then to Montreal or Toronto and maybe to New York City or London. Our grocery store in the town never carried fresh fish in those days, much less lobster, but Mother would make arrangements each spring with the parents of one of her students who were lobster fishermen to save a few one-pounders for us to buy once the season was underway. That was always a high point of early summer for us: driving to the wharf at Arisaig or Ballantyne's Cove, marveling at the stacks of lobster pots and the smell of fresh fish. Sometimes the fisherman would have already boiled the lobsters for us, but on occasion, we brought the lobsters home live in a large pot of seawater to cook on our woodstove. So we would have "our feed of lobsters for this year," Mother would announce proudly as she brought the platter of the cooked, and now red, crustaceans, to the dinner table.

In midsummer, we would repeat this journey to one of the wharves to buy fresh-caught Atlantic salmon, which, again, was scarce for residents, since almost all fish were whisked off on overnight trucks for export. Mother would section the fish into large roasts and poach it for dinner with small new potatoes and freshly shelled peas from the garden. She would serve the salmon with a pat of melting butter and a wedge of lemon on each serving, then the remaining cooked salmon would be the centerpiece of salad dinners over the next day or two, but it had to be eaten in those two to three days since there was no refrigerator or even icebox in those years before electricity arrived.

We did not know of smoked salmon in those early years. It was not until I was teaching at William and Mary in Virginia and was invited out for my first-ever Sunday brunch of bagels and cream cheese that I was greeted with, "You're from Nova Scotia so you must like Nova Scotia lox." I had never heard of Nova Scotia lox and struggled mightily that first time to swallow those salty bites without gagging.

Nor did we know of the varieties of shellfish that even then existed in our inshore waters, including clams, mussels, oysters, and crabs, although we later learned that Malpeque oysters were being harvested in Prince Edward Island and exported to the major cities across Canada. Years later, the local lobster fishermen discovered that a lucrative market existed for the queen crab legs that they used to throw away from their lobster pots or their nets and began to ship these delicacies out to the export market.

We spent many a summer morning making cotton dresses or skirts cut from Simplicity Patterns and sewn on the pedaled

Singer sewing machine we kept set up in the dining room, next to the ironing board that stood ready for use throughout each day. One summer, our mother found a flimsy voile material at Goodman's, a small department store on Main Street in Antigonish, which we could use as an overskirt to the cotton or seersucker base. We loved this store for its collection of buttons and grosgrain ribbons and enticing range of patterns, but best of all, for the pneumatic tubes that whizzed around the counters and up to the cashier's office on the second floor, carrying the written sales slip, the money for the purchase, and on the return run, our change, and a receipt.

I daydreamed constantly about the beautiful swirly dresses I would make, although my finished products always fell short of the imagined. Our little sister, Louise, was the exception; even at age six or seven, she would patiently sew and hem and finish her sleeves with uncanny precision. Louise would go on to make this her lifetime career, first working for Simplicity Patterns, then manufacturing women's clothes around the world for Simpson Sears or the Hudson's Bay stores of Montreal and Toronto, culminating in forming her own company and manufacturing in India.

But we also had our summer games to balance off the berry picking and small chores around the house. There was skipping rope in the small plot of grass to the right of the vegetable garden. We used our mother's blackboard chalk to draw a hopscotch diagram on the gravel road in front of the house, although this would turn to dust and blow away whenever a truck or car passed by. More durable were our pickup games of softball with our neighborhood classmates Edmund and Joe Gaudet, Hughie Dan, and Little Angus.

Angus was almost as tall as I was the summer I turned twelve and a half and grew to five-foot-six inches tall, and he was the first love of my life. He was called "little" because there was a middle-aged man with the same name in the valley who was called "Big Angus."

One day that summer, Little Angus invited me to join him on a fishing trip up the brook. Unlike my brother, he didn't seem to mind if I chattered away, said nothing about scaring away the fish, and he threaded the worms on my fishing hook. Malcolm would say to Donnie and me, "If you are scared of worms, then you can't go fishing with me."

That summer my feet grew to match my height, requiring size 9 shoes. Our Uncle Malcolm, Mother's brother, teased me without mercy when he visited that summer, singing, "Herring boxes, without tops-es, sandals were for Clementine."

Donnie was the early riser in the family on those summer mornings, up with the crows, as our mother would say, reading and rereading her copy of *Black Beauty,* sketching horses in her drawing pad. There were rare opportunities for her to ride a horse, but occasionally, when we were visiting Mrs. Baxter at their farm, John Baxter, the grown son who had taken over the farm after his father, our mailman had passed away, would bring out his quiet old mare and help hoist Donnie up for a ride around the barnyard. I climbed up with her once, but within minutes fell off, a bruised and embarrassed older sister.

"How could you fall off that old nag?" Malcolm asked, shaking his head.

Donnie spent hours poring over pictures of jeans and denim jackets in Eaton's catalog, and one year saved up her allowance for Mother to order her a set of colored glass studs that she could attach to her denim jacket. She would dress in her full denim outfit, wear an old straw hat, and pretend to be riding a horse on the top wooden railing of our fence at the north side of the house, under the old pine tree.

In our early teenage years, we progressed from ragtag games where the girls were part of the boys' team to more organized leagues for the boys and the girls. I had a brief career as the catcher for the girls' team, when in the second inning of the very first game, I whipped off the mask before the ball crossed the plate and the ball smashed into my nose, causing a mighty nosebleed, although no break. My mother, who was coaching, ordered me to the outfield for the next few games but also said that that I could practice pitching, and if I could get the ball across the plate, she might let me start a game as the pitcher. I developed a great left-handed curveball, which, the few times it crossed the plate, always resulted in a strike. But four out of five times, my brother said when he was watching, the ball sailed over the batter's head and into the backstop. He spent his time coaching Donnie, who became a more reliable and effective starting pitcher for our team in those last two summers before I went to university.

For most of those summers, Louise, the youngest, was the quiet onlooker at our games, lagging behind her older siblings when we went running down the road to see if the "swimming pool" we had dammed up in the brook held enough water, even two feet, for us to go swimming.

"Wait for me!" she would wail, and I would usually double back to pick her up, or as she grew older, hold her hand as we hurried down the road to catch up with Donnie and Malcolm. Louise was the quiet one in those years, watching the rest of us with her large brown eyes as we started a game of cards or jump rope, or her auburn head of curls would be bent over her dolls as she dressed and redressed them. In later years, she learned to make clothes for her dolls.

Then there was the summer morning when she was eight that she went with Donnie to the well up at the schoolyard, sharing the weight of the pail of water on the return trip. Did she stumble and fall into the ditch? Neither she nor Donnie could ever recall exactly what happened, but suddenly there were these terrible screams from up the road. I was in the back-yard, so closest to them, and went running. Louise had fallen on a metal spike that had been left upright in the ditch and blood was streaming down her leg. I could see the flesh torn from the gash as I picked her up in my arms and came running back to the house, calling for our mother who had been upstairs doing some chores. Louise was screaming in pain and fright, Donnie was screaming at the sight of the blood, Mother took one look and said, "We're going into town to the hospital. Malcolm, get my purse. All of you get in the car."

I held Louise in my lap for the seven-mile drive that seemed endless, pressing a wet dishtowel on her bleeding leg. Outside the emergency room, Malcolm, Donnie, and I sat hud-dled together on a bench, worried about how bad this could be, while the doctor put a dozen stitches in Louise's leg and or-dered a prescription of sulfa drugs to prevent infection. In those next days, once the pain had subsided, Louise quietly enjoyed the extra attention from her older siblings as we sat with her to play games of Chinese checkers or help while she held a tea party for her dolls.

The main feature of our summer Sunday afternoons was attending the grown-up softball league games, where our valley lads of eighteen to twenty-four played teams of young men from villages around the county. I learned to keep score, how I can't imagine, since we knew nothing of formal notation for scorekeeping except that K meant strikeout. I penciled in HR or 3B and similar for the variety of hits. My scorekeeping must have been fairly accepted because I do not recall any great arguments over how many outs had occurred or tallies of which young man had the highest scores. Malcolm helped me calculate batting averages when we got home on Sunday evenings.

Our trusty conveyance for these activities for several summers, as well as winters, was Mother's blue Plymouth coupe. Considering how small it looked from a distance, that car would hold the five of us, plus piles of softballs and bats and baseball gloves and maybe a catcher's mask, at least one jug of water or for some outings, a jug of lemonade in the small trunk. Mother was always an integral part of our summer games and outings, whether coaching, yelling support from the sidelines, sponging bloodied noses, or bandaging scraped knees.

Meanwhile, our mother had her own goals and assignments. Each summer she enrolled in a course or two at St. Francis Xavier University, and she would drive to the town of Antigonish at 8:30 each weekday morning, returning home after noontime. For most of those years I was old enough to take care of my three younger siblings. We would make our beds, sweep the floors, dust the furniture, and handwash our clothes, hang them on the line that stretched over the vegetable garden, then treat ourselves to a game of hopscotch.

Most of these mornings, Malcolm would dig for worms and go fishing along the brook. For three weeks of early summer and over several years, mostly after Louise had turned six and our young Aunt Norma could stay with us, Mother went to Wolfville in the Annapolis Valley to join a phalanx of teachers from around the province to correct the provincial exams taken in late June by every Grade XI student. This meant extra pay for her. When I was older, I thought to ask her if this wasn't also a great chance for her to be with adults all day and evening for a change.

"Yes," she agreed, but hurried to add, "of course, I missed you four and I always came home on weekends to be sure you were fine."

Those were the days before we had telephones or electricity, so communication was only by letter or postcard. She made several friends from these summers who remained close to her over the following decades.

Mother would also spend a few weeks of those summer afternoons on house decorating projects: new wallpaper for the living room or the kitchen, the dining room, and upstairs bedrooms. Each summer we tackled a different room. I remember to this day the long sheets of wallpaper stretched out on the kitchen table, upside down, and the smell and texture of the paste we smeared on with broad paintbrushes, then rushing with the saggy soggy sheets to the target room wall, one of us climbing up on the stepladder while Mother directed the exact placement. All too often, the wallpaper came in a pattern that had to be matched to each neighboring panel, with lots of scolding and subsequent wails of, "I'm trying to get this match right!" But we could hardly wait to wake up the next morning to inspect the dried wallpaper and the accuracy of our placement.

The walls of our house had been finished with basic gypsum board, so could not be painted. I used to dream of the day when we lived in a house with walls that we could paint. To this day, I loathe wallpaper and would not use it to line the insides of an outdoor privy, should I ever have to live in those primitive circumstances again.

The summer of 1952 was hot and dry. I was twelve and a half, tall, serious, starting to play piano with the violinists at barn dances, and since they would pay me a few dollars each time, I was earning spending money for school clothes and shoes for the fall. We were not accustomed to the unusual heat and pleaded with Mother to take us to the beach on the worst days, getting miserable sunburns in the process. Did we really use suntan oil in those days? Sunscreen was only invented many decades later.

And then the forest fires started, first in Georgeville, about twenty miles away to the northwest as the crow flies, and next on Sugarloaf, the small conical mountain that guards the town of Antigonish. We could see this fire from our front yard, some seven miles away to the east, and at night we watched the flames move up the side of the mountain. By this time, most of the men in the valley had gone to fight one or the other of the fires. The smoke from both fires began to filter into the valley, and then the third fire broke out, over the mountain to our south in Clydesdale, less than five miles away.

By the evening of the third day, the smoke was filling our valley and Mother quietly said to me, "I think we had better pack up some clothes and food and water, in case we have to leave," so I slipped upstairs and found pajamas and a change of clothes for all of us while she made sandwiches and a jug of lemonade for the thermos bottles. "But let's not worry the children just yet," she said. "Maybe they can even go to bed and try to sleep as usual." We decided that we might be safe as long as we didn't see flames coming from the Clydesdale fire, which would mean that the fire was starting to climb over to our side of the mountain range.

Rescue came later that night from thunderstorms and rain, even as Mother woke me, worried that the lightning might start more fires. But the rain fell heavily and lasted the rest of the night so that by morning, we could see from the smaller smoke plumes that the worst was over. By evening the men started to come back to the valley in their pickup trucks. One of the groups from Georgeville stopped at our house to tell us how bad that fire had been, how it threatened the church and the rectory and the one-room school, and how all they had to protect the buildings was their bucket brigade with water hand-pumped from the well in the schoolyard.

The scars of both the Georgeville and Sugarloaf fires could be seen for decades, first as blackened stumps of trees and fields, then in later years, outlined in the bright green of deciduous trees, many of which were the fast-growing poplars that had grown on the fire site, contrasted against the patches of dark green spruce trees that had somehow survived the fires.

Getting Electricity

Not every village in Nova Scotia had been powered with electricity during the years of the Great Depression, as President Roosevelt had been determined to accomplish with his rural electrification program in the United States. Then the war broke out and all materiel and manpower in Canada went to help defend Britain and protect our continent from attack from both Europe and Japan. My village, Pleasant Valley had not been wired for electricity before the war began.

Without electricity, we heated our houses with coal during the winter, supplemented with chopped wood in the kitchen stove. In summer, the fuel of choice was softwood, cut by the local farmers during the winter months from the spruce and pine trees in the woodlands and sawn in a great "sawing bee."

But one family in the valley had a small amount of electricity. This family, who lived up the slope of the hill about a half-mile from our house, had a windmill, built by either the mechanically minded father or his two sons, also reportedly mechanically minded, in the words of the villagers. Somehow, we learned that when the wind blew, the windmill had enough power for three lightbulbs, one for the inside porch, one in the kitchen, and one in the barn where the horse was kept. This seemed an endless mystery to us, as we would look up the hill on a still morning to see that the arms of the windmill were perfectly still or venture out to the back porch during a windstorm to look up the hill and watch the arms spinning wildly. "Ah," we would say, "today it's windy and they have electricity."

But after hearing rumors all spring that we were going to get the "power," and after the weeks of watching the men in the village, supervised by confident strangers, pound large poles into the roadside for miles on either side of our house, the summer morning came when we got electricity.

We watched as the one-ton Nova Scotia Light and Power truck with the enclosed back pulled up outside our house. The man in the hard hat who drove the truck knocked on our front door to tell our mother, "We are here to install the wiring in your house so that you will have electricity."

The men from the power company were competent, quiet in their work, and respectful of our house and the chores that Mother was doing on a summer day. They were also patient with we four children as we followed them silently from room to room, watching them drill holes in the sideboard and the ceilings, pull multicolored strands of covered wire through these holes from one room to another, trying to understand the shorthand calls of one man working upstairs to the man down in the living room as the wires were pulled and positioned and fastened to a plate in the wall to be covered by another plate with a switch.

"Now don't touch anything we've done today," the kindly older man who seemed to be in charge said to us as he was packing his tools in a large metal box and gathering up shards of wire. "We'll be back tomorrow to finish the wiring here, and if your neighbor's house is finished, we might be able to turn on the power along this road by tomorrow night."

We stared in amazement at him and looked around the house at the dangling wires, trying to imagine what the new electric lightbulbs would be like when the work was finished.

"What will we do with our kerosene lamps then?" Louise asked.

"We'll just throw them as far as we can throw them," said my brother, who was glad to be rid of the daily chore of cleaning and trimming and filling the dangerous, old-fashioned lamps.

High School and the Two-Room Schoolhouse

For my last two years of secondary school, I went to a two-room schoolhouse in a nearby village, where once again, and fortuitously, my mother was my teacher. In this schoolhouse, the 9th-through-11th-grade pupils were in one room, separate from the elementary and middle school students in the room next door.

I was in the 10th grade that fall, thirteen and a half, taller than most of the boys in the class, wearing size 9 shoes, a pony-tail, and to my despair, I had sprouted some pimples on my chin.

Each day we drove the eight miles from our valley to this school at Malignant Cove, so named, according to local myth, after The Malignant was shipwrecked on the shore during a storm sometime in the 1800s. My mother drove four of us — Malcolm, Little Angus, Hughie Dan, and me — in her Plymouth Coupe through all the weather challenges of the three school seasons.

More than one winter morning, when the car would slide into a ditch from icy roads, we four would climb out, tromp into the woods along the road to cut branches from the spruce trees to put under the back wheels for traction, then push with all our might to get the car back on the road.

Travel during the rain and mud season of late winter and early spring was seldom better, as the car tires would get caught in ruts caused by ice or frozen mud. Once again, we would pile out of the car to push it to more even ground. Since this was high school and we could have tea or coffee, Mother always packed two thermoses, one with coffee, the other with hot tea, and would have slices of homemade bread, butter, and jam as a treat during the morning ride.

High school was filled with wonders: There was algebra, with its elegant formulas and arithmetic mysteries, and geometry with its intricate angles and exciting solutions. Mary Wallace, my classmate and my contender for top grades, and I could spend hours absorbed in crafting geometry problems, plus the solutions. There was French language, where we struggled mightily to grasp the difference between l'accent a grave and l'accent aigu although never knowing the pronunciation of either or how to pronounce any other words in the basic French vocabulary.

My mother did the best she could without speaking the language, so we plowed ahead with our own pronunciation. But we mastered the grammar and the syntax since this was part of the language that my mother knew well. I did not hear spoken French until I arrived at college.

Literature was my favorite class, even though it was a total pain to have to read Walter Scott's *Ivanhoe*; or maybe history, where we could romp through Britain's various centuries, focusing on one bloody Henry after another and learn to enumerate all of the various Henrys' reigns and the names of their wives. One year we studied Canadian history and memorized the names of the prime ministers starting from the Confederation, but courses in American history were not on the curriculum, despite the importance of this country as our great southern neighbor.

Did I love our science classes best? Since there was no laboratory or any recognizable scientific equipment for us, our only science class was botany. We spent blessed time looking at the stamen and the pistils of a flower or the intricate veins in a maple leaf as we probed our way through the available scientific kingdom in our woods and fields or stood down by the beach on those cold early mornings of late March and early April, marveling at the ten-foot-high, blue-tinted ice shelves that washed in with the winds and the tides from the Labrador Straits.

We did not have the privilege then of knowing much of the science of tides or winds or anything that might hint at oceanography, but we learned the products and features of earth science firsthand., and we learned something of local "scientific" lore. Why did the seagull circle inland some days? Because, our local farmers said, he knows there will be a storm so he's looking for food. Why does the smoke rise straight up from the chimneys on some winter days? Because, the same local savants would say, we are going to have a snowstorm. Do the squirrels have a thicker coat and bushier tail this October? If so, we will have a harsh winter with much snow.

Not only did our mother have extensive knowledge of the English and French languages, and of math, history, literature, and botany, she was extremely capable of covering all of the topics with three grades in that room. During my 11th-grade year, we were four students, with six or seven in the 10th grade and about fifteen in the 9th. There was a set curriculum for each grade and textbooks of varying levels. She would spend fifteen or so intense minutes with the 11th graders on double equation algebra, then leave us with problems to solve, while she taught logarithms to the 10th grade, leaving more problems for quiet work, then moved to the other side of the classroom to put the 9th-grade boys and girls through their arithmetic drills. Her day was composed of these fifteen-minute segments, punctuated by short math tests for everyone on Fridays and essay assignments in literature or history to be ready for her review on the weekend.

With my mother as the teacher, there was no skipping out on homework, no gossiping or complaining about classmates, and absolutely no misbehaving in class. When Bill Miller, who sat behind me, one day dipped the end of my auburn ponytail into his inkpot of black ink, I had to sit silently until I was able to get to the pump in the yard during lunchtime to rinse out my hair. He never apologized, but days later, when he realized that he was not being reprimanded by the teacher and it was most likely because I did not tell on him, he became especially friendly, and the next lunch hour offered me his apple.

I never knew what to call my mother either. Certainly not Mom and not even Mother, and it didn't seem sensible to call her Mrs. MacLellan, as my classmates did. I finally decided I would call her "Ma'am," a term I discovered perhaps by watching John Wayne movies. But Mother objected vigorously: "That's rude; you can't call me that!"

Years later, when she visited me in Williamsburg, Virginia, where I was teaching at the College of William & Mary, and she heard the polite shopkeepers and waitresses in the town address her as "Ma'am," I could not resist reminding her that I tried to address her as Ma'am those years in high school when she was my teacher, and I couldn't figure out what else to call her.

One weekend, Mother permitted me to stay with the elementary school teacher, Tilly, and my classmate Lucille, both of whom lived in an apartment above the school. We planned to travel to Georgeville to see a movie at the Parish Hall called A Connecticut Yankee in King Arthur's Court. Seeing a movie, any movie, was always a rare treat, and this one starred Bing Crosby.

Our main challenge the final year of high school, grade 11, was to be sufficiently prepared to take and pass our province-wide exams. I do not recall that there were any sample exams from earlier years on which to practice, so we depended on the memory of our teacher, my mother, for the format from earlier exams and her ability to devise the right questions and grill us intensely until we were confident and prepped for the exams.

The test was given in the vast gymnasium of the nearby university. The exams were proctored by teachers from the town high school, who walked up and down the aisles looking formidable. We sat for algebra in the morning, French in the afternoon, geometry the next morning, history that afternoon, English literature on the third morning, and social science in the afternoon. It was grueling and frightening, but throughout was the sense that justice would prevail, that it did not matter that we went to a little two-room school with all three grades of high school in one room with one teacher in a village called Malignant Cove. Those exams would be protected in confidence and graded anonymously by teams of teachers from around the province during July. The graders would never know which school or area of the province the exam came from. We would have a fair adjudication.

We waited the agonizing weeks for the formal report cards to arrive from Halifax, the provincial capital. All four of us in the 11th grade passed our exams. This meant that I would be accepted at the university.

Someone Missing, for the Rest of My Life

If you ask me, "What did you miss most in your life?" I will dodge the question and falter, then say something innocuous, but the answer is ever-present, although I will keep it silent.

A father. That is what I have missed all of my life. I have been blessed with an amazing mother, but almost every week, if not every day, as the years have passed, I have missed my father. Certainly, when I was in serious family or marital difficulty or having trouble dealing with some of the men where I worked, I would think, *If I had a father, he would know; he would guide me.*

Or maybe he would just love me with an open mind, care for me, be there when I walked home from school on a cold day, and say, "Welcome home, dear. Are you all right? Are you very cold? Come near the stove where it's warm."

And I would say, "Hi, Daddy. I'm just fine," and burble on about my day and what I noticed and thought about and my interpretation of events, and he would listen. Or I would be home ahead of him, perhaps doing the dishes at the kitchen sink, looking out the window and down the road for his car. Then waiting at the door to say, "Hi, Daddy. Welcome home. Did you have a good day?"

To have a father, a Daddy, with a capital *D*. Maybe when I was older, in college, he would be Dad, as in, "Hi, Dad," when I called home from the dorm room. "I'm doing quite well in English lit, but not so great in chemistry."

And he would say, "Do not worry. Not all of us are good at everything." Maybe he would add something more, like, "Stay with it, though, because you may pick up an important fact that will be helpful later in life."

But I am making up these words in my voice, my modern New York City voice. I have no idea, no memory of how he talked, of the sound of his voice, the timbre, his vocal expressions. I am not even sure what color hair he had. I've always assumed it was black like his hair in the black-and-white photographs that hung for years on the wall of my mother's bedroom. My mother said that he was turning gray very young, but that does not show up in the photos from the summer of 1944, the latest we have.

I learned almost nothing about him in the years after we lost him, growing up with my mother, my younger brother, and two little sisters. Nothing about his personality, what he liked to do, or what type of things he talked about. The subject was too painful in our family. If we ventured a question to our mother, she would go silent or brush it off, saying she was busy. When the anniversary of that fateful day came each February, and we would go to church if our school schedule allowed, or, on Remembrance Day, each November 11, when we would gather with the people of the town to pay homage to those who lost their lives in the two big wars, we four children would stand silently with our mother. Afterward, if we were to ask her to tell us more about our father, what he was like, the tears would begin flowing, and we three girls would no longer be capable of listening even if an answer were to come.

Except for my brother. He did not cry, even when he was very young. His face would tighten, his eyes would look at something far off, and he would stay silent through his sisters' snuffling until our mother would tell us all to be quiet, now, enough of this.

Over the years, an occasional detail would surface about my father. When I was in my mid-forties, battling my cigarette habit and groaning to my mother during a visit about how difficult it was to quit, she suddenly said, "Your father smoked cigarettes, too. He liked Player's Navy Cut." Another year, while watching a movie on TV with her, she mentioned, almost as an aside, "Your father liked Gary Cooper."

My own memories of him from those early days are few but etched firmly in my mind. I remember spending time at the kitchen window with my younger brother, watching for the express train that carried passengers as well as mail to pull into the station up the road. Then we would wait for the train to pick up steam as it puffed down the tracks that were just across the road and up an embankment from our house, to hear it thundering along and maybe blow its whistle.

My mother told me much later that my brother and I learned to tell time by waiting for that train, which was due at three every weekday afternoon, watching the clock to be sure that we would clamber up on chairs at the window well before that time. We waited, excited, telling each other each time that Daddy would be on that train, that he was coming home again.

How we were able to see the train station so far up the road and spot a person alighting from the train, much less identify that person, is puzzling and seems amazing to me now. But one day, during one of our vigils, we saw him, swinging down from the train, waving to someone, perhaps the stationmaster who was also the mailman and the general storekeeper and then see him begin to walk down the road toward our house. "Mommy, Mommy!" we shouted. "Daddy is coming! Daddy is coming!"

Our mother told me years later that she paid no attention to us, was busy with some household chore, or was looking after the baby, Donnie, and figured we were just imagining him. But we could see him. I took my brother's hand and led him, running out the door, through the yard, and starting up the road. This was normally forbidden, as we were taught not to leave the yard because of cars and the train tracks up the embankment. And then we were leaping up into his arms.

We came into the kitchen, triumphant in our great find, our father holding each of us on either hip. "We said Daddy was coming," we shouted to our mother with him laughing at our glee and my mother's flustered joy.

Well, I remember her confused face, and now I can call it flustered. I have made up the joy part, but she must have been joyful, as well as surprised, to see him unexpectedly. I do not remember anything but our excitement and our overall joy.

Years later, when I prodded her for details, she remembered that we shouted to her that he was coming, that she was not expecting him and just ignored us since this was our daily vigil. But she confirmed that our father was given an unexpected weekend off and that he decided to surprise her, and us, with that visit.

We were all expecting him for Christmas of 1944. He had recently been transferred back to the Royal Canadian Air Force base in Dartmouth, near Halifax, so it was possible for him to arrange a trip on the train for a few days' leave, as he had for that surprise weekend visit those few weeks before.

I was turning five that Christmas, old enough to be excited about what Santa might bring but, at the same time, not expecting much. It was wartime, and there were few toys and no dolls or so few that I was told not to expect any, but Mother said, "Perhaps there will be some candy this year."

My father arrived home with his large black suitcase, and I remember thinking how glorious he looked in his air force–blue uniform. I remember asking to try on his hat. But as he

121

opened that suitcase, what amazed us three children were the boxes of chocolates wrapped in cellophane and glistening with red ribbons and red bows. Daddy announced that one of the boxes was for us, one was for his mother and father, one was for my mother's parents, and the last one was for our elderly aunt, Aunt Cassie, who lived up the road and who took care of us sometimes if our mother needed to go shopping in the nearby town.

We were so excited by the promise of those chocolates. But what stays with me was my amazement at his generosity, that he was thinking not just of us, his children, but of the parents and close family, and bringing them an unattainable gift. I think that surpassed my own craving for chocolate or even for a doll.

I do not remember what Santa brought that year, or Christmas dinner, or my birthday. But there is one other sharp memory from that week or possibly from a weekend in the next month when he was also able to come home and when he brought along one of his fellow airmen. I must have been hovering near him all weekend because suddenly the other man reached out with a switch or branch to hit me across the legs and ordered me to stop being a pest and leave them alone. My father reacted fiercely. "Leave her be," he said. And I am quite sure that he then said, "She sees so little of me; let her stay." I so wanted to be near him, and he defended me.

The next memory has been indelible throughout my lifetime. Every detail is seared into my brain and so pivotal to my life and the future of our family that I have never dared to share it with my mother lest her memories would confuse my own. In recent years I have asked her the sequence of events of when our father's plane was lost, and she has told me her memories of when and how the news first came to her. But I never shared my memory of that time.

For me, that first awareness is of a dark, early morning in winter — February, I learned much later — and I am standing in a doorway wearing my winter nightgown, a flannel type that came almost to the floor. My feet are bare and cold because I forgot to put on my slippers. My mother is lying face down on the sofa in the living room. There is no light on in the room, just a shaft of light from another room, maybe the kitchen, although I sense that the light came from behind me and that I was silhouetted in that light because I could see my shadow. My mother is sobbing, and my grandmother, her mother, is leaning over her, murmuring. There are one or two other women in the room, bent over and with their backs to me, probably my Aunt Anne, my father's sister, and my young Aunt Norma, my mother's adopted sister. But in my memory, I do not see their faces, just their shapes, and their obvious pain. I think the radio is on; it was a large brown box that sat on a table in front of the living room window because I could hear the announcer's voice. I started walking toward my mother, saying, "What's wrong, Mommy? What's wrong? Why are you crying?" and then my grandmother was reaching out for me, to put her arms around me.

No one answered my question, but I heard my mother say to the room and her mother, "I must go on because of the baby. I have to think about the baby."

I do not remember knowing that she was having a baby, but I knew with finality that my father was lost. We have never said our father is dead, we have always said "lost," as in, "His plane was lost." And I knew he was not coming back. We would be alone.

Then the screen goes blank. I have almost no further memories from that morning, when I was just five years and seven weeks old, until late August of the next year when I was six years and eight months old and we moved to a new village where my mother would be the schoolteacher and I would begin third grade. I do not even remember my baby sister, Louise, being brought home from the hospital, which occurred just three months after that dark February morning.

Years later my Aunt Anne, my father's younger sister who frequently spent time with us during those years of the war, told me the following story: it was later in the spring of 1945, several months after my father's plane was lost, and she was spending a few days with our mother and we children. One day, as she and my mother were sitting at the kitchen table having tea, the stationmaster arrived in his truck with my father's suitcases, which had been sent on the afternoon train. He silently brought the suitcases into the kitchen, set them in the middle of the floor, nodded his head, and quickly left. Aunt Anne said that she and my mother sat there, stunned, holding their teacups, too numb to move or talk, and just stared at the black leather suitcases with tags that read Flight Sgt. D. A. MacLellan.

I had been playing in the far reaches of the backyard by the little brook with my younger brother and sister, no doubt watching the pollywogs, and only noticed the truck as it was pulling out of the yard. Aunt Anne said I came bounding into the kitchen, pigtails flying, out of breath, then saw the suitcases, and threw myself over them, sobbing and sobbing "as if your heart would break." She meant her heart, too, because she could do little to ease my pain.

My mother stays silent when I ask her about the incident; perhaps, like me, she did not want to remember it. But in recent years my mother told me another incident: one day, some weeks after that February morning when we got the news about my father, she was washing dishes at the kitchen sink and sobbing and I came up to her, put my hand on her arm and asked, "Mommy, are you still crying over Daddy?" My mother said that she resolved there and then never to cry again and cause extra pain to her children. She decided to banish her own pain and get on with taking care of us and fending for our future.

So through our years growing up, our mother sealed away her emotions, just as she sealed away my father's letters and his Royal Canadian Air Force flying pin and epaulets in the brown mahogany chest beside her bed, forbidden territory for us for many decades. And maybe that is why, even years later, she could never talk about our father, no matter how often we might pester her with questions about their early days together and what he was like. Granted, we four could not deal with the subject either, could not talk about him without dissolving into tears, and not just as preteens and teenagers, but well into our twenties and beyond.

There are a few mementos that I have treasured over the years, and no doubt my siblings have done the same: several faded snapshots and the two photo enlargements on the wall of our mother's bedroom, one of her and my father with him

125

holding me at age two and a half while she holds my brother, who is about nine months. The other is their wedding photo, sepia-colored now, mother wearing a flowing satin dress and broad-brimmed hat and my father looking young and earnest and standing with his knees locked. This is visible even under the loose dress pants of the day.

I notice now that my grown son stands the same way, with knees locked. My tennis instructor of short-lived efforts when I was in my early twenties, once said, "Do you know you stand with your knees locked? That's not good for you."

So we lived with this silence as the background to our everyday lives. And in those next three years, as young as we were, we must have been aware of subsequent deaths in the family: my "little" grandmother MacLellan, gone just four months after my father "of a broken heart over the death of her son in the war," the yellowing newspaper obituary reported; my paternal grandfather; and then my young Aunt Isobel, who had taken care of me after I was born, and my mother was recovering from rheumatic fever. I remember these as solemn, sad years, but for my mother, those deaths must have been excruciating.

In those early years, there were many nights that I dreamed my father came home. We would see him coming down the road in his air force uniform and we would call out to our mother, "See? He isn't lost. He is coming home." I did not tell my mother about those dreams, but they would shadow me throughout the day.

There is another searing memory from the summer I was eleven. We four children were picking strawberries for the neighbors in the fertile field behind our house when someone brought us a message that our mother wanted us to come back home quickly, that we had a special surprise visitor. So we ran, stopping once to pick up some of the strawberries we spilled, asking each other who it could be.

I sped ahead, bounding up the back steps two at a time and into the kitchen, and there stood this man, smiling at me. My father? Is this my father? The same smile from the photos in my mother's bedroom. Is this him? Is his hair this gray, this curly? Has he come home again after all?

Heart pounding, breath coming in gasps, the tears started to pour out as my mother said, "Children, this is your Uncle Jim, your father's brother. He has come to visit us."

I think that Uncle Jim then hugged us all and must have tried to understand my sobs. I had no memory of this uncle, as he left for work in Ontario when I was about two years old and there were no photos of him from those intervening years. After he left our house that day, my mother agreed that he looked very much like my father, except that he was not as tall, but that his personality and warm nature were similar.

When we next saw Uncle Jim, many years later at a family funeral in Ontario, I was jolted back to that shocking encounter in our kitchen those years ago and studied him carefully, trying to determine whether that was how my father would look now. Would my father have aged this same way? And would he be as pleased and interested in us, my two sisters and me, now that we were grown women with our own careers and families, as my Uncle Jim was that day, wanting to know about our work, our travels? Throughout the day, he watched us intently, fondly, as if trying to find traits of our father in our looks and actions.

Maybe this is how our father would be with us, totally interested, intrigued with our careers and our lives, doting on our children, singing them Gaelic songs and teaching them to say their earliest prayers in that ancient Scottish tongue, *Our Father, who art in Heaven*, just as he taught me so long ago.

Those prayers in Gaelic are long forgotten. But the few memories I have of my father hold fast, etched in my mind throughout the years.

Donald Angus MacLellan
Record of Service
Royal Canadian Air Force

September 29, 1940: Enlisted into Service, Toronto, Ontario

October 31, 1940: Basic Training, St. Thomas, Ontario

March 27, 1941: Air Patrol, Moncton, New Brunswick

July 7, 1943: Air Patrol, Tor Bay, Newfoundland

January 30, 1944: Mont Joli, Quebec

March 26, 1944: Vancouver and Ucluelet, Vancouver Island, British Columbia

July 21, 1944: Halifax/Dartmouth, Nova Scotia

Donald Angus MacLellan
Record of Leave

April 28 – May 4, 1941: 7 days

June 22 – July 5, 1942: 14 days; Annual

April 5 – April 8, 1943: 4 days

August 4 – August 13, 1943: 7 days

May 17– May 30, 1944: 14 days; Annual

Dec. 9 – Dec. 29, 1944: 19 days; Christmas and Annual

April 18, 1944: Appointed to Rank of Flight Engineer

Jan. 29, 1945: Appointed to Rank of Flight Sergeant

Service Knowledge: Searches for way to improve his service knowledge.

Trade Proficiency: Superior; knows his work and does it well.

Administrative Ability: Organizes effectively and gets things done.

Loyalty: Can definitely depend on his loyalty.

—*c/o/ Trecarten, Commanding Officer Dartmouth, Nova Scotia Station, 26 January*

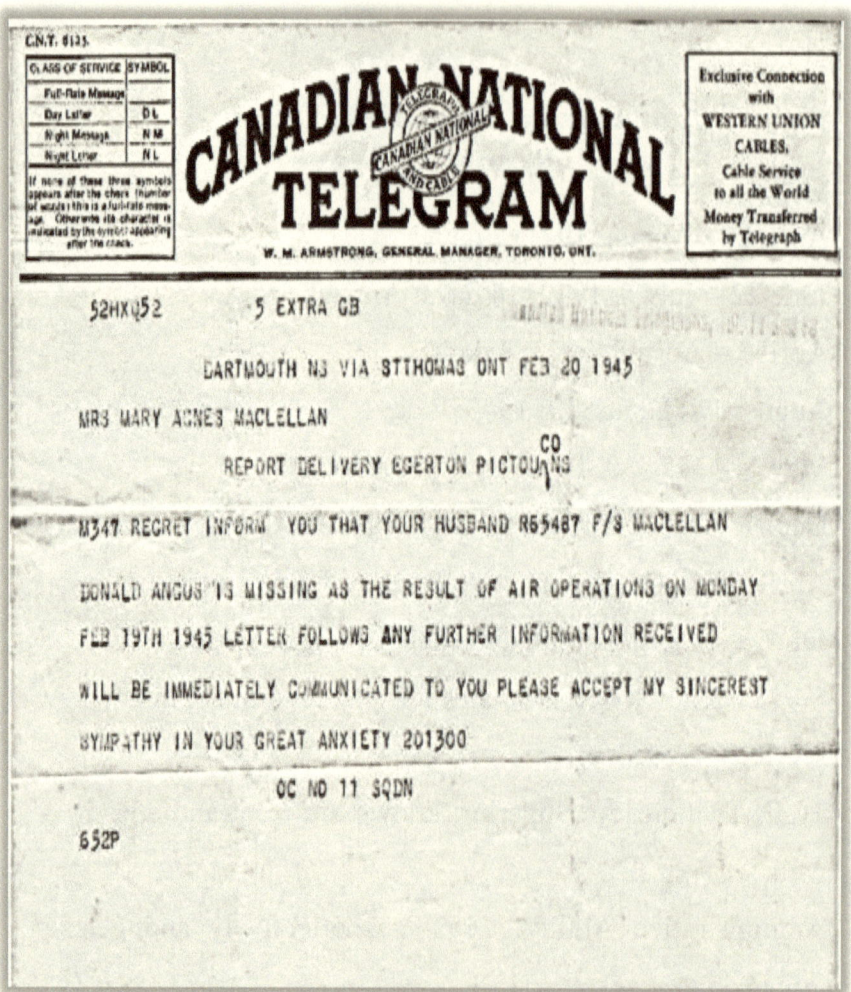

Official Royal Canadian Air Force Casualty Notification

February 20, 1945
MacLellan, Donald Angus
Missing: 19-Feb-45 (Operations) (Canada)

Seven Airmen Missing as Search Is Pressed

Wednesday, Feb. 21, 1945, The Halifax Herald

Royal Canadian Air Force aircraft and Royal Canadian Navy ships last night were combining operations in a search for a missing bomber and its crew of seven long overdue at its Dartmouth base and feared down in the North Atlantic. The multi-engine bomber left its base on Monday for a routine patrol of an Atlantic area and was due back at base late Monday afternoon, the R.C.A.F. disclosed last night.

Little Hope for Seven Airmen

Thursday, February 22, 1945, The Halifax Herald

Royal Canadian Air Force officials said last night only faint hope was held for the lives of seven members of a Dartmouth-based bomber crew which disappeared over the north Atlantic Monday with three Nova Scotians in the crew.

∼

Dartmouth, N.S. 22nd February 1945

Dear Mrs. MacLellan:

Further to my telegram of the 20th instant regarding your husband's most unfortunate accident (sic) of February 19th.

Your husband was engaged in Air Operations over the Atlantic Ocean starting out early Monday morning and extending through the day to early evening. When his aircraft failed to report at the time specified for the completion of the patrol, immediate action was instituted to contact him but without success. Aircraft were also dispatched immediately to carry our (sic) a search. They have been searching continuously for the past two days and nights and no crew members have been found, although wreckage of the aircraft has been picked up.

It has now been decided to discontinue the search as it must be assumed that all the crew members perished in the aircraft.

W.A. Swetman, Officer Commanding, No. 11 Squadron, RCAF

~

OTTAWA, Canada, 26th June 1945, by Registered Mail

Mrs. D.A. MacLellan

Egerton, Pictou Co., Nova Scotia

Dear Mrs. MacLellan:

It is with deep regret that, in view of the lapse of time and the absence of any further information concerning your husband, Flight Sergeant Donald Angus MacLellan, since he was reported missing believed killed, it is now proposed to take action to presume his death for official purposes.

Yours sincerely, Co. M. Wismer R.C.A.F. Casualty Officer, Chief of the Air Staff

~

BUCKINGHAM PALACE

The Queen and I offer you our heartfelt sympathy in your great sorrow.

We pray that your country's gratitude for a life so nobly given in its service may bring you some measure of consolation.

(signed) George R.I.

They Shall Not Grow Old: A Book of Remembrance

MACLELLAN, Donald Angus FS(FE) R65487. From Pleasant Valley, Antigonish County, Nova Scotia. Killed in Action Feb 19/45 age 32. #11 Bomber Reconnaissance Squadron, Dartmouth, Nova Scotia. Liberator aircraft missing.

Please see Hogan D. for casualty list and flight detail. Flight Sergeant Flight Engineer MacLellan has no known grave. His name is inscribed on the Ottawa War Memorial at Ottawa, ON.

Published by the Commonwealth Air Commonwealth Air Training Plan Museum, Brandon, Manitoba, Canada

Many decades later my mother told me the story of the morning of February 20, when the telegram was sent from the Royal Canadian Air Force. The telegram was delivered to the general store up the road, which also served as the post office and the railway station and was run by a longtime family friend, Anthony "Dux" MacKenzie. Dux said later that he could not, just could not, take that telegram down the road to inform my mother. So he walked the quarter-mile to our Aunt Cassie's house. She was our grandaunt, sister of my paternal grandfather, an intelligent woman who had been trained as a nurse and as a young woman had worked as a governess to wealthy families in Brooklyn, New York. My mother said she was looking out our kitchen window and saw Aunt Cassie walking down the road, but slowly, even for an older woman, so mother knew something must be terribly wrong.

Flt. Sgt. Donald A. MacLellan

Mom and Dad on their Wedding Day, September 19, 1938,
with Aunt Isobel and Malcolm MacLellan (no relation).

Daddy and Mom in
Egerton in 1942, with
me and Malcolm.
I am 2 ½ ; Malcom is
9 months old.

Here I am at 2 ½ in
Grandmother
MacLellan's garden
in Dunvegan.

With Dad and Malcolm in Egerton. I was 3 ½
that summer; Malcolm was 2 ½.

Summer 1943 in Egerton. I am 3 ½, Malcolm
is 2 ½, and Donnie just turned 1.

Summer in
Dunvegan.
Donnie is 5.

Donnie at 8, Shirley at 12, in Dunvegan.

Summer in Dunvegan. I am 7 ½, Malcolm is 6,
and Louise is almost 2 ½.

CHAPTER 2

The College Years

Remembering the College Years

For years I have been dreaming about walking down a long, narrow corridor that links two buildings. There is never enough light in the corridor, and while I am not frightened at least in a Hallowe'en sense, I am upset and disturbed about something. There are steep, narrow stairways used to access each end of that corridor, and at the end that is the exit in my dreams, the stairway bends to the right onto a small landing, then abruptly shifts to the left. Then I am walking down a larger corridor, the light is grayish around me, and at the end of this corridor, I pass a large double door made of wood. There is a rectangular glass transom at the top of the door with light coming through. That is the light for this corridor, and it is a grey light.

I walk faster, and as I do, I seem to become more apprehensive, worried, like have I done something wrong? Am I about to be punished for something? Then I come fully awake to check on my surroundings, to be sure that I am securely here and now and that I am securely me, not that apprehensive, worried person.

Those corridors of my dreams have stayed with me for over fifty years now. I don't have the dream every night or even every week or month, but often enough, a few times a year, so that I remark to myself later in the morning that this still happens.

I do believe those images in my dreams are an almost accurate replication of the corridors at the women's residences of my undergraduate college so many years ago.

The women's part of our college was separated from the main campus by the large cathedral of the diocese. Behind the cathedral was a walkway and several stone steps down to the main campus; it took at least eight minutes of brisk walking to reach the campus from our residences, and then another minute to find our classroom. This only applied to our courses from the sophomore year on, since the nuns made sure that all, or mostly all, of our classes in our freshmen year would be held at the women's college. "They want to keep you away from the boys as long as possible," one of the upper-class women said.

The oldest two structures of the three on the women's campus were built of wood, although with strong stone foundations that had deep cellars, where our dining rooms and the laundry rooms were located. The first floor of the oldest building, which dated from the early 1920s, held the formal sitting parlor as well as the nuns' residences. Upstairs on the third floor was the freshmen residence, and this was adjoined through corridors to Immaculata Hall, built perpendicular to the oldest building. It held a large concert hall that we also used for assemblies, and the music rooms, located at the back of the hall, were where I took my piano lessons over the years, starting when I was a seven-year-old and traveled in from Pleasant Valley. The sophomore dorms were on the upper floor above Immaculata Hall.

The newest building was Gilmora Hall, built after World War II and made of the local limestone blocks that were also used decades before to build the cathedral. Gilmora Hall was a long rectangular building of four floors, the first, partially underground with windows placed high on the walls to capture light, was our gymnasium. There was a large room off one end used to store our wardrobe trunks and suitcases. This "trunk room" had no windows and so became a vital place for us during the spring of our senior year, when we took our type-writers there after lights out to frantically finish and type our senior theses.

Gilmora Hall was the residence for the junior women on the third floor and the senior women on the fourth floor. The large first floor, with ceilings high enough to constitute two floors, was designated as a parlor floor, with sofas, arm-chairs, a piano, and for the year we were seniors, a television set, then a novelty for us all. My mother bought the first TV for our family that same year. The main entrance for Gilmora was through a large door "under the Arches," a graceful nod to the gothic arches of medieval Europe, which opened to a small entryway and a room on the right, the office of the dean of women.

This petite but formidable nun, Mother St. Mary Phillippe, held court there, greeting her favorites or admonishing those she accused of unacceptable behavior. She maintained a close watch over all of us who left or entered in the few evenings that we were permitted to be out past half-past seven, making sure that we signed in on the big book on a standing lectern. Her office didn't have a window that looked directly under the Arches, but somehow, she seemed to always know who was held too tight or even kissed goodnight by a boyfriend from the main campus.

Those Arches were to cause ongoing problems over the years. This was likely the site for any of us caught in a first furtive kiss by Mother St. Phillippe as she was opening the door to shoo us in. Once she found one of the young women locked in a tight embrace and in a passionate kiss. That young woman was then "campussed," as we called it, for the next two weeks, not allowed to go to the weekly dance at the Parish Center or downtown to a movie. The young woman was blamed for "this disgraceful behavior," not the young man, with Mother St. Phillippe stating as she frequently did, "It is always the fault of the young woman."

In the fall of our junior year, fresh cement was poured under the Arches late on a Saturday afternoon, forcing us to use the back door at Immaculata Hall for our comings and goings until the cement was dry. That next morning, a Sunday, when Mother St. Phillippe opened the main door to check on how well the cement was drying, she found several designs and sayings sketched into the wet cement: large hearts with "John Loves Mary" written on one; "Roseann, Please Come to Me" written on another. We were all called to assembly in Immaculata Hall after our Sunday Mass in the chapel to be upbraided by an irate dean of women, who told us coldly, "If the young men from the university did this, then it is your fault. It is always the young women who are at fault." Then she campussed all of us, freshmen through seniors, for the next two weeks. Being "campussed" meant that we could not go to the big dance at the Parish Center on the following Saturday night, which, grumbled one of the senior women, left the field of eager young men to the even more eager young women at the nursing school of the hospital.

Gilmora Hall's perpendicular structure was joined by a long, narrow corridor that began at the inside foyer for the Arches and ended at the beginning of the oldest structure, which was accessed by a flight of stairs. These, then, were the corridors of my dreams, one that joined the oldest building to Gilmora and the one that joined the other side of the oldest building to Immaculata Hall. As freshmen and sophomores, we walked the corridor early each morning from Immaculata Hall to reach the chapel — Mass was mandatory each morning except for Saturday — and as juniors and seniors, we walked the long, narrow corridors from Gilmora to chapel and to reach the dining rooms and then the corridor at the other end to reach the large assembly room in Immaculata Hall. I took those corridors each week to have my piano lessons in the music rooms at the back of that hall.

But why the apprehension, the growing sense of dread in these dreams? My waking mind would go back to the four years and be puzzled because those four years were successful and put me on the path to my lifelong career, and I was happy at the university in the last three years, when I established bonds that I keep and cherish to this day. But at the women's residence, over those years, there were several incidents that could well have been the cause.

Freshman Year

This was a year of continuing cold doses of new realities and shocks. The first shock was the attitude of the nuns who ran the women's college of the university. These nuns were from the Congregation of Notre Dame, a French order from Montreal, although most of the nuns sent down to Nova Scotia were English speaking. My encounters that first week were of a group of stern-faced women dressed in flowing black robes with white

pointed wimples who were strict, punitive, and seemingly dis-
trustful of the young women placed in their charge.

Shocking too was their rigid adherence to Catholic rites
and daily insistence on our "proper behavior." In my family,
our practice of Catholicism was developed under our mother's
guidance, but it was never oppressive. The priests in our parish
were mostly kind and considerate. Only one older priest was
grumpy and sometimes gruff and would order his altar boys
around or turn from the altar to glare up at me in the organ loft
if I was slow to begin the "Gloria" or the "Sanctus" in the years
that I was the church organist. But he was never cruel or oppressive. During Lent, our mother led us through nightly reci-
tations of the rosary.

Our travel to Sunday Mass was a distance of four miles,
and for many years, we included Mrs. Baxter, our wonderful
gentle and elderly neighbor from across the brook who was
now a widow. Her gift to us each week for taking her to Mass
was a pint of cream from her farm, so rich and thick that on a
winter's morning when we brought the jar in from the porch,
our mother would say, "You could stand a spoon up in it."

During my two years of high school, when we drove the
nine miles to Malignant Cove and had to attend Mass on a holy
day, my mother, who was also our teacher, would pack a breakfast treat of her baking powder biscuits with our homemade
jam, some apples, and a large thermos of coffee with cream and
sugar. The pangs of the long fast — in those days we were not
allowed to eat or drink before taking communion — would
evaporate when we got back into the car and plunged into these
special treats.

So our religion was not a burden, instead was part of the community. For me, it was a backdrop to what I thought of as my real religion — the woods and hills of our valley, the sparkling stars and the Milky Way on clear nights, the call of crows from the hayfields, the gleaming silver trout in the brook, the croak of frogs from the nearby frog pond on a long summer's evening. We would be saddened by the V-formation and the haunting honks of Canada geese as they flew southwards in the late fall, but then would wait eagerly for those sounds in late winter and would go running outdoors to follow their northward formation in the grey skies. "Spring will come soon," Mother would assure us, "now that the geese are returning."

We were called to assembly following Sunday Mass that first week of freshman year, reporting even before breakfast. The dean of women, Mother St. Mary Phillippe, started her speech with a brief smile, but quickly began a recitation of the house rules and her expectations for our behavior: "No running or laughing in the hallways or stairs; you must attend Mass each morning at seven, except for Saturdays; you will be polite and respectful at all times to all of the sisters who are here for your best interests. You will be allowed out to the Saturday dance, but you must be in before the doors are locked at ten. All other nights you must be in by half-past seven. All lights are turned off at ten. You must be on time for meals; you must do your homework and assignments in the study halls, where you must be quiet at all times."

"Gee, they want us to live like nuns," Chris from Halifax whispered to me. Mother St. Mary Phillippe must have heard the whispered noise and turned to glare at us.

"I expect you to be silent and to listen carefully to everything I say." Her voice was cold. Her smile had long since disappeared. The formidable enclosures and the bewildering, seemingly haunted passageways and dark stairs of the three buildings of the women's college now seemed a fitting surrounding for this voice.

Almost all of our classes that first year were held at the women's college. "They want to keep us away from the guys on campus as long as they can," Roseann muttered one morning, echoing what we had heard from an upper-class woman.

When roll call was being taken the first morning of our French 101 class, the professor, Mother St. Carola, looked over at me when she came to my name and said something in French that sounded sarcastic to me. I did not then understand spoken French, despite our years of learning to decline verbs and acquire some vocabulary. Whatever it was that the nun said, the young classmate from Montreal looked over at me in surprise. After class, I stopped her and asked, "What did the nun say?" My new classmate hedged, clearly uncomfortable to tell me, then said, "She said something like, 'So you are the country girl with the big scholarship?'" I had won a scholarship that was large enough to pay for all of my resident expenses and books for the full four years; my picture announcing the award was in the local paper in August. Did Mother St. Carola see that story?

The next day, my professor of advanced English was none other than Mother. St. Carola. She surveyed our class, her eyes glinting, telling us we were there because we had placed well above the required freshman English in our entrance exams and that she expected "we would justify our presence in her classroom with superlative work." We would be studying fundamental writings in the literature, starting with Beowulf and Chaucer, and would be assigned much essay writing. "And we start now," she said. "I expect a three-page essay submitted by each of you by our next class."

I worked hard on that essay, staying long hours in the library to edit and shape the words and then to rewrite it in my best handwriting on clean, unlined paper. My essay, when returned on the third class, was a mass of notes in red ink, and at the top of the pages, a large letter D, also in red ink. Shock. I went numb with shock. I had never received below an A in my entire school life. Finally, the blur in front of my eyes cleared enough to read her comments. I vowed to understand those comments, however cruelly presented in the red ink, and to learn from all of these corrections. I also vowed that if I were ever to teach classes, I would never use a red ink to correct a term paper or an exam. Green or blue ink would be more compassionate.

Then there was Latin. I had not studied the language in high school, but we grew up using Latin in our Mass on Sundays, so many words were familiar, if not the grammar. The teacher was Mother St. John, a tall, angular woman who strode forcefully in and out of the classroom. She also turned out to be our phys-ed teacher, and she easily ran the length of the gym bouncing a basketball, even in her long black robes. We noticed that, in the gym, she wore sneakers under the robes.

"She must have grown up a real tomboy," Maureen said after the first phys-ed class.

I did, however, take three classes that year on campus: history, because the class at the women's college was in conflict with my English class, and Psychology 101 and Chemistry 101. I was the only girl in Father McGillivary's history class, which was held in a room filled with about seventy young freshmen lads. "Father Long Legs," as the guys called him, was uncomfortable having me in his class. I discovered it was best to sit in the back row behind one of the taller guys, so as never to be in his line of sight.

I enjoyed his lectures but for chemistry class, I disliked every lecture and shuddered at the smell of the labs. I just didn't want to be there. Taking a science was mandatory and I wanted to take geology, but the dean of students, Father Bauer, who was at the registration desk the day I was signing up for my courses, stepped in to say, "Girls don't take geology; they take chemistry instead."

No one had ever told me that I couldn't do something because I was a girl. Later in the year, the upperclassman who was the pianist for many of our concerts and musical productions, Jack O'Donnell, told me that Father Bauer, who was also the musical director for many of the productions on campus, knew that I played piano and had decided to "keep me on campus and not out in the fields with the geologists" so that he would have a back-up pianist for rehearsals.

I forgave Father Bauer then but continued to loathe the chemistry lab and be agitated during the lectures.

Why, I asked myself, *didn't the professor explain how those scientists knew what they knew? Through what process did they discover this compound or that element in the periodic table or something as basic as H_2O?*

Until I could know of the discovery process, I couldn't accept the formulas or the compounds. I gratefully let the guys help me with the labs.

Four of the freshman girls were still fifteen years old as classes began that fall of 1955. Besides me, there were the two girls from Newfoundland, Roseann and Barbara, and Mary from New Glasgow. We heard rumors going around the campus about this and wide speculation as to who these "baby freshmen" were. But except for Roseann, the rest of us escaped notice, partly because, on campus, more attention was now being paid to a young man from Quebec named Brian Mulroney who spoke perfect English and perfect French and was reported to have turned sixteen only a few months before starting college.

The next shock was discovering ethnic prejudice. My roommate in the freshman dorm was Ruth, a French Canadian girl from northern New Brunswick. She spoke English with a strong French accent and frequently groped for the English vocabulary in many of her sentences. Her village was entirely Acadian French, which was the language of her household and the church, and she hadn't begun to learn English until high school. I liked her at once, enjoyed her great laugh, and shared the cookies and sweet pastries that came in the boxes of food her mother sent regularly. I helped her with the English words she needed every day and for her classes, hoping that I could also learn to understand more of her language.

Our dorm was open plan, with rooms separated by five-foot walls, then open to the ceilings. We had curtains instead of doors, so with all that unstructured space, voices, even whispers, carried the length of the hall, down to the door at the end, which was the room of our resident nun, Mother St. John, my professor for theology, Latin, and gym. Lights were turned off throughout the dorm at 10 p.m. and lamps were not permitted, so our rooms would suddenly be plunged into darkness. We needed to have all of our bedtime preparations completed in advance — toothbrushing, face cleansing, or showering — in the big communal bathroom in the other hall that we all shared. In our beds after lights out we could get away with whispering, but anything louder, such as a giggle, would be met by a stern "Silence!" thundered at us from the open doorway at the end of the hall.

"What does she do, stand at her open door and wait for one of us to make a noise?" Maureen from Halifax asked one morning. Then, if we were still awake, we would hear the swish of her robes and her footfalls as she went to use the same bathroom as we did. Another night, I was certain that I heard lighter footsteps going to her door, heard the door open, and then close.

One afternoon I came back to my room from the study hall to find Ruth lying face down on the bed, sobbing, her long ponytail bobbing up and down in rhythm with her sobs. "Ruth, what's wrong? What happened?" I asked, rushing over and putting my hand on her shoulder.

Between sobs, she said, "There were talking about me; they were making fun of me."

"Who are they?"

"The three girls down the hall in the large room." That room held three beds and dressers and was occupied by the three girls from Halifax, one of whom loved Broadway musicals and on Saturday afternoons would play the scores from *Brigadoon* or *Oklahoma!* on her portable LP player.

"What did they say?" I asked Ruth, whose body was still shaking in her misery.

She sat up, her face tear-streaked, and said, "They were laughing at my accent, saying that I talk funny and have some funny manners and that I laugh too loud."

So they were mocking this girl because she was French Canadian, part of us, but different from us. Didn't the Halifax girls meet any French Canadians in their schools, or were those too fancy to have ethnic groups? What to do, what to say, how to handle this? I had never encountered prejudice before. We had several Acadian French families in our town and several African American families. They were all part of the scene, part of the community. I had been elected president of the women's freshman class, so that must give me responsibility as well as some authority to talk to the three girls down the hall, even if they were older.

After dinner, knowing that Ruth had gone to the study hall, I walked down to the triple room and found the three sitting on their beds, deep in animated conversation. I gathered my courage and said quietly, "You have hurt Ruth terribly. She overheard you this afternoon, making fun of her accent." They were stunned silent for a minute. "Of course her accent is different," I continued, "but we probably sound pretty funny to her as well." They said nothing.

I stopped at the chapel on the way to the study hall, said a few prayers for guidance, but also for Ruth that she would recover from this. The three girls seemed to steer away from Ruth for the next few days, and I never knew whether they apologized to her, but they never again made fun of Ruth, as least when she was around and could hear them. Ruth's English improved over the year, faster and better than my French, and she finished the year with good grades. But Ruth never returned to the women's college or to the university.

One night, about an hour after the lights went out, I woke, realizing that I had to make a trip to the bathroom. I tiptoed down the hall, across the corridor, and fumbled to the left for the door to the bathroom, which was closed.

That's funny, I thought, *that door is always left ajar and the lights are left on during the night for anyone needing to go, like me, at this moment.*

I opened the door to find Mother St. John in her white night robes, sitting on a stool and combing out the long, wet hair of my classmate, Muriel, who was kneeling on a towel on the floor, her arm resting on Mother St. John's knees.

"Pardon me," I said, fleeing to the furthest stall. I had to go and could not possibly wait through the night. This was the only bathroom. I flushed the toilet and then had to move past them again as quickly as I could and closed the door behind me. I lay awake for another hour, going back over this scene in my mind.

What were they doing in there? Why was Muriel allowed to stay up so long past lights out? Couldn't she wash and comb out her own hair like the rest of us?

The next day I said nothing to my classmates, but over the next few weeks, I could hear the soft footfalls after lights out and the door opening and closing to Mother St. John's room. Then one morning in April, Mary Ingles pulled me aside after breakfast and asked me to step into the study hall before our classes. She said she had something to talk to me about.

"Do you know that Muriel is going into Mother St. John's room most nights after lights out?" Mary's room was at the top of our corridor, closest to Mother St. John's room. "I've heard tiptoeing many nights, heard the door opening and closing, and then I started to peek out from behind my curtain and saw it was Muriel. Lately, she has been going there almost every night," Mary added.

"Yes, I've heard the footsteps, but I have only seen them in the bathroom," I said and told Mary what I'd witnessed.

For days, Mary and I had private conversations, trying to decide what, if anything, to do. Final exams were beginning the next week, then we would be leaving for the summer. "I don't know what this all means," I said finally, "but it doesn't seem right. I think we have to tell the dean of women."

The next day Mary and I stepped into Mother St. Mary Philippe's office, asked to close the door, then told her what we heard and saw. She said little, listened, and looked at us in silence, her black eyes narrowing. "That's all, girls. Go to your classes now and your final exams."

Neither Mary nor I were to know what happened after that, but we both failed Latin. I had never failed an exam in my life. Over the summer, I was able to study the text by myself in between reading Somerset Maugham and Hugh McLennan, and I took a special makeup exam with another professor on the university campus at the beginning of September. Mary showed up to take the same exam, which was the first we knew that the other had failed Mother St. John's Latin.

"I just don't understand how I could have failed that course," Mary said. "I took Latin throughout high school and always tested just fine." In the fall of my sophomore year, I took the advanced Latin course on campus, taught by a monk from the nearby monastery. I made *A*'s throughout the semester.

In the spring of my freshman year, my date for the senior prom was Ricky, a young man from the village where I went to high school. His younger brother was in the same grade as my brother, Malcolm. Ricky planned to go to graduate school for teacher training and appeared at our house in Pleasant Valley a few days after the senior prom and asked to meet privately with my mother in the living room. He told her he wanted to ask me to marry him. I have always wondered what expressions passed over my mother's face when this question was posed. Afterward she told me that she said, "I don't think that's possible, Ricky. Rosemary is just sixteen." She had spared me from having to deal directly with, and reject, this astonishing proposal.

Late that summer following that first year, when I had returned home to Pleasant Valley from my summer job and was preparing again to leave for college, I stood in front of our kitchen window, washing the dinner dishes and staring down the road that led to the town. I said to my mother, "I do not want to go back to Mount St. Bernard this year. Could I stay at home and go to the university from here?" Tears were suddenly there on my cheeks. I reached to dry them with the dishtowel.

Mother was quiet for a minute before replying with the practical, "But dear, I drive in the opposite direction to school each day. How would you get to your classes? You have your scholarship, so that is paying for you to stay at the women's college." She was right, of course. I finished drying the dishes, stacked them in the cupboard, and went upstairs to finish packing my trunk.

My First Job

During the early spring of my freshman year in college, I followed the suggestions of several of my upper classmates and applied for a job as a waitress at one of the two major tourist resorts in Nova Scotia. Keltic Lodge is a first-class destination with a major golf course and is situated in one of the most beautiful places in Nova Scotia: on a finger of land called Middle Head that bisects the harbor of Ingonish on the northeast coast of Cape Breton Island. The magnificent mountain headland called Cape Smokey looms to the south, and the smattering of small offshore islands to the north is a frontispiece to the distant Cape Breton Highlands range of mountains. These are not mountains like the great Rockies, but more like the Berkshires in the eastern U.S. or the White Mountains of Vermont. They are great, worn-down ancient ranges covered with spruce and pine trees, maples, and birch, known to us as simply as The Highlands.

I was joyful at the acceptance letter from the provincial department of tourism, although I had a tinge of guilt over leaving my younger brother and sisters behind at home and the extra help I could have been to my mother that summer. But this was an adventure, a chance to spend the summer in a beautiful location, and I would have a job, my first job! I would earn and save some money for my sophomore year.

Visions of bountiful tips from grateful tourists outweighed any tinges of guilt.

There was, however, a sobering last line to the acceptance letter. "Because of your young age, you are being assigned to the coffee shop and not to the main dining room." I was sixteen that summer, as tall as any of the senior girls at our university, and quite sure that I looked grown-up, even rather sophisticated. Short of assessing the different dining venues when I got there, I suspected that the tips in the coffee shop would be less than in the formal dining room.

Once there, I discovered my hunch was right when our experienced shift supervisor said, "We'll get some tips and you'll be able to save a decent amount of money, but tips are less here than upstairs," referring to the main dining room. "But" she added, "we will have a better shift system — every other week we'll work mornings and evenings and have the afternoon off for the beach, and on the other week, we'll have the early mornings and evenings off, great for taking long morning walks on the golf course or evening strolls to the village."

I asked her why the management would consider age a factor in assigning new staff to the coffee shop rather than the dining room. "It's those trays," she said. "You have to be able to balance heavy trays, with the dinner or soup plates piled high in their steel covers. That takes great strength and lots of practice. Here, we can carry our trays in front of us."

I tried lifting one of our trays containing a few aluminum ice cream dishes to my shoulder. The tray wobbled, my wrist was much too weak for this, so this coffee shop was going to be the better place for me.

There were four of us on that afternoon shift for our first day of work. Most of the supplies for the soda fountain area and sandwiches and soups had arrived, although not everything was unpacked or yet laid out for easy retrieval — the loaves of whole wheat and white bread were still in their plastic sleeves at the back of the sandwich station, and we had only begun to arrange the water glasses and small dishes for ice cream sundaes when the first customers appeared at the door. I straightened my tartan apron and patted my starched matching headband, picked up the menus, and walked eagerly over to the two couples who were taking their seats by the window, saying in my most polite voice, "Good afternoon and welcome," and described the items that we could offer them for lunch.

I went back to the counter to announce their choices. In whispers, we discussed who should do what part of the four separate orders. Kay, the supervisor, moved quickly to start a pot of coffee and set out the cups and saucers (we had not thought of preparing coffee before now) and the rest of us decided who would make the sandwiches — two would work together, one to open the loaves of bread and the other to add the fillings and later make the desserts, while my assignment was to bring out the place settings and glasses of water and serve the lunches when ready. We were all moving quickly but getting in each other's way, struggling to finish the sandwiches. I was helping to arrange them on the plates and add a few potato chips when we looked up to see a mass of people coming through the main doors of the coffee shop. It was a flow, a stream of people that seemed to have no end.

"What has happened; who are they?" I whispered to Kay, who had worked there for the past two summers and knew the daily patterns.

"It must be a bus tour; they are all supposed to go to the dining room." She looked at her watch and said, "It's 2:15. The dining room is closed, and the bus tour must have been running late, and here they are."

We had not yet served the first table because we had just finished making their sandwiches. Kay looked at the coffee pot, still brewing, only half the pot completed. "Get this mob some menus," she said to me. "We will finish making the sandwiches."

By then, every table in the coffee shop was filled with more people than our total supply of menus, but I took the first handful and headed toward the nearby tables, clumsily doling out two menus to a table and stammering perhaps a quick, "Hello," or something equally inane, then rushing back for more menus to give to the remaining tables. I could see the four pairs of eyes from the first table watching me, impatient, waiting for their lunch. I rushed back to the counter.

"Do we have their sandwiches ready? Is the coffee ready?" I asked and gathered up the first two plates, bringing them to the table. I could no longer remember who ordered the ham and cheese and who asked for the tuna and lettuce on whole wheat, so I had to ask, embarrassed. "I will be right back with the other sandwiches and the coffee," I said, by this time frightened as well as rushed, so that when I reached the counter, I asked Kay if she could serve the coffee and the other two girls if they could start taking orders from the mass of tables. That seemed like a good division of labor, as I went back to the first table with the other two plates of sandwiches and Kay arrived with the coffee pot.

Somehow, between the four of us, we managed to take the lunch orders from all of the tables, aware of the mutterings from the latecomers that they had paid for a proper lunch in the dining room and here they were, subjected to this skimpy menu and too few (they might have added "harried") staff.

I thought, *How are we going to make all of those lunches, and what if they want soup? None of the soup vats were hot yet. Did we have enough bread and fillings for all of the sandwiches? How could we make coffee quickly enough using the regular-size percolators? What if they all wanted dessert and all at the same time?*

That reminded me that our first table had asked for ice cream sundaes for dessert, no doubt one of the most attractive items on our limited menu. Who was going to make those sundaes? By this time, we were scrambling to assemble sandwiches and I was gathering up dozens of place settings, pouring glasses of water and starting out with full trays (carried in front of me) to the many tables. I remember a sea of faces, all watching me closely, annoyed to begin with and clearly anticipating much delay before they would be served their lunch. Over my shoulder I saw that one of the men from the first table was waving at me, so I broke away to speed over to his table.

"You may forget about our dessert. Please bring us the bill," he said. I sped back to the counter and asked Kay if she had the bill ready.

"Go back to those other tables," she said. "I'll take care of it."

To this day, I do not know how we were able to make all those sandwiches, brew and pour coffee, dispense Cokes from the soda fountain and make milkshakes, much less desserts for all those tables. It all happened in a frenzied blur, and a blur it remains over the years. Somehow, Kay kept track of the orders and added up the costs of each bill (we call those "checks" these days) while we other three scurried back and forth, refilling cups and glasses, trying to avoid the critical looks and grumbles over poor service.

When the bus tour customers finally left and the room was suddenly silent, we looked at the tables littered with the debris of crumpled paper napkins, plates with crumbs, and coffee stains. I walked over to the first table with a tray to gather up the items from our first four customers, who had long since left. I stacked the coffee cups and saucers on the tray, then the empty water glasses, and picked up the first sandwich plate to find, underneath, three miniature pennies. I found no other coins as I gathered up the remaining items. Back at the counter, I set down the tray and spread out the tiny pennies for my colleagues to see.

"What are these?" I asked. Each of us in turn held the pennies up to the light to read the value and the origin, for they were much smaller than Canadian coins, even smaller than our ten-cent dime. Kay squinted, turned one over, and held it up close to her glasses.

"These are from Sweden," she said, "and they appear to be pennies."

"But," I said stupidly, "this is Canada. Why would they leave us a tip in Swedish pennies? We can't spend Swedish money in Canada."

No one answered. Words were not necessary. Our efforts to make them lunch and serve it in a timely fashion had been a failure.

"Well," I said, "if this is the way it will be for us this summer, we are not going to make any money. None at all."

Exhausted, we moved about the empty tables, gathering up dishes, glasses, and silverware, taking them back behind the counter, and stacking them in the large dishwasher. We fanned out to wipe the tables, and straighten out the salt and pepper shakers, still silent.

Kay looked at her watch and took off her apron, saying that the shift was almost over and there would be no more customers that day, since the coffee shop was closed that evening. She asked if someone would walk down and lock the door from the inside, then said, "All right, we must get organized. We have to do better, even if we never have to deal with a busload of angry tourists again this summer."

So over that next week, we did get organized and came up with a commendable distribution of labor. One person would be in charge of sandwiches, one would make soups and salads, one would take the orders, do the place settings and bring the food to the tables; and Kay would take charge of the coffee, the soda fountain, the ice cream orders, and the cash register. The rest of us could pitch in making the desserts and cutting the pies as our tasks permitted.

One day in midsummer, the dining room manager came down to observe us at work during a pleasantly busy lunchtime and proclaimed us "the most efficient and still-charming shift crew" he had seen in many years. And by summer's end, we did make some money, as the tips flowed steadily, if modestly, and along with our minimum hourly wages, money was easy to save since there was little opportunity to spend it. All of our meals were provided (plus those mini-chocolate marshmallow sundaes we would allow ourselves when cleaning up from the evening shift, taken without guilt from the almost-empty ice cream buckets). We had comfortable rooms on the third floor of the main lodge building, quieter and with fewer parties than the chambermaids and bellboys had in their quarters down the hill, but perfect for late-night or early-morning reading or sharing stories about our families or our different universities.

That was the summer I read Somerset Maugham, every book of his that was available in the lodge library, and we all took turns reading Hugh MacLennan's Barometer Rising, about the great Halifax explosion of 1917, which was the largest man-made explosion in the world before the atomic bomb was dropped on Hiroshima.

There were also the promised outings during our free shifts. We took those early-morning walks, following the craggy path among the pine groves stunted by the ocean winds to the tip of Middle Head or walking the dewy edges of the greens of the eighteen-hole golf course, well before the earliest golfers arrived. And very early one morning, we hiked the trail up to the highest point on the nearby mountain range overlooking the village and the canyon formed by the small river that wound through the golf course. We could see the great hump of Cape Smokey, the specks of fishing boats at sea, and, we were quite sure, we spotted, through binoculars, great humpback whales breaking the surface and then falling back with a splash to the sea.

Sunny afternoons when we were off shift, we went to the beach, daring each other to go first into the cold waters of the Labrador Current. Evenings off, when there was a full moon and clear sky, we could sit quietly on the lawn chairs near the parking lot and daydream — or rather moon dream — wondering what might lie ahead for us in our next years of college, and perhaps graduate school. I think we grew in grace and maybe even beauty that summer, and we were certainly healthy, as we lived surrounded by the natural beauty and the serenity of those summer days.

On the afternoon of our last shift, I took off my apron and hung it on the hooks by the storeroom door, looked around the empty coffee shop at the soda fountain and the assembly area for sandwiches, and thought, Well. So this was my first job. I earned money to contribute to my next year at college, important help for my mother. I did well at this job, despite that first day, or maybe because we learned well from the chaos of that first day. Perhaps the most important money I earned were those three tiny Swedish pennies from those first customers. Those pennies spoke more loudly than any harsh words ever could.

I walked out of the room, thinking, no matter what happens to me in the future and even if I never succeed at any other job, I have become a good waitress. I can always be a waitress.

The Music Major Learns to Type

I had a week back home with my family after my summer job at the tourist resort, and before returning to college for my sophomore year. I used some of my summer earnings to buy a new sweater set, a skirt, a fall jacket, and the most special item of all, a pair of white bucks laced shoes and white knee-high socks. "All the rage again this year," the man at the shoe store said, "although I hear that this year the style will be to scuff them right away, not keep them white with polish as everyone appeared to do last year." The rest of my summer earnings were to pay for my piano lessons throughout the two semesters.

On Saturday, my mother asked me to accompany her to a wedding reception for the daughter of one of her fellow high school teachers. During the five-mile drive, I told her some details from my summer job, describing how much I had come to love the beauty of Ingonish and the wonderful hikes we would take between shifts at our coffee shop.

As we pulled into the yard and I was getting out of the car, I turned toward Mom to answer a question she had just asked, closed the car door on my passenger side, and then slumped against the car in excruciating pain. I looked at the door and saw that my hand was caught and that when I opened the door, I saw the little finger on my left hand turn paper white then explode with blood.

"Is something wrong, dear?" Mother asked, looking worried as she came around the car, then gasped as she saw the blood spurting from my finger, "What happened?" she asked, then said, "I have a handkerchief in the glove compartment, we can wrap your finger in that." Then she hurried to open the car door and find the hankie, as we called these things.

"Here dear, wrap this part around your little finger as tight as you can, then I'll wrap your hand tightly so that the little finger is straight against your others. That will help stop the bleeding also." She tied knots on both corners, saying, "That should help."

I was still slumped against the car, and the pain was coming in waves.

"What ever happened?" Mother asked again.

"I closed the door on my hand, on the little finger."

"Are you in much pain, dear? I can ask the people in the house for some aspirin. I know I don't have any in my purse."

"No, don't do that. It will just let them know what has happened." I was too young, just sixteen that summer, so she could not say she would run and get me a drink of rum or whiskey. I would have to tough this out all afternoon.

"It is my left little finger, Mom, on my left hand. That's the one I write with, and it's a strong hand when I play the piano."

"That finger does not look strong enough to practice your piano pieces," the piano teacher said as she looked at my left hand the afternoon in early September when I arrived for the first lesson of the year.

"You need to do new types of exercise to strengthen that finger. I suggest you take typing lessons, then come back in three or four weeks and we'll see if you are ready then. I'll arrange things with the secretarial program."

Well, I thought, *typing could be helpful. I could type my term papers this year instead of handwriting them.*

171

The following morning, I presented myself to the nun who was teaching the introductory course in typing. "You are welcome here," she said. "I have placed you at a desk and typewriter in the back row. Just follow along with all the instructions to the typing class."

The typewriter was big, bulky, and black. I tentatively placed all ten fingers over ten of the keys, then the teacher said, "Q-U-E-R-T-Y," whatever that was, and "Keep your little fingers in the air, poised over the shift key on either side and when I say, 'Go,' hit those shift keys."

I did, and then I slumped over the typewriter, weak and dizzy from waves of pain. The typewriter was a manual, the keyboard tough and resistant compared to those I would have years later on my own, a Smith-Corona electric portable or the smooth elegance of the keyboard on the IBM Selectric that our departmental secretary would have two decades later.

How was I to get through this? As the nun brought me a glass of water and stood over me, worried, she asked, "Are you going to be all right?"

I would have to do this three times a week? In early mornings for the entire semester? I clenched my teeth, deciding to concentrate on memorizing the other keys and where my other fingers were supposed to be.

Three weeks later, I found I could look at the typing teacher as she gave us instructions on what to type, instead of looking at the keys. There was still some pain in the little finger on my left hand each time I hit the shift key, but the finger was getting stronger, and I was no longer apt to pass out from the pain.

"This is looking much better," my piano teacher said as she examined the finger when my lessons resumed, testing it by asking me to tap on a piano key. "Now I want you to do scales and arpeggios each day for a half-hour before your lessons to make that finger flexible as well as strong and keep up the typing classes."

By the end of the semester, my little finger was back to full strength and flexibility. I had learned to touch type with high accuracy, and my typing speed was so fast that on the morning when my class took the final typing test, I scored the highest marks for accuracy and speed. The rest of the class was astounded, although I could tell that some were none too pleased. I was an interloper, and typing was to be the foundation of their career.

But the tension was broken when one of our classmates said, "Well if Rosemary can do this in typing, I'm going to take piano lessons!"

Sophomore Year

My premonition of a dark year ahead was to be actualized the fall semester of my sophomore year. Our dorm that year was on the upper floor of Immaculata Hall. Here, we each had our own rooms, furnished with a single bed, a desk and chair, a dresser, and a medium-sized closet.

"You can store off-season clothes in your wardrobe trunks in the trunk room, to give you more space," our young floor proctor, a nun, told us when we arrived.

We all shared a large bathroom at the end of the hall that featured two separate rooms with a bathtub, four shower stalls, and several toilet stalls. There was a long row of washbasins that became a busy — and noisy —place to gather in early mornings, and by 9:30 in the evening, when we were getting ready for bed. That was also a hurried event since we needed to have all homework completed and the lights in our rooms turned off promptly when the bell rang at 10 p.m.

Squeezing in an extra hour of homework was not possible because each of our rooms had a glass panel above the door, a transom we called it, and the nun-proctor would walk the hallways beginning promptly at 10:01 each night to determine that all lights were indeed turned off. Some of us suspected that at least one of our truly studious classmates used a flashlight under her bedcovers to get in an extra hour of study. But we never proved that rumor and she was never caught by the proctor. Those bathroom lights were welcome towards the end of the semester when Mary Cameron asked me to help her study for our philosophy exam.

"It's all Greek to me," she said. I knew that Mary was a whiz at science, so she could always help me there.

"Of course," I said, "but when will we have the time to do this?" We both agreed that we would violate lights-out rules and study in the bathroom, which we did for several nights, perched on the wide window ledge.

All lights except those in the bathroom area at the end of the hall might have been turned off, but the nighttime drama was still a possibility. One night, just as I was drifting off to sleep, I was startled upright in bed by a terrible moaning from somewhere down the hall. This was a deep-voiced moaning of someone who was terrified. I got up, fumbled in the dark for a robe and slippers, and opened my door. Mary Thompson, whose room was directly opposite mine, was just opening her door. We could see each other in the reflection from the night lights in the bathroom. The moaning was louder now that we were in the hall. It was low-pitched and terrifying to me. My skin was crawling. "Mary, would you come with me? We'll walk down the hall and check where this is coming from."

We clasped hands and walked down three or four doors. Maura, whose room was on our way, opened her door and we whispered, "Come with us." Three doors down, the moans were at a crescendo.

"That's Darryl's room," Mary said.

I knocked on the door, turned the knob, and said loudly as the door was opening, "Darryl, it's Rosemary and Mary and Maura. Whatever is wrong?"

Maura reached in and switched on the light. Darryl was hunched against the wall, holding her knuckles to her cheeks, her face white with terror. "There's a mouse. It's under my desk. It's squealing. I think it's caught in a trap," she blurted out between sobs.

I got down on my knees and looked under the desk. "How did a mousetrap get in this room?" Maura asked, not expecting an answer. I determined to ask that question the next day. There, under the desk, was a mousetrap with a mouse, surely caught, and by this time, surely dying.

"Mary, stand in front of Darryl. I'm going to take this critter and its trap to the bathroom," I said, which I did, holding the end of the wooden trap with the now limp creature in front of me, and scurried down the hall to the bathroom where I tossed the dying mouse and trap into a large waste can, covered it with several layers of paper towels, and pushed the metal cover down tightly. We could dispose of the remains in the morning.

"Darryl, why don't you sleep in my room for the rest of the night?" Mary said. Her voice was kind. "There has never been a mouse in my room."

By this time, another ten or so of our classmates were gathered outside Darryl's door and the young nun, our proctor, was coming down the hall hurriedly, dressed in at least part of her nun's habit.

"Everything is okay now," Maura assured the nun, as Mary, along with the posse of classmates, escorted Darryl up the hall and got her comfortably settled in Mary's bed. I walked Mary back down the hall, saying, "Poor Darryl, she's from Montreal and may not be familiar with having a mouse in the house. We always had mice in the country, maybe not in our house, but in the neighbor's barns, and scurrying out of haystacks."

"We all have our terrors," Mary said calmly. "I do not do well with spiders."

But the mouse drama seemed mild to us as the early months of the fall semester progressed. If we thought that the geographic distance between our freshman dorm and Immaculata Hall would stop the nightly visitations by the nun who was still our gym teacher, we were sadly wrong. This time, the nun was coming to Muriel's room. Perhaps five or ten minutes after lights out, I could hear the swishing of the robes and the door opening and closing to the room. I found myself staying awake every night to anticipate this, although I was often asleep before later hearing the door open and close.

Within days, this was the whispered topic of discussion amongst my classmates, with sharp questions from Nadia whose room was next door to Muriel.

"What is going on in there? Why is this happening?" she asked. Nadia was the only one of our classmates who was not Catholic, so she must have been questioning our religion as well as these nightly visitations.

Then one night, Nadia snapped: Just as the door had opened and closed to Muriel's room, Nadia began screaming. Her screams pulled me and several of my classmates out of bed and out of our rooms to see Nadia running down the hall to the bathroom, screaming, then dropping coins into the payphone that was our only telecommunications link, to call her parents in New Glasgow. "You must come and get me now!" she screamed into the phone. "I'm packing a suitcase. Meet me at the back door of Immaculata Hall."

The young nun-proctor was standing at the entrance of the bathroom, her face ashen. "What is going on?" she whispered. None of us answered.

Darryl said to Nadia, "I will help you pack," and led her down the hall.

"Maura, will you come with me to the dean of women right after Mass in the morning and before breakfast?" I asked since Maura was vice president of our class, and I was president. This would be a daunting meeting, but we couldn't live with this situation any longer.

Early the next morning, Mother St. Mary Phillippe looked grimly at us, her small black eyes narrowed, her jaws tight as we told her what was going on at night and also reminding her that the same thing had occurred during our freshman year. She nodded to us, but said only, "Go to breakfast now, girls."

Nadia never came back to our class. She finished her planned secretarial course in Halifax. Mother St. John was not in our gym class the following Wednesday; instead, the sweet nun from the home economics department bounced a basketball, and not expertly, and told us with a shy grin that she would be our new gym teacher. We never saw Mother St. John again.

And Muriel? There was never any acknowledgment from her that anything had ever happened. She went about her classes with the same chirpy voice and pleasant smile, tossing her long dark hair, and went into rehearsals for the lead in the next musical production.

Just over a year later, my summer job doing surveys for the Canadian government took me to northern New Brunswick and to the town where Muriel lived. I found the telephone number and address in the local phone book and called, telling Muriel I was in town. "Do stop by when you can tomorrow afternoon," she said. "We will have tea and cookies."

When I arrived, Muriel was sitting on a swing on their front porch. Her mother was standing behind her, brushing Muriel's long hair. I looked quickly at the mother as I was approaching the steps to the porch. She was a large, ungainly woman, not at all attractive, much less pretty than her daughter.

"I grew up with seven brothers," Muriel's mother told me over tea. "I had to do all the cooking and wash all their clothes.

I never had time to myself, so I make sure my daughters do not do housework."

She looked quite like Mother St. John, but much kinder.

Finding My Lifetime Career

I didn't choose my career in life, it chose me, immediately and without any doubt, at the end of my first class in economics, Economics 201, in early September of my sophomore year.

The economics course was obligatory for all but the engineers, and the registrar's office assigned each of us to a professor. My professor was a woman, Dr. Doris Boyle, distinguished by the fact that she was an American as well as being the only woman professor at the university that year who was not a nun.

Dr. Boyle began taking roll call while we were still searching for our seats in the classroom and struggling to take off our jackets. She held up Paul Samuelson's book and said that this would be our textbook for the year, and we were to read the first two chapters before the next class. This textbook was to become the classic foundation economics book for many decades in many countries. I always chose it for my classes during my years of teaching.

But that was it for the textbook, even if Dr. Boyle remembered at the end of each class to assign the next chapter. Instead of lecturing to the textbook, Dr. Boyle began a long series of soliloquies about the fundamentals of an economy — people at work or without work. She told gripping tales of unemployment during the Great Depression, detailing what President Roosevelt did with his government policies and actions to counteract that terrible economic downturn. She spoke passionately about the importance of family income, of the differences in income levels, of the perils and costs to society of lost jobs and incomes, of the ravages caused by poverty, of the particular difficulties that women and their children faced in those low-income strata. She talked of families desperate for enough food, of going without new clothes or shoes for their children, for years on end.

She spoke about the geography of poverty in the United States, but also in the poor fishing and farming villages of eastern Canada. She thought poorly of most business leaders, "*Cap-it-al-ists,*" she called them, singling and sounding out each syllable, calling their actions cruel in demanding long work hours in miserable factories and paying wages that were too low and benefits — if at all —- that were too few to support families.

She told us stories of how the labor force was mobilized during the war years. She described the fundamental industries of a nation: fishing, farming, logging, and mining; manufacturing and the factories; the export sector; the medical professions; the importance of education and how vital it was to educate not only all children, but particularly the importance of educating girls, stressing how vital the teaching and nursing professions were for women.

I couldn't get to sleep at night with all of the images of the economy she described running through my mind. I had begun university thinking that I would major in English literature and probably carry a double major in music since I was still taking piano lessons and classes in music theory. But this new subject of economics was making my pulse as well as my mind race, sending me again and again to the library on many afternoons and weekends just to read more.

I never looked to any other career possibilities after that course in Economics 201 taught by Dr. Doris Boyle. I went on to major in economics for my BA and to earn a master's degree in economics. I have spent most of my working life as an economist, and I have never been bored one hour of my life since I discovered the field of economics.

Flu Season

I think that most of us caught the flu that winter of 1957, my sophomore year, and although my classmates and I had our separate rooms in Sophomore Hall, the germs must have spread quickly through the dining room or during morning Mass, which was mandatory in our convent residence in those days.

I don't recall that this flu that year had a name, it was just "the flu." The admonition around the women's college and the university was, "It's a bad flu this year, so take care." How we were supposed to take care to avoid getting the flu was never specified. There were no flu shots then, and antibiotics were rarely prescribed, just aspirin and extra glasses of juice. The juice was canned apple juice, since canned orange juice, much less fresh oranges, was rarely available.

There was a small infirmary in the women's college, with maybe five or six beds watched over by a nursing sister. The infirmary filled up quickly as the flu broke out, so most of the young women who came down with symptoms were confined to their bedrooms. The parents of those who lived within a hundred miles or so were asked to come and take their invalid home.

I do not remember whether I caught the flu that year. Growing up, there always seemed to be some type of flu making the rounds each winter, with varying degrees of severity. Those flus didn't have names either, but I clearly recall the winter of 1953, when I had just turned thirteen, and my entire family came down with all of the miserable symptoms: fever, aches, intestinal cramps, loss of appetite. We four children were the first casualties and were all sick at the same time. Our mother held out longer, carrying trays of juice or hot porridge up the stairs each morning, taking temperatures, changing the bedsheets Then it was mother's turn to catch all of our symptoms, and I, as the eldest, staggered out of bed to take care of her and take over nursing and cooking duties for the younger ones.

By contrast, the early symptoms of the 1957 flu appeared to be average: high fever and aches but without severe intestinal distress. If I did suffer then, any symptoms must have been mild and of short duration. This became an important detail in the winter of 2009-2010 since in order to ration supplies for the vulnerable children and "at-risk" groups such as pregnant women, those of us over sixty were not given the scarce doses of vaccine for the H1N1 virus. The premise was that my generation would have built up antibodies from the 1957 flu. During the 1957 outbreak, I only remember carrying trays of food up to many of my classmates who were suffering and not of being ill myself.

Then, one night, there was an intense commotion on the floor — feet running, doors opening, lights being switched on, urgent whispers that carried down the hall. I pulled on a robe, found slippers, and rushed down toward the noise. Several nuns were hovering around the door of my classmate Barbara's room. They had dressed hurriedly, with some wimples askew. Several of our other classmates were also hurrying down the hall. The nursing sister from the infirmary rushed out of Barb's room saying, "We must call the doctor. She has a fever of a hundred and six." I tried to look in the room, but there were too many black robes blocking the view of her bed.

One of the girls whispered, "Should we get her a glass of water?"

"Yes, go ahead," said the nursing sister, so she and another girl rushed off, glad to do something in their fear and anxiety. The wait seemed endless before the doctor and the nurse arrived from the hospital, pushing a wheelchair and moving us away from the door. We could hear scrambling movement and voices saying, "Be careful," and "Easy now," and then the nurse backed out the door, pulling the wheelchair, with the doctor following, holding Barb's wrist and looking at his watch. Barb was slumped over, flushed with fever, eyes closed. We watched in silence as the group moved down the hallway, the tires on the wheelchair squeaking on the polished wood floor.

"Go back to your rooms now, girls, and pray for your classmate," said one of the nuns. The next day we learned that Barb was in a coma, and her condition remained the same for the rest of that week. We organized nightly prayer vigils in the chapel.

The winter days gave way to the windy and wet early spring so common to eastern Nova Scotia, with no reported change in our classmate's condition. The province-wide newspaper carried reports of severe illnesses and several deaths that were said to be caused by this still-nameless flu. There was yet no change in Barb's condition. When the semester's final exams were finished and we all packed our trunks to leave for the summer vacation, we held one last vigil and two girls in our class were elected to visit Barb in the hospital, to look through the tent that encased her bed with all of the attachments for breathing tubes and heart monitors.

Sometime during that summer, the doctors found a new treatment that finally brought Barb out of her coma. She was then moved to a specialty rehabilitation center, where she had to be taught to walk and talk again, and to get help in reading. I did not see her again for many years, but the news from afar was positive — Barb had recovered, had finished her secretarial course, found a good job, married, and became the mother of a son.

I visited her around that time and found her cheerful and grateful for her recovery. She told me that she had no memory of the many months in the coma or much memory of her months in recovery. She was most proud of her son, spoke of how well he was doing in first grade, and described him as a bubbly little boy, a great talker, smitten with his collection of toy dinosaurs.

Then several years later, there was another severe flu season. Where was I by that time? California. I had mild symptoms but worried more about my little son who was just turned one and a half. But his bout with the flu was relatively milder than the attack of croup he'd had earlier in the winter, which thoroughly frightened both my husband and me. I could be found in our kitchen late that night, boiling the kettle and pots of water while my husband frantically sought advice from the pediatrician over the telephone. I was told to drape a large towel over my head and hold the baby's face over the steam until his throat cleared and his breath became even.

The word came a few weeks later from one of my classmates, Thelma Power, who had grown up in the same town as Barbara. "Barb has died," she wrote. "She contracted severe symptoms from this winter's flu, fell into a coma, and there was no hope, not this time."

So H1N1 is here. It is a strange appellation, but the CDC in Atlanta insists this must be the name, that it is not "swine flu" as the great devastation after World War I was called, and, after the fact, as the 1957 flu was named. I obsess over my little grandbabies — have they had their shots for the regular flu as well as the two doses of the H1N1? Has my pregnant daughter been given her shots? And my daughter-in-law? What about my son? He was quite ill earlier this year; he must be in line for the scarce supply.

I have this sudden image of the long, dark hall of our sophomore floor, with the shaft of light pouring out of that one door that is ajar, of dark robes scurrying, and of frightened girls rushing to help, but being helpless in the end. And I think of Barbara's too-brief life, that too-short respite between the seasons of flu.

The Senior Prom in Sophomore Year

By the time of the senior prom my sophomore year, I had a powerful crush on my date, Doug MacDonald, a tall, blond, shy geologist with a great sense of Cape Breton wit when he grew comfortable enough with his classmates, although never with any girls who might be nearby. He was known to launch into a Gaelic-tinged tale or anecdote about one of the many brothers from his large family. Around him, I was the one who became bashful and tongue-tied, unused to this mesmerizing state of infatuation.

He seemed caught up in that infatuation too, and while I have no memory of that prom, what we might have talked about, or of the color of my gown, except to recall that it was floor-length and full-skirted with an organza top layer and that I had dyed-to-match pumps. What I do remember is that at three in the morning, there I was, tramping through the snow and mud of early May on Nick Delaney's field, Doug following close behind me, up to my ankles in the cold, wet, snowy, muddy field, my dyed-to-match shoes already ruined and the skirts of my fancy dress soggy and mud-splattered. That's how we looked when Nick Delaney opened the door after our many poundings and rattling of the latch, Doug in his wet tuxedo, my corsage long since wilted.

"Our car is stuck in the ditch. Could you help us get it out?" I asked Nick Delaney.

Nick Delaney was the noted hermit of the valley. He lived with his mother on a subsistence farm some three miles from town, midway to our house. He was spoken about, but no one ever reported having spoken to him. His long beard, silence, and solitude were barriers to all, and here I was, face to face with Nick Delaney at 3 a.m. on this cold, miserable morning, asking for help. Did he even know I existed, that I was one of the "Teacher's kids," as we were called behind our backs?

He stared at us, apparitions that we were, and growled, "Wait a minute," then closed the door. Shortly after, he reappeared in boots and a heavy jacket that covered his overalls and said, "I'll get the horses."

Doug and I trudged back to the car, where the couple who were our prom companions were huddled in the back seat, trying to stay warm. "Did you get help?" they asked.

Help shortly arrived. Nick Delaney came down the hill leading his two horses, positioned them in front of the car and attached a hook from the whiffle tree to the bumper. Then he urged his horses to pull away. After a few tugs and snorts, the horses finally pulled the car out of the deep muddy water-and-ice-filled ditch.

How was I going to explain all of this to my mother, who, no doubt, was awake, worrying why I wasn't home when I had said I would be home by 2 a.m. at the latest. My explanation as Doug and I arrived at the kitchen door in our muddied, ruined clothes, was so beyond any normal excuse we might have offered that mother brushed it aside and said to Doug, whose face was red with embarrassment, "You and your friends must have a cup of coffee before returning to town."

Mother said almost nothing to me the next day but listened with a light in her eyes as I told my younger siblings the story, with them pestering to have every detail repeated two or three times. They were astounded.

"Rosemary spoke to Nick Delaney! He hitched up his horses and pulled their car out of the ditch at three in the morning!"

Whatever mother was thinking, my encounter with Nick Delaney became the talk of the valley for the next few weeks.

I never saw Nick Delaney again, but I have always remembered his willingness to help us, these strange town-and-gown-looking people, at that awful hour of the morning.

Dear shy Doug. He and I were to get into another embarrassing situation that summer after my sophomore year, when he came out to Pleasant Valley in his ancient Model T Ford, which he assured my mother had been "fully overhauled and restored by him." Those were a lot of words from him, and he blushed red to the hairline of his blond hair saying them. My brother and two sisters were scampering around the car, excited to see this ancient specimen, exclaiming over its shiny finish and its strange boxy shape. They no doubt added to Doug's misery.

After standing there in numb embarrassment, wishing that my younger siblings with their giggles and sly looks would just evaporate, I finally found my tongue. "We are going around the Cabot Trail," I said, "but we'll be back this evening before dark."

"Can this old car climb those steep mountains?" my mother asked Doug.

"Yes, I am certain it can. We will be okay. I will take good care of your daughter," Doug said.

So we set out, the car chugging down the gravel road of our valley with an occasional hiccup and lurch. Along the trip, just before we reached the Canso Causeway that would lead us onto Cape Breton Island, we stopped at a gas station to refill the tank and were soon surrounded by everyone who worked at the filling station and at the next-door garage, plus other motorists who pulled in when they spotted the old car, marveling at its look, peppering Doug with questions.

What did Doug and I talk about during this trip? We were both shy and tongue-tied, as my mother would say when she was encouraging one of her students to speak up in class. "Come on now," she would say but kindly, "are you tongue-tied?"

We were both infatuated with each other, so most of the time we probably smiled, ventured a few words, stole glances at the other when we didn't think we were being watched, and blushed some more when discovered. I did ask him about the job he was to soon start in Northern Quebec, working as a geologist with a large mining company. Did we stop somewhere to have lunch or at least to buy a sandwich and soda to have in the car?

The Cabot Trail begins at Cheticamp with the entrance to Cape Breton Highlands National Park and begins a long climb up and then down the high range of ancient mountains. At Pleasant Bay, the road switches back and forth down the mountain, with beautiful views form the crest of the bay to the village below. More mountains loom ahead, then the road levels to a high plateau before beginning the descent into Ingonish. By this time, the ancient car was heaving and jolting, with new sounds of clanging alternating with loud burps.

"We'll stop at the garage in Ingonish," Doug said. "I'll take a look at the engine and the tailpipes. Besides, we'll will need to fill the gas tank again."

Doug was still bent over the engine, talking with the garage mechanic when I returned from the store, but then he stood up, reached for a rag to wipe his hands, and said to me and the mechanic, "I think that does it. It is running smoothly now."

We climbed Cape Smokey without problems and successfully navigated the steep and winding descent. But an hour later, on the long climb up the mountain near St. Ann's, the old car coughed and rolled to a stop. It was now just after sunset, in the long twilight common to Nova Scotia in the summertime.

I thought, *This old car has just died. It just couldn't do another climb.*

Doug and I just sat there, neither of us speaking. I could feel his embarrassment even in this dusky light, and I was too embarrassed to ask him what we should do now. Instead, I asked, "Would you like one of the sodas?"

"Yes," he said. Then, "Let me find a flashlight. I'll see if I can find the problem."

Finally, after many minutes that seemed like hours, we saw the lights of a car starting up the long slog of the mountain. The car stopped beside the Model T and the driver got out and said, "Can I help?"

"Could you push us to the top of the mountain?" Doug asked. "I think the engine would start then and we would be okay. There's enough gas in the tank to get us to Antigonish."

So that is how we finished "the trip around the Trail." It was about 3 a.m. when we reached my home in Pleasant Valley. Mother appeared at the back door in her housecoat as we drove into the yard. She probably had not slept at all.

"We had a breakdown on the mountain after St. Ann's," Doug said shyly. "A car came along and pushed us to the top, then the engine restarted."

"Well, you are safe and you must be hungry," Mother said. "Rosemary, get some biscuits and jam and some milk. And young man," she said to Doug, "you can sleep on the chesterfield in the living room. It's too late for you to try driving home in that car."

I only ever saw Doug MacDonald on two other occasions. Later that summer, he wrote to invite me to stop by the dance hall in Judique for his brother's wedding reception.

When we arrived the dance hall was crowded. Dancers were on the floor dancing to the music from the three fiddlers and the piano player who were up on the stage. The groom and his lovely bride were leading the dancers, both flushed from the pace and the excitement that was palpable in the hall. Doug saw me come through the door and came over. He put his arm around my shoulders. "Can you stay for a dance?" he asked, nodding and smiling at my mother and to my brother and sisters.

This was a different Doug. Handsome in his tuxedo, he was obviously at ease around his many brothers. He introduced me, trading quips amid the winks and nods from them, as in, so this is the girl you told us about? Doug's arm was still around my shoulder, a strange, thrilling sensation.

It was a year later that I next saw Doug. After that wedding, he moved to Northern Quebec to take the job with a large mining company, where he could use his geology and engineering degrees. He wrote me a few letters during that year, my junior year, but the correspondence fell off during the late winter and spring months when I was ill and hospitalized with hyperthyroidism.

I was able to work that summer on an interesting project for the Canadian government, travelling throughout western and northern New Brunswick. My energy was returning after the long illness, but I was still heavy with the thirty pounds I had to gain in the hospital.

I finished the project at the end of August and drove the three hundred miles from the northern part of the province to my home in Antigonish. Sleepy and still groggy the morning after I'd arrived, I sat in our living room, sipping a cup of coffee, my long hair a tangled mess, wearing an old tank dress to cover my overweight body. The doorbell rang and Malcolm, my brother, went to answer it. When he came back in the room, he said, "There's a guy at the door here to see you."

I padded down the hall to the door in my old slippers and there stood Doug: tall, sunburnt, his blond hair still in a crew cut. I had no words. I just stood there and stared at him. Finally, I asked, "Would like to come in for a cup of coffee?" He nodded and I led him down the hall to our living room.

What was there to say? He kept looking at me with surprise. What was he thinking? That this did not look like the same girl he took to his senior prom? Perhaps I said, "I just came back from my summer job," or maybe I said, "My health is better," but I wasn't sure if he even knew about my illness.

There was nothing more to say. I knew that this was the end of our shy romance. There would be no letters, certainly never a phone call, not with that distance. and he would leave with this last vision of me: overweight, unkempt, badly dressed.

Thyroid Illness

The first symptoms appeared the winter of my junior year. I would feel faint and lightheaded during early-morning Mass in the chapel and my pulse would race. I told myself that I'd feel better after breakfast and after resting for an hour in the afternoon. My schedule was packed, and maybe I was doing too much. I was deep into the more advanced economics courses, most of them taught by the young professor just back from getting his PhD at MIT, the Massachusetts Institute of Technology. I had been elected president of my class again that year and also was chosen to join the board of the Student's Co-op Society, which ran the bookstore, the coffee shop, and even the dry-cleaning business on campus.

I was enjoying this new challenge, learning to analyze the financial statements, such as they were. I was also in the chorus of *Oklahoma!*, in rehearsals all winter for an early-spring production, and I was one of four women chosen to dance the dream sequence. But I noticed that my legs seemed to get ever weaker and shakier, and I would need to find a chair to sit in when we were backstage after dance rehearsal. Nonetheless, I was able to perform in the production, which was well received on campus, and the cast and production crew were invited to perform in Saint John, New Brunswick, over spring break.

But then one morning in chapel, I fainted. The world went dim in front of my eyes and I slumped to the floor. I don't remember being lifted or carried out of the chapel, but I do remember sitting slumped in a chair in the Mother Superior's office while she telephoned my mother, telling Mother that she was worried about my health and that several of the nuns had noticed that I had lost weight and appeared to be very tense. Maybe she said "high-strung."

Mother Superior must already have called a doctor, for soon, young Dr. McDonnell appeared in her office, carrying his black bag. He put his stethoscope over my heart.

I don't remember who took me to the hospital, probably my mother, but soon enough, there I was in a bed in a private room, and that's where I would stay for the next three weeks.

I was confined to bed and not permitted to walk; they fed me high-calorie meals and snacks five times a day. "You need to put on lots of weight, Rosemary, to help offset your hyperthyroid condition," Dr. MacDonnell told me.

I had no idea what the thyroid was or even where it was. Dr. MacDonnell described the function of the thyroid and what happens to the body when the metabolism goes out of whack. It had taken several days of tests before he told me the diagnosis, saying, "This is highly unusual; we rarely see this illness in this hospital."

I asked what could cause the thyroid to deviate from of its normal pattern. "We're not sure about that," he said kindly. "But we do have several methods to try and correct the syndrome." He continued, "You certainly are quite a rare case, Rosemary, but what is even more unusual is that we have another case with the same symptoms here in the hospital."

I found out from one of my nurses that the other person was the dean of men at the university, confined to a room down the hall. "We are giving him chocolate milkshakes with two scoops of ice cream midmorning and midafternoon, just like you are getting," the nurse said.

Over the course of those next three weeks, it seemed that every doctor attached to the hospital came to visit me, to stand at the end of the bed and look over my chart. Dr. Gorman, the chief surgeon, came in one morning carrying a paperback copy of *The Brothers Karamazov*, telling me that the author, Dostoyevsky, was an epileptic, and that he, Dr. Gorman, believed that the author gained great insight into human nature during his epileptic fits.

"You are probably gaining keen insights yourself during this hyperactive state you are in," he said. "Don't worry, though. We will get you stabilized, and everything will be under control. You will be better than ever." He pointed to the book again. "You'll find this book fascinating, but I suggest you write down the names of every character and then their nicknames; otherwise, it all gets confusing as to who is saying what to whom."

My sweet mother came frequently, maybe not every evening, because her schedule was busy, what with teaching high school math, taking my brother to his hockey games or my sisters to their high school basketball games. She would stand by my bed, holding my hand, trying not to look too worried, telling me news of the family and of our neighbors and one evening told me that I was not to worry about my college courses since I had taken all of the mid-term exams and had done well on them. She had spoken to the dean of women, who said that all of my professors would pass me in my courses, even if I were not back in time to study and take the final exams.

I don't remember if any of my younger siblings came to visit, maybe they were too young to visit in the hospital, but Mother would bring me handwritten notes from each and maybe a sketch drawing from Donnie. Concerned for me, my classmates from Gilmora Hall sent a delegation each week, telling lighthearted anecdotes of the latest events and college rumors.

Then one evening, one of my classmates, Peter, appeared. He said he was most worried about me and proceeded to pace back and forth around the three sides of my bed, reciting poems, then saying some prayers. He then announced that he was in love with me and said how anguished he was that I was ill and hospitalized.

I barely knew Peter. We may have been in the same economics or philosophy class, and I think we were both on a campus-wide committee for some type of planning, for what purpose now long forgotten.

By this time, Peter was becoming ever more overwrought.

He's in worse condition than me, I thought, *and if he doesn't leave soon, I'm the one who will suffer.*

I reached for the call button and pushed it. The nurse came running into the room. "I am very tired," I told her, "and I must rest now." The nurse looked at Peter, pointed to his jacket on the chair, and said, "You must leave now. She needs her rest."

After the door closed behind Peter, I burst into tears, and in between sobs and sniffles, told the nurse what had just happened. She reached for the phone and called the nurses' desk, requesting that the senior nurse on duty come to my room.

"You are not to worry about that young man," the senior nurse said after she had been briefed on what had occurred. "We will tell the main reception desk that if he should he come to the hospital again, he is not to be let in."

I did get better, and finally, one day, I was released, but for several days prior to that I needed help walking and moved slowly up and down the hall, leaning heavily on a nurse and an orderly. I had gained thirty pounds, which together with the daily doses of Phenobarbital, brought my pulse rate down to a normal range. Mother brought an old pair of sneakers for me to wear on the trip home, since my swollen feet would not fit into my winter boots.

For the next few days, I stayed at home with her, getting lots of affectionate stares from my siblings. Donnie made her special brownies for me and Louise helped to shampoo and brush out the tangles in my hair.

Mother drove me back to Gilmora Hall and to the warm welcome from my classmates. I was able to attend the last few classes of my various courses, but was excused, as promised, from taking the final exams. I read in the campus newspaper about the successful performance of *Oklahoma!* in New Brunswick. The campus production had traveled without me of course.

The semester was just finishing when the campus mail brought a letter from the Canadian government, telling me that I had been selected for a summer job in economic research and that I was to report to a federal office in Truro, Nova Scotia, on May 15. I had applied for the position back in the winter and had forgotten completely about the application. But here was a summer job, much needed, and in economics. I could put the thyroid illness and the long hospitalization behind me.

A Memorable Job Interview

Before filling out the application to the Canadian government, I had been tempted to go back again to the beautiful tourist resort in Cape Breton Island where I had my first summer job. Certainly, I was not going to learn anything new if I went back to last summer's job in the local garage and automobile showroom, where I was assistant to the firm's accountant. Even if I did get to meet Artie Shaw, who was touring Nova Scotia with one of his wives — was she the seventh or eighth?

The garage owner was thrilled when the great bandleader brought his giant black Lincoln in for servicing and knew all about his music and, apparently, his marital history. I did find some excuse or other to walk out to the grease pit where Mr. Shaw was standing with the mechanic, looking up at the undercarriage of his car. On the way I walked past his wife who was looking at the cars on the showroom floor. Was she wearing a fur jacket? That is what I remember. Granted, we are quite far north of the U.S. border, but still, it was July and around here, the teenage boys and girls start wearing their Bermuda shorts as soon as the daytime temperature reaches at least 45 degrees, usually in mid-April.

Aside from that celebrity visit and the fact that the garage owner let me drive one of the used cars home to our valley some evenings instead of having to catch a ride on the milk truck, it was a dreary summer of double-entry accounting and preparing the weekly payroll with the exact dollars and change to stuff into small brown envelopes and distribute to the staff every Friday morning.

So here I was with a unique new summer job and told to report to a regional office in Truro, Nova Scotia. Having this job in Ottawa, Canada's capital city, might have been more exciting, but this job was in my chosen field of economics and promised to still be a great experience.

Somehow, I found a rooming house for the summer on a safe street, and, my mother determined, with a safe family. On a Sunday afternoon I packed my few summer skirts and dresses and a bunch of books and my Brownie Hawkeye camera and left on the bus with great anticipation. This would be a real grown-up job. Maybe I would even get to write some reports, and since I had learned to touch type during my sophomore year, I could type them up as well.

On arrival, I took a taxi from the bus depot to the landlady's address, which was a gabled Victorian house on a street guarded by towering elm trees. This would be a pleasant place to spend the summer, I thought, and convenient, said the landlady when she welcomed me in, telling me that I could walk the few blocks to work and would therefore not need a car.

Monday morning I found the office building, climbed the stairs to the second floor listed on the doorbell, and knocked on the glazed-glass door panel. An older woman's voice called out, "Come in."

The room, as I entered, seemed vast and almost empty. The woman who had answered my knock sat at a desk near the door, hands resting on her typewriter. Across the large room, in front of windows, were two other desks: one angled in the corner, and the other, a large brown desk, occupying the center of the longest wall. A short, wiry man was standing by the angled desk, and a large man with black hair, a thin moustache — and a stern look — was seated at the large desk, holding a document in front of him.

I said, "Good morning," and waited politely for their response. When I was met with silence, I introduced myself and added, "I'm here for the summer job in economic research."

Again there was no response until the woman behind the typewriter said, "Good morning, dear. Have a seat here beside me. You need to fill out some paperwork." She pointed to the straight-back chair next to her desk and then rattled through several folders for several lime-green forms that she then passed over to me, saying: "You will have to fill in all of these forms, so make yourself comfortable. Do you need a pen?"

It was not going to be comfortable filling out all of these forms without a desk or table to use, so I positioned them on top of my purse and said, "Thank you. I have a pen."

The two men were now talking to each other in whispers that grew in volume. Although I could not make out the words, I got the sense that they were not in full agreement on whatever the subject. I lowered my head over the forms and began to fill in the questions on my birth date, address, and education up until now, including some detail on which economics and statistics courses I had completed. Still, neither of the men spoke to me and both were by now intensely whispering to each other.

I finished all of the forms and passed them back to the woman, who smiled warmly as she looked them over quickly and said, "I will give these to the boss."

She walked across the room, placed the forms on the desk in front of the seated man, then walked back saying to me, "Would you like a cup of tea?" Since this was an uncomfortable place to drink a cup of tea, I thanked her but declined.

"Well, just make yourself comfortable until they are ready to speak to you."

The conversations across the room now appeared to focus on the papers I had filled out. I was still not able to hear their words but was curious by now as to what was so engrossing to them and why they did not talk directly to me about my application.

So I waited. By this time, I had been there more than an hour. I scanned the room not knowing where to look. I could see practically nothing through the windows, just the tops of some trees and a few clouds in the sky. The woman had gone out the door and returned with her cup of tea, then resumed her typing. I had nothing to read, no newspaper, and, of course, no book, since it would not look right to bring a book to my first day of work.

The voices across the room rose in volume and tempo, growing more animated. Then the small, wiry man said loud enough for me to hear, "In that case, leave it to me. I will handle this for my project," and began to cross the room toward me.

"Good morning," he said and introduced himself. "I know we have kept you waiting a long time. Perhaps we could go out to the corner tea shop and discuss your summer job? It is almost lunchtime."

Up close he looked grandfatherly and was clearly trying to be polite in a morning that was largely absent of good manners. "A cup of tea would be fine," I said, glad to be freed of that room.

When we reached the tea shop and were being seated at a small table by the window, I looked quickly at my watch to find that it was past 11:30 in the morning. I had waited there for over two hours and no one except the kindly woman had spoken to me until now. Suddenly I thought of the tourist resort: By now the leaves would be out on the trees and the daffodils and tulips would be ready to bloom. The tour buses and the station wagons piled with luggage would be pulling up to the front entrance. The fog banks would be clearing over Cape Smokey.

I waited, in growing misery, for the tea to arrive and for the man to explain whatever was apparently wrong. He poured milk and added three cubes of sugar to his tea, stirred the sugar, then set down the spoon and looked at me directly for the first time.

"I apologize for the bad manners this morning. You must not have felt very comfortable." I did not know how to respond to that, so I just nodded.

"But we do have a problem. You see, you were chosen for this position by the federal government office in Ottawa, not at this regional office. And the man whom you saw, who directs this region, is not comfortable that you are a..." He paused here, and seemed to search for words, "a girl, a young woman. You see, he only hires men, and he had planned for a young man to be working here this summer, one he could send out around the county conducting surveys."

"I could do surveys," I said quickly. " I grew up in a county near here. I could do that."

"I'm afraid he will not budge. He insists he must have a young man."

"But my credentials were good enough for this position," was all I could think to say, because a hot, noisy wave was taking over my brain and my heart was pounding. I was not going to be allowed to do this job because I was a girl, even if he did correct himself and call me a "young woman."

No one had ever told me that I couldn't do something because I was a girl. Growing up the oldest of four children and the tallest and the strongest in my class, I was expected to do whatever was necessary, as were all of the other girls in my grade in our village. Whether I was strapping on the old army knapsack to ski to Purcell's farm for the milk or driving the tractor for the neighbor's haymaking in late August, no one ever mentioned the fact that I was a girl.

All of the women in our valley were important. They all had their assigned tasks on the farms — they milked the cows, tended the chickens and the eggs, were in charge of the sows and their litters, and in addition, did all of the housework and brought up their children. They sewed, knitted, and made beautiful quilts for sale. There were some winters when most of the cash income for the families came from the women's tasks, while the men were up in the lumber camps cutting wood and had to wait until spring when the wood was delivered to the lumber mills to be paid. My mother was the best example in the village. She was the schoolteacher, a widow, bringing up her four children without a man in the house.

My head was rushing so, I almost missed his next words: "But I have my own project, my own surveys to do, different from his. Can you drive a car? Do you have a driver's license?"

I told him that I got my driver's license at sixteen and drove the family car frequently, also tractors and the neighbor's pickup truck when needed.

"And would you be agreeable to traveling through New Brunswick [the province next door] and staying in motels or rooming houses? Would your parents let you do this because you would be working alone?"

I didn't respond right away, trying to grasp what he had just said, so he continued, "I just don't think it is possible to change my colleague's mind so that you could work here in this office. But if you worked on my project, you would have a government car and an expense account and you would report only to me and to my office in Ottawa, where I will be most of the time this summer, directing this project in other provinces as well."

Then it came into focus: He was offering me a different assignment, one that would liberate me from that oppressive office. I would be traveling. I would have a car and an expense account.

"And what would I be doing? What surveys are you conducting?" I asked.

"You would take on this assignment? It doesn't frighten you?" he asked again.

"Of course I will take it on. I'm not at all frightened. It sounds most exciting."

"Very well then," he said. "Let's walk down that street where we keep the government cars, and you can choose one you like. And then we can go back to the office so I can tell you about the details on the surveys I am conducting and what you will be doing. And I will also explain how you can file your expense accounts and your weekly reports to me."

As if to put me at ease before going back into that office, he said kindly, "You must not be too upset by him. He is a good administrator and a good regional director. It is just that his wife is very jealous. Even though they have eight children, she will only let him hire a secretary who is a grandmother. He knows that his wife could never have you working for him this summer."

There was much to think about this revelation, but that could wait. I had a job, and suddenly, an exciting job, with a promise of adventure and challenge. The sting of the morning's rejection would not ease quickly, and I would need to think about this "problem" of being a girl, but not today. Today, I would pick out my car, get my instructions for the surveys and my expense account advance, find a map of New Brunswick, go back to the rooming house to pack my suitcase, and thank the landlady for her one night of hospitality. I was off to be Canada's first traveling economic research girl.

This experience ended well. The summer was one of adventure and challenge. I traveled alone, found charming, safe places to stay, usually in bed-and-breakfasts with nice landladies, but sometimes in roadside motels. (This was two or three years before the movie *Psycho* was released, one that terrified most young women including me into a lifelong avoidance of staying in a motel alone.)

As the project director told me, we were trying to calculate the amount of food imports, of products that could be grown in the Maritimes. At times I worked in dusty railroad depot offices to track down the information needed on carloads of agricultural products brought into New Brunswick from other provinces or from the U.S. Once I had to have the RCMP (the Royal Canadian Mounted Police or "Mounties" as they're commonly known) escort me across a picket line near the dockyards in Saint John. Every so often I would arrive in a town where one of my classmates lived or was working for the summer, so it was not entirely a lonely time of reading books and writing in my journal.

Most surprising of all, at summer's end, when I arrived back at the original office to meet with the project director who had flown down from Ottawa to accept my final report, this kindly, grandfatherly gentleman was there to greet me and to hear about my experiences collecting his survey data. He said, "We have a surprise today. The regional director, whom you met at the beginning of the summer, has asked us to lunch. He wants to thank you for doing such good work."

Facing Down the Football Coach

The expression "beard the lion in his den" was fitting. There he was: big, bulky, formidable, sitting behind a large, formidable desk and guarded by his bulldog, whose ugly face and rippling muscles alone would strike fear into anyone. Our mission was to interview the football coach.

During our senior year, Clare Bennett and I were both writing for the *Xaverian Weekly*, our campus newspaper. The editor thought there could be an interesting, even important, story about the College Placement Office and how it could be helpful to our graduating class. The college placement officer was also the football coach, full time on the placement issues now that his football season was over. We were told that the football team seemed to respect him and perhaps even like him, but his reputation around campus was fearsome, just as he looked in the photographs of him printed in the college and local papers: Don Loney, St. F.X. football coach, a big, bulky man, scowling, pipe clenched between his teeth, guarded by his equally fearsome bulldog.

"Why us?" Clare and I both howled in unison. "He doesn't like girls! He probably won't even talk to us."

"Well, he has to talk to you," the editor said. "College placement is his responsibility. He needs to tell the seniors just what he is doing, or plans to do, to help everyone find a job." The editor picked up his phone and asked the campus operator to ring Mr. Loney's office and arrange for our interview. "But beware of his dog," the editor warned as we picked up our notebooks and pencils. "That dog doesn't like women either."

"So what questions are we going to ask him?" I asked Clare as we walked across the square to the administration building. The college placement office was on the second floor. "And what if he decides to answer our questions with just a yes or a no? Then we won't have a story to write."

"Why, that could be the story itself," Clare said. "Can't you see the headline? 'College Placement Officer Has Nothing to Report.'"

Our giggles were short-lived, as we had reached the main entrance of the building. "We had better write down a few key questions before going in," I said, "in case we are so nervous that we can't remember what questions to ask."

"Or so terrified," Clare said.

So Clare thought of three questions, and I suggested another three that might be important, jotting these down in my notebook. We were sharing this encounter and both our names would be on the byline, when or if this interview would be accomplished. We were in this together.

Clare knocked on the frosted-glass panel of the office door. We heard the dog growl, then a gruff voice yelled, "Come in!"

We stood just inside the door. I glanced quickly at the dog, which was sitting in front of us, guarding the desk, his mouth in a fierce scowl, his muscles rippling throughout his body. I didn't know whether it was better to look right at the dog or not look at him at all.

We introduced ourselves and said we were there to interview him about his work as college placement officer and learn what kinds of advice or guidance he was offering to the graduating seniors.

"Sit down, sit down!" he said, waving with his pipe toward the two chairs that faced his desk.

I don't remember which one of us ventured the first question, only that it was halting and awkward, with many ums and uhs. His answer was brief, but polite. He looked at us both, waiting for the next question. This one emerged in a sturdier voice and was perhaps a better question: "What resources do you have for a graduating senior when one comes in for advice?"

He set his pipe down in an ashtray, cleared his throat, and began to quietly describe the range of resources he had for the seniors, such as information on job openings with the federal government or with major banks in Canada; he even had a list of high school teaching jobs. Something remarkable was happening here. His voice was no longer gruff, but was mellow, and his face was reflecting an obvious interest in this work.

Our next questions were more specific: Did he arrange interviews or provide help with writing a résumé? How many students did he see each week? His answers were patient and thorough. We were both writing notes quickly, going on to the next question. We had a story! Clare and I thanked him as we stood up and we were further surprised when he stood and reached across his desk to shake Clare's hand, then mine.

"Good luck with your article," he said. "I look forward to reading it."

I decided to smile at the dog as I opened the door.

"Was that a twinkle in his eye as he shook our hands?" Clare asked as we were going down the stairs.

"Maybe," I said. "Who would believe this? Do we really believe what just happened in there? Not only did he not growl at us, but he was also polite and helpful."

"But I don't think the dog smiled back at me," I said as we hurried back to the newspaper office to write our article.

Some thirty years later, when I was visiting my mother in Antigonish for the week of her July birthday, I suggested that during my visit we take a drive toward Canso and the Eastern South Shore of Nova Scotia. Mary Cameron Foshay, my classmate from our freshman and sophomore years, who now lived nearby, was having a midmorning coffee with us and, like me, was enjoying my mother's homemade baking-powder biscuits and raspberry jam.

"If you go," Mary said, "why not visit Don Loney in Sherbrooke? He's been living there for the past decade or so, ever since he retired from the university. He likes to have visitors and I know he will show you his paintings, which are very good."

So Don Loney was an artist? Not just a football coach?

"I'll call him and let him know you are going to Sherbrooke," Mary said. "We are old friends from the days that Ernie played on his football team." Ernie, Mary's first husband, had passed away three years earlier.

So Mother and I had our plans set. We would drive down the coast below Mulgrave into the small town of Canso, famous for being the first North American site for transatlantic cable, established by The Western Union Company in 1881 followed by the Commercial Cable Company in 1884. Both companies continued to operate these cable links to the UK and to Europe until the late 1950s and early 1960s.

These days there was not much to see in the small town whose economic base was suffering from the closure of a fish-processing plant, but we found the monument celebrating the first telegraph system. I took a photo of my mother standing beside it, telling her that I remembered that she taught us about Canso long ago in our grade-school class history of Canada.

We made one other stop before reaching Sherbrooke, at the convent of the Sisters of St. Martha in Port Bickerton, where Mother St. Hugh Marie was now retired from teaching, but helping out in the community. She and my mother had been long-standing colleagues, teaching at the regional high school in Antigonish. The nun insisted that we stay for a cup of tea, telling us about the challenges for their social work in that poverty-stricken community.

We resisted having any cookies with our tea, since we were invited to have lunch with Don Loney at his house. "No problem at all," he had told Mary on the phone. "I like to cook for visitors, and, of course, I have known Agnes [my mother] over all these years."

I wondered if he remembered me when he greeted us at the door. "Of course, I hear about you in New York City, the Big Apple," he said, holding out his hand when I introduced myself. I decided then that I was not going to ask him if he remembered that long-ago interview for the campus paper, instead listened to his conversation with my mother over a delicious lunch of cold poached salmon and potato salad.

He talked about his paintings as he walked us around his living room and hallway where about twenty were hung on the walls or resting against easels, saying he had begun to paint first when he was a young officer in the Canadian Navy, then had started again during the off-season of his football coaching days. "I really enjoy having the time to spend painting, now that I am retired," he said. I still expected to see him take a pipe out of his mouth before speaking to us, but there was no sign of a pipe or tobacco or ashtrays in his neat house.

I did venture one question: "Is it lonely here in the winter? Sherbrook is just a village and aren't you often snowed in?"

"Not at all lonely," he said. Mary had told us that he was a lifelong bachelor. "I've made many friends here, and, of course, I go up to Antigonish and the university for events or for dinners there with friends."

"Come," he said to us. "I would like you to meet one of my friends here and you can see his smoked salmon plant. He makes the best smoked salmon in Canada."

Later, as Mother and I were driving home along the St. Mary's River, known for its salmon fishing, and along the lovely drive past Lochaber Lake, I told my mother about the interview those many years ago and our terror in approaching Don Loney in his office, of "bearding him in his den," where he was guarded by his fearsome bulldog" and then, to our surprise, finding him much less gruff than we feared, and even helpful. We both laughed as we pictured this gentle giant of a man, spending his days cooking, making friends, and painting beautiful pictures.

Graduation Day

It is May 17, 1959, and it is graduation day. All week long we played the song "Graduation Day" by the Four Freshmen on the small record player in our room. Florence, my roommate, sang out "It's a time for joy, a time for tears," with loud enthusiasm and completely off key, much to the delight of our classmates passing by our open door. All of the doors on the senior floor stayed open that week, as all of us were freed from final exams and from producing our senior honors theses.

And we were overjoyed once we had notification of our graduation. Our senior prom had just been restored by the dean of women, as were the surrounding dinners and lunches of graduation day which would be shared with our parents, who had descended on the university campus well-dressed and coiffed and appearing as triumphant as we looked to each other.

Maura, who had just been elected as our life president, and I, the senior class president, had spent a tense hour in Dean Mother St. Mary Phillippe's office, pleading for this restoration, telling her repeatedly that there was no way any of the senior women knew what the senior men were up to the previous Sunday, when we were giving them a guided walk-through of our senior floor following the formal tea we held for them, as was customary, in our main lounge at Gilmora Hall.

"But didn't you see the boys open your dresser drawers?" the dean asked.

"None of us saw anything," Maura said. "We have quizzed each one of our senior girls, and all said no, they did not notice anything untoward."

"Of course, there are many more of them than us," I said, trying to add a convincing detail, "We are just thirty women, but there are over two hundred men, not counting the engineers, and most of them came on invitation that afternoon."

The dean brushed aside my arithmetic and went directly to motivation.

"But you must have known that they were taking your underwear from your dressers, and hiding them inside their blazer jackets or somewhere, then hanging everything on outdoor clotheslines around the campus for everyone to see, all of the priests, even the bishop!" She almost spit out her *s's* at this point, she was so angry, before finishing her point, "They must have had a reason for doing this disgraceful act."

Of course the guys had a motivation, they were paying us back for the prank that two of the senior women, one of whom was me, played by crashing the men's "Roast of the Gals" event on St. F.X. Day, back on December 3. This was an annual event, and the rumors always flew around campus of some of the things the men had said about the women. But over the years none of the women had been able to gain access to the auditorium where the event was always held, so to know what scurrilous things might have been said.

But that December 3 of our senior year, Clare Bennett and I slipped into the control room behind the main stage of the university auditorium. The shy young man from the town who was managing the on-stage microphone and public address system had agreed to tape the proceeding for us. What is more, he had given us a microphone so we could cut into the speeches. Our bribe to him was a packet of ten tickets to the local movie theater and a chocolate cake from the best bakery in the town.

Pandemonium broke out in the auditorium when our voices first came through the loudspeaker system, Clare and I taking turns saying, "Now Brian, you can't possibly mean that," or "Brian, you know you have a big crush on Roseann."

Brian Mulroney, our classmate, already called "the Silver-Tongued Orator," was the main orator for their event, with his deep-voiced speaking skills and confidence honed from the many debates and political rallies he held as head of the student Conservative Party during his four years. Decades later none of us would be surprised when he was elected prime minister of Canada. But at this point in their roast, the yelling and stomping, "Who are they? Go get them!" had even shaken Brian, the great orator. We could hear footsteps pounding towards the control booth. Clare and I grabbed the spool of tape from the frightened young man and dashed out a back door and down a back flight of stairs to run as fast as we could through the fields of Bishop's Bowl and to the path behind the cathedral to a back door at Gilmora Hall, where two of our classmates were waiting to open the usually locked door.

Of course the "Great Panty Raid," as it was being called on campus, was payback for that escapade five months earlier.

We dared not say any of this to Mother St. Phillippe. Maura and I took turns trying to find other arguments, explaining that this was springtime, and each of us used a variation on the theme that "the young men could surely be expected to act up in a way that your young women would never dream of."

I stressed the economics of the event: the senior women all had their prom gowns made by local seamstresses; they had bought new shoes and purses; their escorts had bought corsages for the prom.

"And besides," Maura added as the last argument that she could muster, "think of all the parents who are arriving already, here for their daughter's graduation, what would you tell them? Wouldn't they say that this was not something the senior women did, but a prank by the senior men?"

The argument about the parents worked. Mother St. Mary Phillippe relented and said she would restore all of our graduation privileges.

"But you can tell those young men that I am not pleased by their behavior," she said. She had just called them young men now, which elevated them from the scornful "those boys" she had called them earlier in the conversation.

At the senior prom, several of the guys told us how they managed to raid our dressers and not be seen: if two of the women were standing near each door — these were double rooms so each of us had a roommate with twin beds and two dressers — then two or three of the guys would cluster by us, talking away, while another eight to fifteen of the group walked around the room, looking at our books or any posters or prints on the wall. This moving group would shelter two guys who would pull open the dresser drawer, find the underwear, and stuff bras and panties inside their blazer jackets.

"Well, at least my name isn't written on any of them," Florence, my roommate, said later, "and at least they got my panties from the dresser and not from the laundry bag."

On May 17, 1959, I walked across the stage in the auditorium in my new black patent leather pumps, my academic gown covering the new, fitted, white brocade dress that I had the town seamstress make for me. I struggled to genuflect in front of the Bishop because of the pencil-slim skirt on the dress, as he handed me the blue tube with the temporary certificate of my graduation. The larger blue leather-bound tube with the formal diploma printed in Latin would arrive some weeks later.

So my college years were finished. The past three years with all of my classes and activities based on the university campus were filled with laughter and with friends, filled with my exciting courses in economics, nourished by the classes in English literature I was able to squeeze into the schedule. I was leaving with a long reading list that I promised the English professor, Fr. McSween, that I would surely read even if it took the next ten years. "Well, maybe not more of Ezra Pound or Gerard Manly Hopkins," I told him with a laugh. "I think I've had quite enough of both."

While I was packing my trunk for the last time, in the same room that weeks before I visited after lights out to type my senior thesis, I thought back to the great massed choir productions we held before Christmastime, the wonderful arrangement of "T'was the Night Before Christmas" or the octet of four women and four men (I sang the alto part) chosen to do a tight jazz arrangement of "Night and Day." I would miss my choral buddies, my friends on the Student Co-op Society board and the *Xaverian Weekly* newspaper, my economics professor, my classmates. The university had provided me and my classmates with a solid education, with a range of activities to test our mettle and develop leadership skills, and above all, from the priests and the lay faculty, a loving environment in which to learn.

Following the graduation ceremony, my mother had arranged a lunch for me and my younger brother and two sisters at a restaurant a few miles south of the town. She had invited Kathleen to join us.

"She was your 7th-grade teacher and is so proud of you," Mother said.

Kathleen lived with us that year she taught us, which was a double dose of misery for all of us. Behind her back we called her "Miss Grouch" because she scolded us incessantly and never smiled. Malcolm rolled his eyes at the news of our luncheon guest, but he was polite to her, as we all were. Kathleen gave me a silver rosary in a small leather pouch that I still have; somehow it has survived all of the geographic moves over the decades, although the rosary is rarely said these days.

Mother gave me a Waterman's ink pen with nibs and ink cartridges, a special gift that cost about $20, a substantial sum in those days. When these fluid-ink pens became fashionable again in New York City during the 1980s and 1990s, prices ranged upwards of $250. Mother's gift pen has long since disappeared, and in the early days before disappearing, was no doubt cast aside for the newly invented ball-point pen.

I remember little of the senior prom itself, mostly the excitement of getting dressed in my blue satin gown with the blue voile overskirt, especially made by the seamstress who also made my white dress. I had dyed-to-match blue pumps, carefully done at the town shoe repair shop. I waited near the door of the Arches, trembling in anticipation and new love for my escort, John C. or "J.C.," as he was known on campus, to arrive. Four decades later, he wrote a letter that arrived in a large brown envelope containing a copy of our graduation prom photo. You were so beautiful, he wrote.

I looked like a deer in the headlights, I thought, but he was certainly handsome, heart-stoppingly handsome.

I floated through that senior prom in a daze. The music by our own college band, The X-Men of Note, playing the great music of World War II and the late 1930s, added to the magic of the night. After the prom we drove to Buddy Sweet's house at Mahoney's Beach. Buddy ran the Wagon Wheel, our hangout diner by the bridge that connected the street past the college to Main Street.

The Wheel, as it was known, specialized in giant-size cinnamon buns, the source, we came to believe, of the extra weight we gained in sophomore year and not to be lost until the rigors of final exams our senior year. Buddy was hosting this after-prom party for a group of the senior guys, many from the football team. John C. was a favorite of his, as was I. Buddy seemed thrilled that John C. and I had found each other.

Our romance had exploded out of nowhere six weeks before graduation, shocking the entire campus, as well as ourselves. He was the rollicking, dashing, all-American, a hero of the football team, whose wide grin and enthusiastic laugh made him a standout on campus. He would have been the man-about-town if our campus social life ever allowed such breakout behavior. And here he was, suddenly dating me. I was not exactly a goody two-shoes, but I was more serious and studious, although fully involved in campus leadership positions and activities. I had refused to "go steady" throughout the four years of college and I always had dates for the big proms, but I was determined to never be known as anybody's "girl."

How that suddenly changed is lost in time to me, but I vividly remember walking downtown with him to the Wagon Wheel for coffee one afternoon and encountering some of his football buddies, who yelled out, "J.C., are you really dating Rosemary MacLellan?" at which point John C. put his arms around my waist, lifted me up and slung me over his shoulder, yelling back to the group, "She is my woman now."

That scene ricocheted around campus, even reaching Mother St. Phillippe, who called me into her office. "I am sure that everyone is exaggerating," I told her, and fled back to my room.

Where was home after the prom party? Perhaps I was staying with my roommate, Florence, at the Claymore Motel. I certainly have no memory that John C. drove me home to my mother's apartment on Church Street, because I would remember having had to wake her up at five or so in the morning.

Whatever the location, certainly the ending was chaste. The nuns of Mount St. Bernard succeeded in terrifying most of us on the prospect of unwed sex, nor do I have any memory of the next day or days, when John C. would have left to go home to the U.S. Did he have a job that summer? He was to start law school in New York in September. I worked at the local radio station that summer and left Antigonish in late August to begin my master's in economics at the University of New Brunswick in Fredericton. We did correspond that year — all those letters and my journals were lost some years later.

We did not meet again until Labor Day weekend 1960, more than a year after our graduation, when I visited with him and his family at Hempstead Air Force Base on Long Island as I was en route to Williamsburg, Virginia.

Graduate School, My First Apartment, and Fiddleheads

By late spring of 1960 I had finished my coursework and oral exam for the Master's in Economics at the University of New Brunswick in Canada, and now had to begin research on a thesis, part of my commitment for the degree and to the Ford Foundation for the scholarship they had awarded me for this year.

The seven months of graduate classes, all seminars, had been intense, exciting, and had flown by. My days were spent trudging up the steep hill from my residence to the graduate wings of the University of New Brunswick in Fredericton, often negotiating banks of drifting snow in the long winter months or the endless days of slush, rain, and mud in what purported to be the early weeks of spring. But all weather discomforts would dissolve when our various seminars begin, crammed with new aspects of economics.

In the seminar taught by our major professor and dean, Professor William "Bill" Smith, the six of us in the master of economics program, all Ford Foundation Scholars, sat in rapt attention, busily taking notes. We gathered closely in a crescent circle in front of his desk, watched as he lit one cigarette after another, rocking back and forth on his swivel chair (and one day after class, we shared the worry that he might catapult backwards through his fourth-floor window), as he swept us through the history of economics in the 19th century, particularly of England and the British Empire, complete with a parallel review of major historical events and politicians, and the reasons why industries and regional economies went into decline ("Most often," he said, "it is the third-generation effect"). Most days, two-hour seminars went into three hours, and once, almost to a full four hours. We never wanted it to end.

We had three full-time economics professors for the six master's students that year; two of the three were visiting professors from Cambridge University in the U.K., and our dean, Prof. Smith, a Canadian from New Brunswick, had received his PhD from Cambridge. I found myself thinking that if my undergraduate major in economics was slightly removed from MIT because of the freshly minted PhD professor from MIT, then now, we were steeped in once-removed Cambridge. Every day of these seminars I felt fortunate and gifted by this level of instruction.

The rules of that master's degree were that we would take the intensive classroom courses and seminars in the first year, which ran from early September to mid-April, then use the second full year to research, write, and defend a thesis.

Nuts to that, I told myself when classes ended in mid-April. I can't spend an entire year writing a term paper, even if it is a thesis. It is just a big term paper with lots of footnotes and a big bibliography. I resolved to do it all that summer, so I could start the job in September that I had just been offered.

I would do the research and write the first draft of the thesis during May and June, draw the graphs and edit while it was being typed up in July, and do my oral presentation of the thesis to the faculty committee by mid-August. I could then leave by Labor Day for the College of William and Mary in Williamsburg, Virginia, where I had been offered a position as an instructor in economics and research assistant in the newly formed Bureau of Business Research.

Exhilarated by this plan, which would clearly take concentrated effort to complete, my next challenge was to find an apartment for the mid-April-to-late-August months, where I could do my work in quiet and without too much effort, especially if I could find a furnished apartment and move in and go directly to work.

Within days I had found an apartment that was for sublet in the summer months and was indeed furnished and had kitchen utensils, and I found two other young women, both recent graduates and mid-master's like myself, to share the rent.

We happily settled in, bringing our boxes of books, clothes, and linens and were soon comfortable in the two upstairs bedrooms and the "bed-sit" arrangement that I made at the edge of the living room downstairs, behind a moveable screen, since I was the announced night owl who worked late at night and slept late in the morning.

We were all going somewhere interesting in September. Marcella, who was on a paid research project for the political science department during the summer, had just won a Rotary Fellowship and was off to the University of Melbourne, Australia, to work on her master's degree. May Ann was going to the London School of Economics to begin a PhD, also in political science, while I was headed for Virginia.

Our apartment had its own entrance down a gravel driveway towards the rear of a single-family house, with its own sign at the sidewalk that read 122½, clearly indicating that a separate residence existed.

Early one morning, shortly after we had settled in, our doorbell rang to reveal a man selling life insurance. May Ann found great amusement at telling the baffled insurance salesman, "Sorry, we won't be here to use it. One of us is going to England, another to Australia, and the third to the United States," she said as she ushered him off the front steps with a pleasant smile.

I spent the last two weeks of April encamped at the university library, looking up research materials for my thesis, with occasional visits to the economics department to seek guidance from my major professor. I worked out the completion schedule with him, with several interruptions on his part, all sounding the same: "Are you sure you can meet this timetable? It is not really necessary, you know, you can take the full second year to do this thesis. Everyone else does it that way."

But I was sure it was possible and made arrangements with the senior faculty of the school of arts and sciences to set a date for my thesis presentation to the special committee. And then I went back to my apartment, suddenly exhausted from the year of intense study and this past two-week whirlwind of planning and organizing and researching. I noticed a book resting on the top of one of May Ann's boxes of books called *Gone with the Wind*, and thought, I should take a little break and read a chapter or two in this book. I always knew of it but never had the opportunity to read it.

So for two days and for most of the next two nights, I curled up in my little bed-sit corner of the living room, engrossed in Margaret Mitchell's book, emerging every few hours to make a pot of coffee and some scrambled eggs and toast, only to retreat soon after to read the next chapters.

Then I found another novel, perhaps from Marcella's supplies, and settled in to absorb that, and I was only sidetracked one Saturday morning and pulled out of a late sleep by persistent rings of the doorbell. I found a housecoat to wrap around my nightgown, patted my hair down from its flyaway state, and opened the door an inch or so to see who was ringing the bell.

"Morning," said a voice with a pronounced English accent. "We brought you a surprise."

'We' turned out to be the two lads from Oxford who were doing post-graduate work in forestry here in the midst of rural New Brunswick. I barely knew them but did know of their existence and paid what slight attention I did since it seemed incongruous that Oxford grads would be studying forestry and not political economy or literature or already running for elected office in England.

"I am Joe and this is Clyde," he said. "We met at the graduate school social a few weeks ago." I struggled to remember and then recalled the forestry discussion, when I had said, flippantly, "But you don't have big forests in England anymore." He replied, saying something to the effect that that was why they were in the wilds of New Brunswick, so they could go home and plant some forests.

"We hoped that you could cook these for us since we don't have a kitchen," Joe said.

I looked down at his feet to see a large, galvanized tub filled with some wet, green curlicued plants.

"Are those just budding ferns?" I asked, feeling stupid and sleepy and suddenly aware that I was still in nightclothes and bare feet and they were in rather damp and soggy outdoor clothes and jackets and large rubber boots that were splotched with vegetation.

"These are fiddleheads from the banks of the Saint John River, and we got up early this morning to pick them from the riverbank," Joe said. Clyde just smiled in agreement.

I had never heard of fiddleheads. I knew what baby ferns looked like, curled up tightly as they emerged from the ground in the earliest days of spring, then bloomed out to be feathery green in the summer months. I never heard that they were edible. "But how do you cook them, and why would you eat them?" I asked, my stupidity growing with morning grogginess.

"It is really simple. You just get a large pot and fill it with water and sprinkle in some salt and when it is near the boil you dump in all of the fiddleheads. They'll cook in about ten minutes. Then we can serve them with butter and more salt if you have butter," Joe said.

"And some white wine," said Clyde, uttering his first words as he pulled a large green bottle from the pocket of his large jacket.

I had never had white wine, since most types of alcohol were still illegal, and no one drank wine at that time. When you could buy something legally at the Liquor Commission, people seemed to drink dark rum or Canadian rye. I had never been to the Commission store since you had to be twenty-one, and that summer I was just twenty.

"Well, come on in," I said, inbred manners taking over from my sleep-deprived state. "Let me wake up my roommates and put on some water for these things and a pot of coffee. Make yourselves comfortable in the kitchen while I get dressed."

So I made coffee and we talked a bit about graduate school while the large pot of water came to a boil. Joe pulled over a chair in front of the stove while Clyde and I hoisted up the galvanized tub to help Joe pour in large quantities of the fiddleheads. When Joe announced they were "done to perfection," we five sat around the kitchen table, smearing butter and shaking salt on our breakfast repast, which we washed down with the bottle of white wine and laughter.

I went back to reading novels from the stash of books I found in my roommates' collection, reading most of the days and well into the night until the late morning came when Marcella, at the stove making coffee, said, "I thought you were going to finish your thesis this summer. Aren't you going back to the library for your research?"

I looked at her blankly, and then asked, "How long have we been here in the apartment?"

"Almost a month now. Tomorrow will be May 15," Marcella said.

I thought of my carefully planned out schedule and came close to panic. I had started with two good weeks of research, but I had now used up half of the month of May reading novels when I had planned to finish the research and be well into the writing.

"Yes, that is my plan," I said as I headed for the shower to get fully awake and hopefully alert and get to the library before the day was over.

So the next weeks in our apartment became almost military in our devotion to schedule, to research, to my writing the first drafts, to May Ann completing her project and her plans for LSE and application for study in the U.K., while Marcella worked diligently to finish her summer research project and write her report while also finalizing the endless stream of documents for her visa application to Melbourne.

Suddenly, in the midst of drawing some graphs for my thesis, I realized that my visa documents had arrived days before from the U.S. Consulate and lay there on the desk, unopened.

"Hadn't you better get your visa application into the mail?" Marcella asked. She had become my conscience over these past weeks as I had plunged into the research and writing and struggled with editing the first draft of my findings. She had even offered to read the initial pages, although she warned me that she had no knowledge or interest in my peculiar subject of "Price Fluctuations of Potato Producers in New Brunswick, Prince Edward Island, and Nearby Counties of Maine in the U.S."

I tore open the thick legal-size envelope to discover multiple pages of forms to be filled out and questions to be answered. I groaned. "I can fill out the personal and family stuff, but what about those questions? I can't sit still for those, and it will take hours, which I don't have," I added.

Marcella reached for the package of forms and rifled through the pages. "There is a due date of three days from now to return these," she announced, "or you will miss your window for the application, and you will miss your visa. I will help you."

And that is how I got my U.S. visa application in on time. Marcella interviewed me for the pages of questions and filled in my answers, and I filled out the personal pages. She walked with me to the post office to mail it out first class, and I went home in gratitude to complete the editing and graphics and typing the first draft of the thesis. I had found a professional typist with a new typewriter who was skilled in preparing master's theses, so that part would be well completed.

What did we eat that summer besides fiddleheads and who was the primary cook of the meals? Were we conscious of healthy foods and did we eat enough fruits and vegetables, considering the amount of brain work we were all doing? This aspect of our summer in that first apartment is a blur. Perhaps there were times when we could eat our noonday meals at the cafeteria on campus when we were at the library or doing research in our academic departments. I think that I was the only one who knew how to cook a basic meal, such as roast chicken or how to fry fresh fish and prepare potatoes and vegetables. But with our schedules, whether during my weeks of almost all-night reading or our subsequent weeks of diligent work, it is hard now to imagine how we managed in those days before fast food outlets or nearby cafes or any type of prepared foods to get ourselves fed and stay healthy and energetic. Somehow, we ended the summer fit and lean, and, I think, ready for our respective adventures come September.

But I still remember the endless and passionate conversations over endless pots of coffee, long into the evenings when we would come back to the apartment from our days at the university. The topics ranged (and frequently raged) from Canada's stodgy political environment to the fledgling civil rights movement in the United States and what would Senator Wayne Morse of Oregon or was it Washington State plan as his next move? Marcella was finishing a research paper on Lord Acton ("Power corrupts, and absolute power corrupts absolutely") and May Ann, conscious of her imminent move to London, was still rehashing the state of affairs of the U.K. and its colonies in the declining days of the empire, especially after the mess at the Suez Canal. They teased me that I was fixated on fluctuating potato prices and the plight of local farmers, the topic of my master's thesis, and was not reading anything else since I finished *Gone with the Wind* and the other novels that spilled out of our unpacked boxes.

There was the one subject that drew us all into fervent discussion: a cover story in *Time* magazine that summer of 1960 that trumpeted the move to suburbia in the United States, with its split-level houses, the station wagon in the garage, and the devoted-looking wife and apron-wearing mother of two standing with her husband and children and carrying a soup spoon or other utensil for stirring, smiling sweetly. Or was it a smile of desperation?

"That is desperation," said Marcella with no equivocation. "How could she be anything other than desperate? She is locked into that sterile housing development. Look at that picture. Everything is all same, same, same." Her vehement words echo down through the decades. May Ann could not believe that all of these women in the photos "just stayed at home."

"Why aren't they working? My mother works, your mother works, Rosemary." Then she hesitated, perhaps remembering that Marcella's mother had passed away in recent years and we didn't know whether she had been a working mother, although we knew of Marcella's illustrious grand-aunt who had nursed the workers on the Panama Canal through the epidemic of yellow fever.

"You turn into a vegetable," May Ann concluded.

We all resolved never, ever, to move to the suburbs, promised each other that we would find our careers and our husbands and bring up our children in cities, where there was energy and culture and endless possibility.

So the summer ended. I defended my thesis and passed and was given a temporary diploma to prove I had completed the master's degree until the formal parchment would be mailed. My visa arrived for entry into the United States. All three of us found a weekend around mid-August to visit our respective homes and pack up our childhood artifacts and say our farewells to families and friends, then returned for one long weekend of last-minute packing, laundering all of the linens and towels to take to a local charity, and transport boxes of books that could not be transported to our far destinations to the dean of women's office for distribution around the women's dormitories for the September arrivals.

Marcella left first to begin the first leg of a long journey by ocean liner to Australia, followed by May Ann the next day, flying first to Montreal, then across the Atlantic to London. The following morning I carried my suitcases down the front steps, then went back to check the suddenly empty and quiet spaces before closing the door and turning the lock with the old-fashioned, four-inch key, sliding the key under the mat for the landlord to find, and then crunching along the gravel walk with the heavy suitcases to the waiting car. As it pulled away, I looked back with fondness to the locked door of my first apartment, as the car headed to the airport and to the waiting adventure in the United States.

Leaving Home

Mother drove me the hundred or so miles to the town of Amherst, near the Nova Scotia border with the province of New Brunswick, where I would get a bus to the college town of Fredericton and finish off my few days left at the graduate university with the important task of defending my master's thesis before a faculty committee.

The drive was pleasant in the mid-August afternoon, not too hot in those days before air conditioning in autos became standard issue in Canada. I do not remember that we talked a lot during the two-hour drive, just some brief exchanges on housekeeping items, such as, did I remember to take along all of my paperwork for the United States immigration and border crossing people? Did I have all of the items I needed for the meeting with the faculty committee? Was I able to pack everything I needed for the first four months, and was I sure that I was coming home for the Christmas holidays? Did I have enough Canadian money? And where would I be able to get American money?

It is not that Mother was the type to nag at me or to be overly systematic in organizing our lives. As the first-born daughter, I was used to taking over many of the household duties and taking care of younger siblings. And now as someone who was about to gain a master's degree, she expected me to have everything thought through and safely packed. But we needed to make conversation to break the long and painful silences. I was leaving home, leaving her, leaving my younger brother and two teenage sisters, leaving my beloved province, leaving my country.

She was much too careful of her own emotions and much too practical to make a big fuss over me, much less to say too much of how she felt about my leaving. Years later she told me that she was heartbroken over my decision to take this job so far away, to be leaving her, but that day she said little, concentrating on her driving, and asking the bread-and-butter practical questions.

I dared say little else either, except to fill in details on the practical aspects of this leg of the journey. "Yes, I am a bit nervous about the thesis," I said, "but my major professor tells me not to worry, that my thesis report is just fine, and that I will be able to answer their questions without difficulty."

Once I said this, I realized that this was not the question she asked me. She just wanted to know if I remembered to bring along all of the necessary background papers. I had answered what was on my mind and then realized that this was a depth that she did not want to probe.

We pulled into the bus station at Amherst, and I busied myself with getting the two large suitcases out of the trunk of the car. The suitcases were new, bright cherry-red, and distinguished looking, my mother's gift to me for this graduation and for my departure. I hoisted my shoulder-strap purse on my right shoulder and the tote bag with my thesis material on the left shoulder, leaning over to pick up the two new suitcases. Mother was just back from parking the car. "Let me help," she said, but I gave her only the tote bag, thinking that I was the tall, young, and strong one.

We walked to the ticket window, and while I was rummaging in my purse for money for the trip and asking the station agent about the time of departure, Mother produced a $10 bill from her purse and said, "Dear, I am buying your ticket to Fredericton."

"But Mother, I have the money for this," which she knew I had, but this was so like her, using the cost of the transaction as a way to distract herself from the emotion at hand.

"And you did say one way, didn't you?" asked the station agent.

"Yes," I said, "this is a one-way ticket."

"The bus boards in five minutes," said the station agent as she passed me the ticket and to Mother, the change from the $10.

"I was hoping we would have time for a cup of coffee together before you had to leave," Mother then said, the closest she'd come to revealing her true feelings the entire day.

"I guess not, not if it's only five minutes," I said, sounding, I thought, quite stupid, but there seemed to be so few of the right things to say, especially if we could not bring ourselves to say them during the two-hour automobile ride. On some level I was almost relieved to be free of the strained small talk.

We watched as the bus driver loaded my two new red suitcases into the luggage compartment under the bus and then mother walked with me to the open doorway.

"Take good care of yourself," she said, "and good luck with your thesis and your flight to the U.S. Be sure to write us." We seldom phoned in those days, long-distance calls were expensive, something you only did when people died. I gave her a hug, then, holding her slim shoulders, I whispered, "You be careful too, Mom. Take good care of yourself."

Did I say I would miss her and my siblings and my hometown? I doubt it, since the memory that has lasted over the years is of getting on that bus with a full throat, holding back tears, finding a seat by the window, waving at her while the bus backed out of its traffic aisle. And the strong memory of crying all the way to Fredericton, during every mile of the two-hour journey.

Starting at St. Francis Xavier University.
I was 15½ that September of 1955!

My freshman year piano recital, October 1955.

My *Christina* moment, Keltic Lodge,
Ingonish. Summer 1956.

My college classmates, Thelma Power, Mary Thompson, and Pat Carrigan in downtown Antigonish in Fall 1956.

Dressed for the Spring Prom, sophomore year, 1957. That's me in the middle of the back row.

Trout fishing in Pleasant Valley with
English Prof. Father Bannon and Malcolm
(he took the picture). August 1957.

My serious look to the future.
Graduation, May 1959.

CHAPTER 3

A Young Academic in the Early 1960s

My First Professional Job

My first job when I finished graduate school was to teach economics at the College of William & Mary in Williamsburg, Virginia. I was twenty years old that Labor Day weekend when I boarded a propeller jet plane from Halifax, Nova Scotia, to Boston, on the first of several legs of this long-distance journey, much longer in every way than one would consider in these early decades of the twenty-first century. I did not know anyone at that college, or in any other place in the state of Virginia. I had never taught anything before, and I was so young by any standards that my junior-year students turned out to be the same age as I was.

The prospect of the first job in a foreign part of another country was alluring. This, after all, was not Boston, where so many Maritimers had chosen to work and live during the first half of the twentieth century. This was the South, of the United States, where there were reported to be still-active vestiges of slavery and dreadfully hot summers compared to what we were used to in Maritime Canada. I told myself that I would arrive without any preconceptions since my knowledge of the region was so vague as to require a visit to the map section of the university library to study the detailed layout of the state of Virginia and the Tidewater region, which included the peninsula where Williamsburg and the college were located. I had never heard of the College of William & Mary, though I knew about that king and queen from my schooling in British history, so that required an hour or so in the reference section of the library, looking up universities in the eastern states of the U.S.

My two roommates that summer, when we were all writing our master's thesis or doing predoctoral research, kept up a running joke about the "the Canadian who would be expected to arrive in Virginia in an Eskimo mukluk jacket and sealskin boots and say oddball greetings like, "Nice day, eh?""

At Boston Airport I changed to a shuttle flight to New York's LaGuardia Airport, there to be met by a boyfriend from undergraduate college who was attending law school on Long Island. His family welcomed me to a (well-chaperoned) weekend at their large house on the grounds of Hempstead Air Force Base. They took me to my first-ever visit to a Broadway play and a baseball game at the famous Yankee Stadium. And on that Labor Day Monday, we rode the Long Island Railroad into midtown Manhattan to watch the great parade along Fifth Avenue.

The next morning, Tuesday, when I woke early for the third leg of my journey to Virginia, the family told me that the weather had turned crisp from the late-summer temperatures of the past weekend, so I decided to wear my newest dress for the trip and the arrival in Williamsburg. The dress was a sky-blue, long-sleeved, form-fitting knit. This was my newest and proudest acquisition as I prepared for this next important chapter in my life since it was in the latest style of pencil-thin dresses or skirts that came just below the knee. The weave on this dress was somewhat large, looking as if it were handmade, although I would never have been skilled enough to knit the rolled-down collar, almost mini turtleneck in style. I also had new black leather pumps with high, pencil-thin heels and a fetching new black suede purse. I felt like a pert young professional, ready for the world of work, fully ready for this new adventure.

The flight out of New York's Idlewild Airport went non-stop to Washington, D.C., I pulled out the airline magazine from the seat pocket facing me and studied the fold-out map near the back pages for the coastline of New Jersey, Maryland, and Delaware. I was anxious to see the U.S. Capitol building and the Washington Monument when we approached Washington D.C. As the plane began its banked turn towards National Airport in D.C., the flight attendant strapped herself into the empty seat beside me. "Is this your first trip to Washington?" she asked.

"Yes," I replied, "and that must be the POT-o-mac River," I said, stressing the first syllable and acting pleased to show off my newfound geographic knowledge.

"It certainly is," she said, and then added kindly, "but down here we pronounce it Po-TOHM-ic."

Upon arrival at the airport, I concentrated on finding the right corridor and gate for the next part of the journey, which was on a different airline to a place called Newport News. I again studied the map that I had taken from the plane's seat pocket (at the invitation on the cover). At least I could pronounce this place correctly.

There was a good view of the great harbor at Newport News, called Hampton Roads on the map, with plenty of naval vessels as well as cargo ships visible below us as we made our descent into the airport. I was now excited, but also anxious about finding my promised ride for the thirty miles up the highway to Williamsburg and to the university-sponsored house where I was to live with several other young women faculty for this next year. Standing near the baggage carousel was a man wearing a lightweight suit and conductor's hat with a handwritten sign that said Miss MacLellan. As I came up to introduce myself, he said, eyeing my wool dress and suede purse, "I hope you'll be comfortable, ma'am. It's very hot today."

I came through the main door, which he held open for me, to be met with a blast of heat unlike anything I had ever encountered.

"Yes, it's hot-t-t-t," he said, in what seemed to be three syllables. "Weatherman says it's now 98 degrees."

I rode the almost hour-long drive with the window of the car halfway down, hoping without any success to find a cool breeze. Instead, my wool dress was becoming glued to the satin slip I was wearing underneath, beads of perspiration were rolling down my forehead, and my neatly set hairdo was blowing apart in the hot wind coming in from the open window. I was so uncomfortable that it was difficult to respond politely to the pleasant conversation of the driver, who was asking me where I was from and why was I moving here. I mumbled thanks to him as he pulled up in front of a two-story house with a wide veranda. He brought my two large suitcases up the steps and onto the porch.

The screen door was swung open by a petite young woman with a wide smile, wearing sandals, and loose, almost too-large Bermuda shorts, topped by a white short-sleeved shirt that was worn on the outside, shirttail loose. She stopped short, looked at my wool dress and my flushed and perspiring face, laughed loudly, and said, "You must be the Canadian." I may as well have been wearing that mukluk jacket and sealskin boots.

I was thrilled by this, my first job as a college professor at a historic Virginia institution. Well, professor is a generic reference here since my actual title was "Instructor," the lowliest rung on the full-time faculty hierarchy. My appointment was also to be the assistant research director of the newly formed Bureau of Business Research and to help create a Virginia Business Index by establishing a series of economic and business indicators for ten Virginia cities.

But I was faculty and full time, and there I was, a full-fledged member of the economics department in that memorable fall of 1960. John Kennedy was campaigning for president and this college had just revolutionized the age structure of the ancient faculty by hiring a large crop of recent graduate students, including several young women. I was one of those young women and the emphasis here is on "young." The average age of the incoming faculty with master's degrees was about twenty-five, while most of the young men with PhDs were closer to thirty, especially if they were in the sciences. I was twenty years old and guessed that I was the youngest of this young crop.

The College of William and Mary celebrated its long history and traditions with frequent faculty gatherings and parades. The highlight of that early-fall semester was the dean's reception for faculty, an event that required me to dress in my best black sheath cocktail dress, slender high-heeled pumps, a string of pearls, and short white gloves.

The faculty formed a long line to be introduced to the dean of the faculty and his wife. The dean was a tall, slender man in his early sixties with a full head of snowy white hair and a pleasant expression and smile. He towered over his wife (I always thought of her as "Mrs. Dean," although she must have had another name), a rotund, dimpled little woman with a warm smile and a rather clammy handshake.

I was first introduced by the sergeant at arms to the dean, who shook hands graciously and welcomed me to the faculty, to Virginia, and to the United States. The dean then introduced me to his wife. "This is Miss MacLellan. She comes to us from Canada, and she teaches economics," he said.

"Oh, my dear," said Mrs. Dean as she clutched both my hands in hers and beamed at me. "Home economics! How nice! You must be a great cook!"

During my second year on the faculty, the scene was repeated in an identical fashion. The dean introduced me to Mrs. Dean as being a member of the economics department, whereupon Mrs. Dean exclaimed (for all nearby to hear), "Oh my dear! Home economics! How very nice! I'll bet you are a great cook!"

At the beginning of the fall semester of year three, I, by now a hardened and prematurely graying member of the economics department, braced in anticipation of this annual rite with Mrs. Dean. Surely, she would have grasped some sense of the young women faculty by now, and while it was still important to be polite, to try to match the graciousness of these charming Virginians, I also bristled somewhat at the thought of maintaining these fictional stereotypes. But when Mrs. Dean said to me with her customary enthusiasm, "My dear, home economics! I'll bet you are a great cook," I held my hands in hers for an extra half-second, smiled happily, and replied, "By this time, I am getting pretty good!"

We were five roommates in that faculty house, four of us new, young faculty members: the friendly young woman who had met me at the door came from Joplin, Missouri, and taught English with her broad Midwestern twang; there was a young woman from Czechoslovakia who spoke English with a heavy accent and who taught German; an intensely silent, rather mysterious older woman, perhaps in her mid-to-late-thirties, who had an administrative job at the university rather than a faculty position and who, she told us, was waiting for her apartment that was located just outside the town to be ready after some renovation work; and a cheery, tanned and freckled teacher of tennis, golf, and synchronized swimming in the physical education department, who came from southern Georgia and had a deep drawl and a drawerful of unusual (and usually incomprehensible) figures of speech.

During those early weeks, we were polite to each other amid the babel of accents. In those years before a multicultural experience was the norm in most sections of the North American continent, and well before political correctness dictated appropriate behavior to ethnic and international groups, our politeness was based only on our upbringing of good manners.

But the amicable atmosphere began to unravel with the unaccustomed odors of fresh garlic being cut and sautéed in the common room kitchen by the young woman from

Czechoslovakia as well as by the unusual silence and standoff-ishness of the older woman with the mysterious past, who left after three months, just as silently and without explanation. Later we were told that she had recently been released from a woman's prison and while living with us was, in fact, still on probation and under surveillance.

We never did find out why she had been imprisoned, but we thought that she must be a mother since at times we would find her looking at pictures of a little girl and boy that she carried in her purse.

By now, three of us were steering away from the Slovakian woman, not just because of her heavy accent, which made conversation difficult, but from the even heavier stench of garlic. This bulbous herb was completely unknown to many of us in North America in those long-ago days. If I was experiencing the shock of adapting to a new country, at least I spoke the same language as the two other young women, however varying our accents and figures of speech. The Slovak, as we began to call her when talking about her, needed not only to adjust to a new country and new accents, but also adjust to living in a vastly different system than Communism, which dominated her country for most of her years growing up in Czechoslovakia.

Then one day, I walked into the kitchen to make a sandwich for lunch and found her sitting at the kitchen table, sobbing. "What's wrong?" I asked, kneeling beside her at the table. "Are you ill? Has something happened to you?"

She said nothing to me, nor did she look at me for some time, her head bowed, her face covered by a handkerchief.

Finally, she raised her head and looked directly at me, and said, "I am not happy here. You people don't like me. You make fun of me. I want to go home to my own people."

So she had picked up on our whispered criticisms and sensed our closing her out from most dinnertime gatherings and conversations. I felt instant remorse and guilt for contributing to her misery and searched for what to say to her. Finally, I decided to tell her the truth about what we were thinking and saying about her: "We have been critical, you are right about that. We have trouble with your accent, and so we don't understand all of what you say."

She looked at me in astonishment. "You have trouble with my accent? I have trouble with all of your accents. None of you sound alike or say similar things in English, and it is nothing at all like the English I learned in my schools."

"There's more," I said. "We also have trouble with the foods you cook, particularly with that onion-looking item you call garlic. That does not smell right to us, and the smell stays in this kitchen and gets on our clothes."

Her astonishment suddenly turned into peals of laughter. "You don't like garlic? The whole world eats garlic! It is good for you. It keeps you warm and healthy in the winter, so you don't get so many colds."

All of this was said in a heavy accent, but I was listening intently and understood everything. I was also grasping for a solution to this situation that was painful for her and embarrassing for us. "Why don't you cook a dish that's special in your country and that has garlic in it and invite us all to share with you? Then we can experience it for ourselves. And why don't you join us on Friday afternoon when the young faculty members are having a picnic down at Jamestown? We all bring something — a bag of potato chips or some chocolates — and we can all get to know one another."

I had no way of knowing if the other young women of our house would even consider joining her at the table much less sample the garlicky dinner dish, nor could I imagine her willing to mix with the crowd of young faculty, considering that she had trouble speaking to the three of us, her housemates. But she brightened and accepted my apology and said yes to both events.

Only the young woman from Missouri came with me to the "Garlic Dinner," as she called it. The Georgia woman found an acceptable excuse, claiming late practice with her synchronized swimming team; the mysterious one stayed in her room. I choked down the ground beef and garlic and onions dish, hiding as much as I could under the mashed potatoes, but that evening, I could no longer smell the garlic, not on my sweater or skirt nor in the kitchen. I decided that was because I must now also smell like garlic.

I do not remember how the Slovak woman got to the picnic in Jamestown, perhaps I arranged for her to travel with one of the few faculty members who had a car. Another car was picking me up since my assignment for the picnic was to buy two six-packs of beer. Virginia was close to being a dry state in those years, except for the 3 percent beer that was served in the restored colonial tavern, a public spot that could only be patronized by those twenty-one or older. The few delicatessens that sold beer were strict about the twenty-one-year-old age limit. I worried about being able to buy the beer since I would not be twenty-one for three more months.

I picked out the two six-packs, set them gingerly on the counter, and waited until the retailer finished with another customer before he came over. He looked intently at me, then asked: "I must see your identification. You must be twenty-one years by your latest birthday before you can buy beer in Virginia. Please let me see your driver's license."

I stalled for a minute, fumbling in my purse. If I showed him my driver's license and he could do even the most basic math, he could certainly see that I was underage. My fingers found the small card case of cards in my purse. I still hesitated before pulling out the case with my license and picture and then noticed my newly imprinted faculty card with my photo from the university. Summoning all possible dignity, I set the faculty card on the counter firmly and said, "Well, thank you for the flattery, but you can see that I am on the faculty of the university, which must mean that I can buy beer."

He blushed and apologized as he quickly took my $10 bill to the cash register and brought me back the change. "I am so sorry, ma'am. You please come back now you hear?"

The Young Faculty, Learning to Teach

We were about thirty strong, this young faculty group that reported to campus early that September of 1960, and we were a new demographic group, a major departure from the existing faculty, who dated primarily from the Depression Era, or in a handful of cases, from the post–World War II, GI-Bill soldiers who went on to finish their bachelor's degrees to matriculate with master's and PhDs in the arts, sciences, or business.

About eight years separated us from that latter group, with few arrivals in between, so we were an anomaly for that era and certainly for that campus. And we were a diverse group, both in origin and in our academic fields. Several of us were international (still regularly called "foreigners" in those days), including one young woman from Edinburgh, Scotland, who taught German (we teased her endlessly, asking if she spoke German with the same thick brogue as her Edinburgh English); a pert young woman from Bristol, England, who also taught German, as did the young woman from Czechoslovakia, each with their own inimitable accents; and me, with my eastern Canadian accent that was not quite British, Scottish, or American.

The young men included the "Don Juan" of the English department, a newly minted PhD in romantic literature who embraced — figuratively and, we suspected, literally — the beautiful young senior women who regularly invited him to chaperone their sorority parties; or the quiet, bespectacled newly minted PhD in physics who was teaching a mysterious subject called the philosophy of science.

Another young woman, a native of the town of Williamsburg, who had just returned from two years of graduate work in Italy with tales of amorous Italians fond of pinching her bottom as she walked down the street, taught philosophy as well as Italian. During that first year, with all of the new-faculty receptions and parties, my Georgia-born roommate and I became good friends, or at least close colleagues, united in our youth and mildly impetuous attitudes against the older and more staid members of the faculty firmament.

As the new arrival in the economics and business administration department, then under one director, I was assigned the courses that the older faculty no longer wanted to teach.

"Aha," the department director said as he looked over my college transcripts, "You have taken economic geography and done very well with it, so you can teach our course in that," which fixed my fate for the first semester. Here I was, fresh out of graduate school, well imbued with the latest knowledge on economic development policy and practice, the history of economic thought, and several aspects of international economics, and I was asked to teach economic geography.

This was a subject that I loved in college, and I loved geography from my earliest years in secondary school. The thought of traveling and knowing about the various countries and regions of the world was dear to me. I did not, however, have the vaguest idea of how to teach economic geography. What was I supposed to do, open a physical geography atlas and say, "Here are the major wheat-producing regions of the world? Here are the great rice-growing regions of the world? Here is where major oil companies are drilling for oil? Here are the major iron ore deposits of the world?" Not that I had any choice, so I said an enthusiastic "Yes, of course."

As a matter of fact, I did not know how to teach any subject, even the more advanced topics of my senior year in college or the graduate courses. How did one prepare a syllabus for a course? How did one prepare a lesson? How much homework should one give? Should you allow questions in the lecture? Should you make every effort to initiate a discussion? How in the world would one concoct a midterm or final exam? And how stringently should it be graded? I knew nothing of the U.S. academic system at college, was baffled by the grade-point average and was unsure as to how one assigned an *A* or a *B*, much less the plus and minus ranges that came with each letter. In my college system, we received numerical grades, which somehow, and somewhat mysteriously, were translated into summa cum laude and magna cum laude and down the line when we graduated.

The young faculty commiserated on this topic in those first weeks. We were all fresh out of graduate school, where most of us had no teaching assistant job much less full-time teaching experience. The older faculty members and the administration seemed content to just "throw us in the pond and see what ripples we would make" as the young Byron of the English department quipped. And since our fields of endeavor were usually different, except for the contingent that was teaching European languages, we decided that we just had to make it up each Sunday evening as we prepared our lectures for the week.

I prepared pages of notes for my introductory class in economic geography, which was way too much for my fifty-minute class, but I figured I could use the balance for the second lecture.

The class, which eventually totaled about thirty students, filed in, the young women pert and smart, taking their seats and opening their textbooks, pens in hand. Most of the young men were more casual in attitude, strolling in, chewing gum, taking a long look at me as they sauntered to the nearest empty seat.

"We do not chew gum in this class." I heard my mother's voice and my mother's intonation as I said this, which surprised me. "We will now have roll call. Please introduce yourselves. The registrar wants to make sure that you attend class so I will have to take roll call at the beginning of this and every class."

My voice may have sounded somewhat steady, but my knees were shaking. I got through the roll call without too many mispronounced names, although my few gaffes brought chuckles. I did not laugh; this was too terrifying. I described the course I would be teaching and the textbook they would be using and told them to buy it in the bookstore if they had not already purchased it. Then I plunged into my lecture on why the study of economic geography was important, how it fit into overall economic knowledge, and how it gave us information on what commodities and minerals the U.S. both imported and exported.

I turned back toward the blackboard to see if there were any pull-down maps, but there were none and no brackets for mounting them either. What was the department thinking? How could one teach economic geography without a map, especially a map of physical geography and one of the climate types, and one depicting the major mineral and oil deposits in the U.S. and the various agricultural regions? And, even worse, I was suddenly at the end of my typed notes. I looked up at the big clock on the wall. It was 11:17, which meant that I had been in class for seventeen minutes. This class was supposed to last for fifty minutes. I could not think of another thing to say, except to mumble, "That is all for today. Please read the first two chapters of your textbook for our next class."

There was nothing else could I do under those circumstances, I told myself as I gathered up my notes and the piece
of chalk and my purse. In the subsequent semester and following year, when assigned to teach this course again, I could never
get through those notes for my first class. It would take me at
least two full sessions before I would cover all of the points in
that lecture.

Whatever it was that struck me in that first class, I realized
that I needed to find out just how much basic geography my
class knew. Could they find London or Paris on a blank map of
Europe? Did they know the major countries in Africa? What
did they know of the Asian countries, particularly Japan or
Laos, and Vietnam, where there was some political agitation?
There was not much point in asking details about China, which
was a large red blob on my own atlas, or the Soviet Union,
which sprawled over the atlas in somber forest green with little
identification of cities or even wheat-growing areas. I decided
to design a quiz that had some blank maps and a list of cities
that they would have to match with countries to give at the beginning of the second session. The results of my quiz were both
astounding and sobering: Not one student in the class of thirty
identified more than 10 percent of the places and countries.

After class, I walked down the hall to the director's office,
asked for an appointment, and when received into his office,
asked politely for wall maps. "What kind of wall maps would
you like?" he asked, puffing happily on a pipe.

"Sir, my students need an entire set of world maps, both
political and physical, for each of the continents, plus the world

map. And if these were maps that I could pull down when needed, that would be even better."

He puffed away, thinking about this for a while. I suddenly remembered the yellowing wall map we had in my one-room school in Nova Scotia and my teacher (usually my mother) pointing with her long ruler to France, Italy, or England, Egypt, the Belgian Congo, or the Argentine pampas, where they grew wheat and raised cattle, as the farmers did in western Canada. There were blank maps of countries in our Grade 5 geography book where we had to fill in the capitals and recognize the outline of the countries in all of Europe and Latin America and several in Africa. By the spring of our fifth-grade year, the teacher expected us to correctly place the capitals and the great ports of Europe.

"Very well," the department director said between blue puffs of smoke, "this shouldn't take too long. I believe they are in storage. It is just that no recent professor has asked for them."

I got my maps. I learned to pull each one down depending on whether I was doing physical geography and identifying regions for agriculture or mineral deposits or needed to spend time on the actual political boundaries and the major cities in each country.

The following year, when I was teaching the course for the second time, one of the students in the class who was due to graduate that May and who, as an ROTC cadet, was to report to the U.S. Army immediately after his graduation celebrations, launched into a spirited debate about the political issue of the day, which was the crisis in Laos. I no longer recall how we segued from a discussion over trade with Southeast Asia based on their economic geography to politics, but there it was, an actual discussion by a student with some views on a subject.

"Well," he said with rising confidence, "when I am wading ashore on the coast of Africa to defend these people of Laos...."

"Mr. Gustafsson," I said, cutting him off at once and pulling down the map of Asia. "You are going to be in for a big surprise: Laos is not in Africa. It is in Southeast Asia and there is no shore. Now let's get back to studying our economic geography."

Discovering Culture in America

My first encounter with a formal cultural event came two months after I arrived in America and the state of Virginia on the night after John F. Kennedy won the presidency of the United States. This was my first election — not that I could vote, since I was a resident alien with a green card and not a citizen. I had never voted in Canada either because I was too young when I finished graduate school.

None of us was in good condition that night after the election, since we were all up until 5 a.m., waiting for the final count, and I fear had drunk too much Canadian Club or bourbon and ginger ale — neither familiar to me — during the long, exciting night, when about thirty of the new, young faculty gathered around someone's black-and-white TV with a grainy screen to watch the returns and the election commentary. Most of us had to report for work in the morning, either to teach a class or in my case, to appear at 8 a.m. for my full-time job as a research assistant.

The concert that night after the election all-nighter was the first in a series of classical offerings by the university for its faculty and students and featured Marcel Marceau, the great French mime. I had read of him, but never saw anything quite like this performance — silent and masterful. But the silence was not a great asset for that evening after the election all-nighter; I think I fell asleep with my eyes open, despite enjoying the new experience. Not all was lost because I still remember his persona on that stage these many years later.

Our next concert, some weeks later, featured a young rising star in classical music named Grace Bumbry. She was unknown at that time even to those few on our young faculty who professed a considerable knowledge of classical music. This type of concert was quite unfamiliar to me, as we had no opportunity in eastern Canada to see such a caliber of performance when I was growing up. I was thrilled by her rich mezzo-soprano voice and by her stage presence.

Later that season we heard a quartet playing classical music, but what I remember that first spring in Virginia, during our second semester, was suddenly announcing to a Friday-evening cocktail hour hosted by one of the young faculty, "Sorry, I have to leave now. I must get home to watch Steve McQueen in *The Bounty Hunter* on TV."

My words were met with astonishment and probably some measure of scorn. I was leaving a cultural gathering of young intellectuals (if martinis and academic chitchat are culture) for a common TV show? But leave I did. Steve McQueen was a dashing new actor, one I thought would be a major star, and I considered that was as much a "cultural offering" as anything we had seen all year.

But driving home that early-April evening, I became vividly aware of another form of culture: the panoply of spring in Virginia, this early and glorious season of japonicas and crocus, forsythia, daffodils and tulips, and flowering pink dogwood and bounteous azaleas, each in turn or maybe all at once surrounding every house in this small city and lining every street and thoroughfare. In Nova Scotia, spring is a painfully slow and erratic affair. In early April there might be some welcome warmth in the sun, but the wind stays cold, and most disappointing of all, we would likely have occasional days of spring snow. "Good for fertilizing the fields," was a common refrain, but perhaps this was just a brave rationalization. "You must wear your jacket and a scarf and your gloves," our mother would admonish. "You can be fooled by a few minutes of warm sun, but you will all catch your death of cold if you take off your jackets."

Years later, I would use the same words to urge my two growing children, anxious to shed their winter jackets on the first warm sunny day in April. "Keep your jackets on," I would say, hearing the echo of my mother's voice, "or you will catch your death of cold."

But not in April in eastern Virginia. Here, one could shed jacket and scarf and try out their new spring wardrobe and sandals and be alight and alive in the spring glory. This indeed was culture of the highest order of nature.

Adjusting to Life as an Expatriate

I was a few weeks into my early faculty challenges and cultural adjustments before the reality set in that I had left home, had left my mother and three younger siblings behind while I set off on my personal adventure. The agonies of guilt almost overwhelmed me then and would shadow my life for many years to come.

Certainly, I needed to have a job after graduate school, but I could have stayed in my hometown and taken the offer at the radio station with the new TV addition starting there. I could have looked for an academic teaching job somewhere in Nova Scotia or anywhere else in Canada. I never did, because in the uncertainty of what I was to do in those last months of graduate school, my professor asked me what I wanted to do. "Teach university," I said. He thought about this for a few minutes, then said, "I think you should go to the U.S. It might be easier for you to get a position. Just don't tell them how old you are unless you are specifically asked, of course."

So this was the decision path: He was gently suggesting that I might have trouble getting a position teaching college or university in Canada because of my age. He didn't hint at the fact that I was a young woman and not a young man, although, later, I came to think that might also have been behind his suggestion.

The early road of an emigrant is a mixture of pain and longing and excitement over the new and the untried and the challenge of figuring out whether you can understand this new culture, this new atmosphere, and then whether you can prevail, even survive in its midst. Those first months were not at all a mixture but a wild pendulum swing of deep longing, regrets, guilt, of questioning what I was doing here and what had I been thinking; of wondering how my brother was doing in the engineering college and with his hockey games; what my sister's experience in college — she was now a sophomore — was like. Did she like her courses, did she have a boyfriend, did she make the basketball team? And my youngest sister, was she still being benched by her high school basketball coach because of her red-haired temper? Was she still working weekends at the co-op grocery store checkout counter, greeting everyone by name? Were the few pimples disappearing from her freckled face? Who was helping her with her homework?

But this agony was not every day, maybe not every other day, for my life in Colonial Virginia, in the restored town of Williamsburg, was a blur of new activities at the university, a steep mountain of challenges in learning to teach my undergraduate students, going to faculty meetings and weekend brunches in the King's Tavern. I was still under twenty-one that first fall, so not even eligible for a 3.2 percent beer, the only offering permitted by the town elders.

Then there was the excitement of occasional weekend visits to the large department stores in Richmond, Virginia's capital and largest city, and a shopping mecca compared to the small, quaint stores in Williamsburg that sold candles and scent cachets and cookbooks of Colonial-era recipes where the *F* looked like an *S* and vice versa.

There were beautiful clothes to choose from that year of 1960, pencil-slim skirts that came fashionably below the knee, elegant shoes also with pencil-slim high heels, the perfectly fitted little black dress, and the eye-catching strands of faux pearls (still expensive, so we had to save a certain amount from several paychecks to then splurge on the purchase).

Just before Thanksgiving that year I bought a leopard-spotted hat with a soft floppy brim, modeled I was sure after one Audrey Hepburn wore in a movie. I wore this hat on my journey home for Christmas vacation, feeling instantly that I was totally in fashion, looking just like a spiffy working girl, although perhaps not at all like a college professor.

Perhaps it was these shopping trips that brought out the greatest pangs of guilt over leaving my mother. Shouldn't I have been working close to home, saving most of my money to share with her as she was buying clothes and books for my siblings and food for all of the drop-in visitors and boyfriends as well as the family? Our college education was paid for and each of us had a monthly spending allowance from the Canadian government, which was their monetary tribute to the family for the loss of our father in those final months of World War II. And, as I did during my college years, all three of my siblings worked during the summer, which bought most of the clothes needed for the year, plus yielded some extra spending money for cosmetics or LPs or movie tickets. And if I were working and living nearby, I could stop in on evenings or weekends and make dinner for the family or do the laundry and ironing or take the family car in for a tune-up.

Although if I gave these anxious thoughts some space to furl out, I would then remember that my mother was perfectly capable of doing all of these tasks by herself, as she always had, fitting everything in with her high school teaching job, getting together with her friends to play cribbage or bridge, briskly rolling out a pan of baking powder biscuits or a carrot cake, parceling out the remaining chores to the three youngsters left behind, who would likely grumble the same way they had in the last few years, as in: "But I have to study for an exam," or "But I have to get ready to leave for a (hockey) (basketball) (volleyball) game."

I set aside a certain amount of money every paycheck, except for the first, which was subsumed by household expenditures of furnishing my room — sheets, pillows, a blanket, towels, reading lamps — for the airplane ticket back to Halifax for the Christmas holidays. I would have at least ten days off from teaching my class and from the research work that was part of my job assignment. I would wear my new red wool suit and black wool cape and high-heeled leather boots and my faux-leopard-skin hat that looked like an Audrey Hepburn original. I would have stories to tell and accents to replicate and open up a treasure trove of recipes and tales I had heard about Jack and Jackie Kennedy. I surely would be considered almost an insider to the U.S. presidency and its vivid politics.

There was no family to meet me at the airport: no mother, no brother, no younger sisters bubbling over with their stories while also clinging to me and my tales of adventure. There was no mother, looking relieved and happy to have her prodigal daughter back again and to find me looking spiffy, up to date, in the U.S. fashions of the day. Mother, it turned out, was helping to run the holiday fair at her high school; brother was away playing hockey; college sister and high school sister were each working for a few days at their summer job sites, earning some extra money for their Christmas shopping. My family was too busy to meet me at the airport, so sent an old family friend, but not one of my dear respected friends, to meet me for the two-hour ride to my hometown.

It appeared that my family was doing just fine without me, while in those first four months in Virginia, I was suffused with the nagging guilt of an emigrant. Later I was to ease any nagging guilts by making plans that each sibling would, in turn, visit me in Williamsburg in the summer and then travel home to Nova Scotia with me in whatever car I would buy.

That next summer, I sent Louise an airplane ticket from Halifax to Newport News, with detailed instructions on how she was to make the two or three changes of airline and gates for the journey. Louise was seventeen and close to finishing high school. When she arrived, I took her to a large empty parking lot on the William and Mary campus so she could practice driving the little red Sunbeam Alpine. That next morning, as I readied for work, I passed her the keys and a map of the area and told her she could drive to Jamestown ("carefully watch that speedometer...") and then to Yorktown, where she could find a place for lunch. Then she could meet me at the business administration building at 5 p.m. and we could go for another drive and then to dinner. Louise had passed her driving test the summer before and had plenty of opportunities to drive our mother's car during the past year. Years later, Louise marveled that I would trust her with my new little red sports car and its stick shift in this new country.

The following summer, Malcolm came to visit and drove home with me in the sports car, and then the third summer, my

sister Donnie arrived for her introduction to Colonial Williamsburg. We planned for an overnight stay in Washington, D.C.,
where we saw a Broadway play that was on tour and then on to
New York City for two days of just being tourists.

Donnie and I drove from Washington to New York City
with the top down on the little sports car. It was a hot, sunny
day, both of us were dressed in Bermuda shorts, t-shirts, and
wearing straw hats that tied under our chins against the strong
winds that buffeted us despite the windshield. Somehow, we
navigated our way into the city and through the crowded streets
of Manhattan to find the hotel that I thought would be appropriate as well as safe for us to stay in, the Barbizon for Women.
The doorman took the keys to the sports car as he helped take
the luggage out of the trunk and we walked excitedly through
the lobby, carrying our suitcases, eager for adventure in this
storied great city. The older woman behind the desk looked up
at us, peering over half-glasses, leaned over to look at our outfits, and said sternly: "You cannot come into this hotel dressed
like that. You will have to go someplace else."

"But we have a reservation," I said, digging the paper out
of my purse, "and we have just been driving in a sports car with
the top down, so we needed to dress like this."

"No matter, you are not permitted to come into this hotel
without being properly dressed."

I knew of no other hotel or how I would even be able to
find one in these circumstances. Granted, we must have looked
like sunburnt raggedy girls, but there must be some solution.
"Do you have a ladies' room on this floor?" I asked as politely
as possible.

"Yes, of course, we do," she conceded.

"Well then, if you can just direct us to it, we will take our suitcases along and change in the ladies' room. We have nice dresses in our suitcases that we can put on and then we'll come back to the desk and register."

And that's what we did. Donnie, throughout her life, has registered at many fine hotels and, no doubt, at some motels with her daughters on vacation as they were growing up. I have had the same opportunity over the years, and I've stayed in some wonderful hotels in Asia and Europe as well as in the U.S. and Canada, but this unwelcoming arrival was the one we would talk about over the decades.

A few years after that episode, I noticed that the Barbizon for Women no longer existed. By the mid- or late 1960s, they must have exhausted the population of young women who would appear at the registration desk in their little black dresses, strings of pearls, and white gloves. But we truly must have looked unsightly arriving at the front desk, sunburned, splattered with insects, windblown almost beyond recovery despite our straw hats, wearing crumpled and probably crumb-covered shorts, sweaty t-shirts, and sagging socks in dusty sneakers. Small wonder the receptionist reacted as she did.

The Amphitheater

That second semester of my first year I was assigned to teach American economic history. It seemed to be a rather absurd assignment since I was still a recent arrival in America, and while we learned a great deal of the subject when I was studying

Canadian economic history — the U.S., after all, was the large and powerful economy to our south and most political and economic developments in Canada were influenced by what was going on in the U.S. — this was going to be a stretch. I went off to the bookstore to find any book on U.S. history to read alongside the economic history text I would be using.

The morning of the first class, the registrar's office phoned to say that the room designated for this course had been changed from one in our business administration building to "a larger room over in the chemistry building," because my new class "was a large class." I asked the departmental secretary about the room number in the other building. She looked at a classroom guide and said, "That room is the amphitheater, which they use for the big freshman Chemistry 1 class."

I made my way across the campus quadrangle and up the steps of the imposing chemistry building and walked down the hall until I found the door with the designated room number. I opened the door to a wall of faces, a wall that extended up the risers toward a high ceiling and curved around, as in an actual amphitheater, and extending upwards from a podium in the middle of the floor. That podium, it appeared, was for me. I was to stand there (clutching the sides) and teach upward to this sea of faces. It would take me half the class to go through roll call.

I was terrified. I thought of flight. Perhaps it was not too late. I could go right to the airport and wait there until I could find flights back to Canada. Maybe the radio station in my hometown with its new TV station would still have the job they had offered me; even going on camera was less terrifying than this.

Somehow, I got through the session, my ears ringing as though in some type of force field, my voice going dry, my legs trembling. The department head was apologetic. "I did not put an upper ceiling on registration for that course," he said. "We never get more than ten to twelve students for this course, so the people at the registration desk had no reason to cut off registration, and now you have a hundred twenty students."

From the young faculty network, I learned that the word had spread among many of the students that a new, young female faculty member was teaching the course, and so the football and basketball teams decided that the class could be fun and maybe an easy A grade.

Throw in the lacrosse and tennis teams as well, I thought as I began to prepare the lecture for the second class.

This entire semester would be a challenge. How was I going to manage this crowd? What if I got a run in my stocking or my slip was showing, or some button came undone on my blouse? I would be under constant scrutiny, just like something in a petri dish that a chemistry student peers at through a microscope.

My only comeback to this crowd — and it needed to be subtle — was to teach them the Canadian version of the War of 1812. I assigned the chapter from their text on this interesting phase of history as well as economic change underway in the U.S. and reminded the assembled horde to read it carefully. For the next class, I brought my newly prepared notes and taught the entire 1812 to 1814 war period, including the burning of Washington, from the Canadian point of view. At the end, when I had just finished pointing out that the "renegades" had gone up to Toronto — then called York — and burned that fledgling town in retaliation, I asked: "Are there any questions?" There was no response. I asked again, "Any questions?" It was clear that no one had read the chapter or remembered anything from their high school history on this war or how and where it was fought. "There is an extra lesson here," I said. "I have just taught you a view of history that is not shared by your country, at least not in the history books I have read here. What I have taught you is 'truth,' but from Canada's point of view. You must read your own history and be able to counter anyone with a different account of why something happened."

They did look sheepish, all 120 of them, sitting up there looking down at me. But they also got back at me, in a way, although they were not to know the circumstances of why I showed up one day wearing my academic gown. I gave no explanation, kept on with the lecture as usual, but it was a near incident of acute embarrassment that I was covering up under that black gown, for just before leaving my office for class, I scrunched down to put away a file in a bottom file drawer only to hear the unmistakable sound of fabric tearing — and a long tear from the length of the sound. When I stood up, it was clear that the back seam of my pencil-slim skirt had given way and there was now at least a five-inch opening at the back of the skirt. I had no sewing kit with me, and besides, there was no time, it was already 10:50 a.m., leaving me only ten minutes to get across the quadrangle and to my class. I looked around the office in growing panic. What to do? I couldn't just cancel class; we were always expected to be there presenting our lectures unless truly ill. Then I spotted the academic gown on a hanger at the back of the room, in a ready state for the many formal processions we seemed to have at this university.

What the heck, I thought.

I had heard they wear these gowns at Cambridge and Oxford. So I pulled on the black academic gown, carefully fastened the front hook-and-eye combinations, grabbed my folder of notes, and dashed off to teach American economic history in the chemistry building amphitheater in my Oxford don gown.

The One-Time-Only Frat Party Chaperone

That first spring, I was asked to chaperone a Saturday-evening party at one of the fraternities. I knew nothing of fraternities since they did not exist in my undergraduate school, and I was too busy with my graduate work to ever take notice of their existence on that campus. But when politely asked if I would please chaperone the fraternity party on Saturday night for whatever the Greek three-syllable name, with promises that the party was well regulated and would end early, I immediately said, "Yes, of course," thinking that it must be something we young faculty were expected to do.

Saturday evening, I dressed carefully, wearing a suit jacket over a slim black dress. I combed my hair back and wore little makeup and no jewelry. I was trying my best to look professorial and serious. I found my way to the street address on fraternity row and was greeted politely by the fraternity president. "Good evening, Miss MacLellan. Would you like to come into the patio room and meet some of our fraternity officers? And what would you like to drink?"

"Thank you, I will have a soft drink. Any kind," I said. I do not like any kind of soft drink, but I did not think they would have orange juice. He guided me towards the bar. I wondered if they were allowed to have a bar. Was this not supposed to be a dry campus in a dry state? But there, beside the bar, was a giant galvanized tub with lots of ice and plenty of beer in cans and a few bottles of orange juice. My young host saw me looking at the tub of beer.

"This is perfectly legal," he said, anticipating my question. "We are technically 'off-campus,' across the road from the official boundaries of the campus, so we are allowed to have beer." I suddenly remembered the rumors amongst the young faculty that the giant-sized watermelons we saw the students bringing to the football games during the fall semester had been injected with gin or vodka using hypodermic needles from the science labs.

"Oh, I would like one of those bottles of orange juice," I said.

"You can sit here on this sofa near the window, which will give you a good view of the party, since you are, after all, the chaperone," he said, still polite, but with more than a small twinkle in his eye.

I sat down, wondering what I was now supposed to do, either for these young men or with myself. What exactly did chaperone mean? If some of the boys got into a fight, was I to break it up? If one of the boys started to mistreat one of these lovely co-eds who were now arriving, was I supposed to intervene? What should I do if someone drank too much of that beer and suddenly threw up?

Several of the young women came over to speak to me, asking me what I was teaching and if I was enjoying the campus and Virginia. They were followed by a series of young men who stopped by to introduce themselves, saying they hoped that I was enjoying the evening. I clung to the corner of the sofa.

As the evening moved on, I noticed that the trips to the tub of beer grew more frequent and the tenor of the evening grew louder. Someone put on a record and a few of the students got up to dance. The young women had disappeared from my side and my view and were either dancing or off in other corners, deep in conversation with some of the young men. I had finished my orange juice and then had accepted a Coca-Cola, as a young man sat down beside me.

"I hear your name is Rosemary," he said. "Would you like to dance?" He clearly had been one of the beer drinkers, because his voice was thick, and he hissed the *s* in my name.

"No, thank you," I said, hoping I sounded quite prim, as I was beginning to be nervous about all of this. He smiled at me, got up, and then returned with two other young men.

"We would like to dance with you, Rosemary." I sat there, stunned. Then I realized that by this hour of the evening and the stage of the party, they no longer remembered or even knew that I was their chaperone. I was the same age as most of the juniors, maybe even the seniors, at the party, and I had not been given a badge that identified me. It was time to go, and quickly. I stood up, patted down my dress, and picked up my purse. "Gentlemen," I said as politely and firmly as I could, "the evening is about to end, and my coach awaits. Please make sure that everyone gets home safely." Then I fled with what little dignity I still maintained.

The only other time I agreed to chaperone an event was the spring prom of my third year of teaching, when I commandeered my more-or-less boyfriend, George, into accompanying me to the prom held in the sunken garden of the campus. I did a tour of the dance floor, wearing my chaperone badge, with George as my protection. This time, as a chaperone, I thoroughly enjoyed myself.

Discovering the Foods of Virginia

One of the great discoveries of those first two years was the food of colonial Virginia. I had never heard of "Johnnycakes" or Smithfield ham or ham biscuits, which were small tea biscuits baked with a slice of the salty Smithfield ham inside, or grits. In my second year on the faculty, I shared an apartment with Millie from southern Georgia who taught tennis, golf, and synchronized swimming and who had been one of my roommates in the faculty house our first year. This was a lovely duplex apartment, built onto the side of a glorious colonial house. We had our own entrance, a fireplace, and a wonderful pink dogwood tree that was overgrowing our private entrance, so that in spring, we had to gently move some branches aside to get through the outside door.

When the colder air of late autumn finally arrived, I decided it was time to cook a hot cereal for breakfast, so I bought a box of Cream of Wheat. The next morning, my turn to cook, I invited Millie to a hearty northern breakfast. She sat down at the table as I poured the coffee. She looked intently at the bowl of white cereal at her place, then got up, excused herself, and headed for the kitchen, returning with the butter dish and the saltshaker. She then proceeded to slice a few patties of butter into the Cream of Wheat in her bowl, pour on some salt, and then said, pleasantly, "Why, thank you for the grits."

"What do you mean, grits? This is Cream of Wheat," I said as I spooned brown sugar and poured cream into my bowl.

"Why this is ground white corn," Millie said, "and we usually have it with a breakfast of sausage and eggs."

"No, this is Cream of Wheat. It is made of wheat, and we have it with brown sugar and cream," I said. There was nothing else to do but laugh, and for each of us to eat the breakfast we knew. But there was never any doubt or translation needed about the special seafood and the preparation of that seafood in coastal Virginia. The best and soon to be my favorite was called Crab Norfolk.

I had never heard of crabmeat in Nova Scotia. Our local lobstermen pulled traps filled with succulent young lobsters or nets with Atlantic salmon, fresh and natural and delicate pink. But crabmeat? Many years later I learned that the fishermen on the Northumberland Strait finally realized that the crabs they had thrown out of the nets those many years were worth something and could be called "Queen Crab" and could command a high price in the fish markets of Toronto, Montreal, or Boston. But this was the early 1960s and specialized foods were still a rarity in Nova Scotia, and I was sitting at the Yorktown Inn and being told by my hosts for dinner that I should order Crab Norfolk.

The green salad was served first, and then the salad plates were gently pushed to the left side by one waiter while a second waiter appeared with a tray of small covered pewter pots. He smiled at us and warned us in a gentle voice, "These pots will be hot." The waiter beside me then uncovered the dish and peered in before he smiled at me and reminded me again that the pot was hot. Then he bowed slightly and left me to contemplate this special dish from the kitchen.

I can still remember today, years later, the aroma wafting from those pots. There was the hint of lemon, then of a moderate dose of garlic — in slices sometimes, carefully diced at others — a sprinkle of salt and fresh parsley. And there it was, spooned onto the plate, gently steaming, aromatic, a triumph — lump crabmeat from the Chesapeake Bay. This was accompanied by a baked potato and either fresh asparagus or green beans. The simply prepared dish enhanced the natural flavor and texture of the crabmeat. For me, this was a revelation in cooking style as well as an introduction to a new type of seafood. This was indeed food for the gods.

These days in New York City, I can buy lump crabmeat from Virginia and can try to re-create that dish. But while tasty and appealing, it is never quite the same. Maybe it was that pewter pot that made the sautéed crabmeat extra flavorful, but maybe it was the sheer freshness of the crabmeat and the skill in its preparation.

Then there were the Thanksgiving dinners. I remember these first for the gracious generosity of the hosts for their invitation to join their families for this special dinner. In Canada, the major family gathering time was the Christmas holiday; the newly designated Thanksgiving weekend in Canada, to be held the same weekend as the U.S. Columbus Day seemed to have more to do with university alumni events than with Thanksgiving.

Next was the unique food. The turkey and its preparation for those Thanksgiving dinners in Virginia was familiar, except for the stuffing, which, in Virginia, was accented by adding chestnuts and perhaps savory sausage. The vegetables were distinctive and different from any then served in my part of Canada: puréed sweet potatoes or yams, collard greens, and yellow and green string beans with toasted almonds. For dessert, there was both pecan pie and pumpkin pie, both novelties to me.

Everything I had been told about the American observance of Thanksgiving was embodied on those dinners and remains the pinnacle of achievement as I have gone into my New York City kitchen these many years to prepare our Thanksgiving dinner.

Then, one day in spring, Millie was taking her turn in the kitchen to prepare breakfast, appearing at our little dining room table with a plate of spicy sausage patties, fried eggs, and grits. She passed me the butter dish and the saltshaker. I looked at the grits, then at Millie, and said, "Excuse me," and went into the kitchen to bring back a bowl, brown sugar, and cream. So once again, over more than a few giggles, we each ate the breakfast that we knew.

My First Car

My first car was a sports car, a small red Sunbeam Alpine from the British company Rootes Group. It was part of a flood of imported sports cars that were arriving in the U.S. by 1960: MGs, TR3s and then TR4s, Austin-Healeys, Sprites, and the advertised "Cadillac of imported sports cars," the Jaguar XKE, an ostentatious presence of glitz, long needle nose, and tailfins, costing multiple times what the other cars cost, and driven, the small sports-car snobs said when gathering for an afternoon sports car rally, by "rich kids who knew nothing about the inferior transmission in the machine they were driving."

I took no part in the sneering contests because I knew nothing of inferior transmissions systems or whether this statement had any veracity. I was much too smitten by my special little car. This was the first Sunbeam Alpine sold in the state of Virginia, and it was a beauty.

The first time I saw this little red car at the dealership on the outskirts of town, the salesman waxed in flowing words about its torque and its maneuverability, its rapid-fire acceleration from second to third gear and then to fourth, and its dexterity on turns. I had no idea what torque might be. I knew almost nothing about cars except how to drive, and I had very little experience with a stick shift, just from the old pickup truck where I learned to drive — its gears had growled anyway so it didn't matter how delicately I tried to go from first to second. So, except for the part of "dexterity around turns," I just had to believe what he was telling me. I would read the instruction booklet later, and for now, would try to figure out the rest of his sales pitch.

There was no doubt that I immediately loved this little car, but my main preoccupation right then was if could I afford it. I had been saving furiously from my salary for the last six months to be able to buy some kind of car, and I was quite sure that I had enough to make the down payment and that my teaching job at the university would be enough to warrant an installment plan. The sticker price was $2,700, half of my salary that year. That still sounds exorbitant, but my taxes were very low, including Social Security taxes, and my share of the rent in our university-owned faculty house was $15 per month. The next year, when I was to share an apartment with one of the other women faculty, my rent would rise to $27 per month, but maybe I could still afford the car, since my salary would go up to $5,600. I walked around the car once and then again.

"Sit in it and try the steering wheel," said the salesman. The leather bucket seat was a new experience, and it was comfortable. I studied the dashboard, which looked like the pictures I had seen of the cockpit in a small airplane.

"See that dial?" the salesman asked. "You can check your rpm's on that dial." I didn't know what an rpm was either, but I could learn.

"We recommend that you buy seat belts for it since you will be driving most of the time with the top down," the salesman added, "and those will cost you $30. We will install them for free." Seat belts were not standard in those days; the cars that first featured them were small European sports cars like this one.

"Also, these cars do not come equipped with a radio. We suggest that you go to the electronics store and buy a special portable radio with a sleeve. This way, you can detach the radio each time you park the car at night, so the radio does not get stolen. Anyone could cut through the soft top, you know," he said, adding, "Come, let's put a couple of gallons of gas in it and I will take you for a spin. You can practice changing gears and get a feel for the car."

I paid cash for the few gallons of gas that he put in the car, then he stepped out, gestured with a swooping arm toward the driver's seat, and said, "Go on, you drive, and you will see just how great it handles." So with a few more detailed instructions on handling the clutch and changing gears with a light touch, he said, "Let it float," and we were off for a trial run on one of Williamsburg's small back roads, ideal, it appeared, for this type of car.

"See what I said about the way it handles on the turns?" he asked in a voice that showed he was almost as excited as I was. I was driving gingerly with my heart thumping and was too busy maneuvering the car and the stick shift to talk to him until we were back at the dealership. I was already smitten.

Yes, I would buy this car, I thought, and then said aloud, "Yes, I will take it."

I may have whispered those words, but nonetheless, he ushered me into the office and pulled out a sheaf of crisp, new papers to arrange for the down payment and the five years of installment payments. I was calculating the down payment plus the cost of the seat belts, which were now being installed in the mechanic's bay, and scrutinizing the balance in my checkbook with relief, thinking, *I am okay. I will have a little left over*.

Then the salesman said, "Oh, we have to give you registration plates and that will cost another $20."

My heart sank. I could do this, but if I did, there would be only $2 or $3 left in my checking account and that would have to last me until payday on Friday. This was only Tuesday.

So I filled in the paperwork for the installment loan and wrote the check for the down payment, the seat belts, and the registration, my heart now doubly thumping.

"Congratulations!" the salesman practically bellowed in joy as he passed me the keys. "Enjoy your sports car!"

I drove home gingerly and only looked at the gas gauge as I pulled into our driveway. It seemed to be registering empty, but then I was too excited to read it carefully. I jumped out to run into the house and bring out my roommates to marvel at my new car.

"Oh, look, it is a convertible! Take us for a ride," squealed Jocelyn. I got back into the car, put the key in the ignition, and turned on the starter. Nothing; no sound. I tried again. Still no sound. Glenda, our new roommate, also arrived to admire the car, looked over my shoulder at the dashboard, and said, "I think it is out of gas."

My new little car was indeed out of gas. I was almost out of money in my checkbook and had spent almost all of my remaining cash on the gallons of gas at the dealership, which we had used up on my test drive and my drive home.

In those days, before checking account overrides, and with a depleted saving account (shifted over to checking for the down payment) and with too much pride to ask any of my roommates for a loan of $20, I had just enough cash left to buy a loaf of bread and a jar of peanut butter. That would have to do for lunch and dinner until Friday. Again, this was Tuesday.

Meanwhile, my new car would sit in the yard, gleaming red, offering exciting prospects. I could sit in the bucket seats and study the dashboard, practice putting up and taking down the soft top, and attaching the tonneau cover, which protected the seats and dashboard in case it rained. I could read the instruction booklet. But I could not move my new car out of the driveway.

On Friday, payday, I arranged to meet my roommate Glenda. She drove us to the bank in her little putt-putt of a car so that we could deposit our checks and take out some cash for spending money. We went to a restaurant for a hearty lunch, ("Hey, it's not peanut butter!" I said) and then Glenda drove me to a gas station where we bought two gallons of gasoline, which she hosed into the station's borrowed can. We drove home to our driveway, where Glenda, the more expert, poured the gasoline into the tank of my shiny, new, red sports car.

We both laughed happily when the engine sputtered to life, and as she rode with me to return the gasoline can to the station, we talked about the adventures we could have on the weekend and in the coming months.

And so began an exciting five years with my special little car, my red Sunbeam Alpine from the Rootes Group of the U.K., and the first of its kind in the state of Virginia that April of 1961.

The Rootes Group has long since gone out of business, and by now may be long forgotten. The sports cars of those early days are also a distant memory, existing for me in an old black-and-white snapshot as they were, lined up for a sports-car rally I joined one day in 1962. Perhaps no one remembers the Sunbeam Alpine or the Jaguar XKE for that matter, except for a few museums. And me. But one day in the late 1990s, as I was walking along a narrow street in Soho, London, with some friends, a man drove past us in a perfectly restored red Sunbeam Alpine, top down, dashboard gleaming in the afternoon sun, shifting from second to third gear.

"Wait!" I yelled and started running to catch up to the car. What was I planning to do, one of my friends asked later, jump in and ask him for a ride? The driver did not hear me. I stood there, breathless, as the little car turned the corner and disappeared down another narrow Soho street.

Maybe it was not the ride around Soho that I wanted, but just to sit in the bucket seat, strap on the seat belt, look at the dashboard, and remember those long-ago days in Virginia.

A 1960s Cocktail Party

We attended our first big cocktail party in late April of that initial year as the spring semester was winding down. The host and hostess were of the early post-war faculty, now in their mid-to-late forties, lively and personable, and living in a ranch house a few miles away on the outskirts of town. They sent us a map with detailed directions of the winding country roads of Tidewater Virginia. These were perfect roads for sports-car rallies, our great pastime in my second year on the faculty. Our hosts welcomed us warmly as we each arrived in our separate vehicles, and I tucked my small new red sports car near the hedge by the children's playground.

Our dress for the evening was of the new Kennedy era: for the young men, well-fitting suits with either blue or red ties, and for the young women, our best little sleeveless black dress with a string of pearls, perhaps pearl-drop earrings, black pumps, a black clutch purse, and elbow-length gloves, either in black or ivory to match the pearls. The hostess took my black lace shawl to a nearby closet while the host arrived with a pitcher of frosty martinis and a perfectly shaped martini glass.

Canapés were passed around — pigs in blankets, tiny crab cakes, and this being Virginia, miniature ham biscuits made with the savory and salty Smithfield ham. The hostess came around with a plate of deviled eggs, freshly made and sprinkled with paprika, as we all stood around in small groups, chatting amiably, with cool jazz playing on the hi-fi in the background.

By this time, eight months into the academic year, most of our group were already good friends or at least on pleasant speaking terms. As the party got underway, two of the more outgoing young men had already attracted their own circle of interested admirers, all chiming in on the topic of the day, most likely the newest proposal from our young president. I entertained my small group with the tale of my recent stint as a chaperone for the Saturday-night fraternity party. Only Gwendolyn of the chemistry department held back from joining in the lively conversations. Plump, bespectacled Gwen was shy, most always noticed (if at all) hovering at the edge of any group, much too bashful to offer an opinion beyond an occasional nod of assent, blushing if anyone asked her a direct question.

As the party progressed and the voices grew louder and more animated, the host turned up the volume on the record player, which raised further the volume of voices and the level of merriment. The cocktail party was a success, and the host smiled with satisfaction as he walked around to the various clusters with another pitcher of martinis. One of the young male faculty members was telling a story about his English class and one student's valiant attempt to recite Chaucer in his southern Virginia accent. There were peals of laughter, except, I suddenly noticed, from the shy Gwen, who seemed to turn ashen and stumble toward a nearby armchair.

"Wait!" I started to say as I noticed the plate of deviled eggs that someone had set down on the chair, but I was too late. The pale and flustered Gwen had already sat down and the yellow whipped yolks with the red paprika dots were already oozing around the edges of the broad backside of her black dress. I rushed over; no one else had seemed to notice this except me, and it was clear that Gwen would be mortified beyond recovery if this became the next focus of laughter and jokes at the cocktail party. I stood in front of her and whispered, "Gwen, don't move; I am going to get my shawl. We will wrap it around your waist and move quietly out the door to my car. I'll say goodnight and thank the hostess. You just back quietly out of this room."

I found my shawl in the entryway closet, brought it over to Gwen, looked around for my clutch purse with my keys and driver's license, and said to the hostess, who was nearby, "Many thanks. I must go now. I have an early tennis game tomorrow morning," and fled out the door toward Gwen, who was walking down the steps of the house.

"Gwen, I am going to drive you home. Where do you live?" I asked as I moved her toward the convertible. "Don't worry about the shawl. Keep it with you. You can wash it in cold water and give it back to me on Monday."

"Oh," she groaned, "I am so embarrassed, and I don't feel well. I think I am going to be sick."

"No, you are going to be just fine," I said as I took her elbow and helped her into the car. I did not want her to be sick in my new car, not on those leather bucket seats. "And don't worry. No one else saw you sit down on the deviled eggs, just me, and I will not tell anyone." Gwen burst into tears. "Please tell me where you live," I said as I turned on the ignition and the lights and began to slowly back the little car down the driveway to the road.

Gwen gave an address on a street that was unfamiliar, but she said, "It is very near the Williamsburg Inn," which would mean a cluster of narrow brickstone houses on small streets with indecipherable colonial street names.

As the car nosed out of the driveway, I suddenly swooned, head falling forward over the steering wheel. "Are you okay?" Gwen asked in alarm. I lifted my head, shook my head, and stopped the car for a moment to rub each eye. There seemed to be something clouding my vision and there was a terrible buzzing in my head. Gwen might remember which street she lived on and what it looked like, but we had to find the town first. Where were we now? How did I get here? The town was five miles away and I had left the directions on the shelf in the entryway closet. I said nothing. Gwen was already distraught and kept repeating that she did not feel well that her stomach was in upheaval.

My stomach was also in upheaval. It went with the buzz in the head and the blurry eyes. How many martinis were poured into my glass? I had never had martinis before but thought that there had been several refills. I didn't remember how many.

I turned left out of the driveway and headed down the dark road, hoping this was the right direction, for if not, I would be heading for the North Carolina border. A mile or so down the road I asked Gwen if anything looked familiar. We came to an intersection, and I had to make a decision: Do I go left or right? Keep going forward? I decided to keep going forward because it was easier to drive that way instead of having to turn at the intersection. Two or so more miles down the dark, wooded road, we came to a traffic light and some streetlights.

"Gwen," I said, "does this look familiar? Are we nearing your home?"

"Yes," she said, peering ahead and then looking over the top of the windscreen. "I think that street ahead leads to my street; we cross the intersection here and then we take a left...."

We did reach her door after that intersection, and I watched as she climbed the stairs to her front door, found her key, and opened the door. She waved a thank you to me, then disappeared inside.

I looked at the street and thought: *My head is spinning. What is this street name? And where is this street in relation to my street? I have to get home, and soon. What if the state police were roaming about tonight, looking for partygoers like me? I wished I had a driver. This is just not safe. I should not be driving. I got Gwen home safely, but can I get myself home safely?*

I turned the car around, took a left at the intersection, hoping it was the correct way. Except for my headlights, the road before me was very dark. There was no moon and only the occasional streetlight. I drove slowly, deliberately. I did not want to wreck the car or get arrested, and I promised myself I would never, ever drink martinis again if only I could get home safely.

I drove down a few more streets, made a left turn and another left turn, and finally recognized the street leading to our cul-de-sac. My roommate was away for the weekend. Had she been with me, we could have helped each other on this trip home, but home I was. I stumbled out of the car and hooked on the tonneau cover. Once inside, I looked out the window at my new little car. It was intact; I was intact. Gwen was intact (if not the deviled eggs).

Never again, I told myself over and over as I climbed the stairway to my bedroom, head spinning and stomach churning.

"Never again," I said to the world at large that next morning. "I will never, ever drink martinis again; I will never, ever drink anything alcoholic and then drive my little car." I still do not know how I found my way home that night.

Taking Chances, Growing

Over the summer of 1961, as I began to prepare for my second year at the College of William and Mary, I was invited into the department director's office to discuss a request he had received from a private company, a pulp and paper plant located some thirty miles north of Williamsburg. "How would you like to teach a course in statistics to the engineers of the pulp and paper up the James River? You studied statistics in college, so this should be easy for you," he said.

"Why do they need to know statistics?" I asked, wondering to myself how much I remembered since it had been more than three years since my junior year when I took that course. How would using statistics improve their production process? I didn't see the connection, at least not then. Perhaps I had forgotten too much or maybe did not learn everything thoroughly in that one course.

"They told me they need to improve their quality control on their production run," the director said, adding, "and they will pay you for this. You can drive up after classes are finished here and teach their course in the evening."

"Yes, I can do this, and I will take it on," I heard myself saying. Was it the challenge, something quite new where I could learn a practical and useful application beyond knowing how to do both the mean and the median on my final grades for the classes I was teaching?

"And," the director continued, "now that you have agreed to take on this extracurricular task, we would like you to teach the statistics course here in the department. The economics and business majors need to have a good grounding in this field."

So over the summer, I reviewed textbooks for the two classes and looked for case studies that might help the pulp plant assignment. In early September, I made an appointment with the vice president of the company and drove the thirty miles in my small red sports car to the pulp and paper plant, which came suddenly into view as I rounded a turn. Its smokestack was tall and belched out thick, gray smoke that spread over the parking lot and headed toward the river. Why did we never see that smoke on the horizon from Williamsburg? And the smell! I began coughing, nearly choking on the sudden sulfurous stench. I had no protection. I was driving with the car's top down since it was a pleasant late-summer evening.

I stopped my car at the barrier arm guarding the entrance to the parking lot. The guard asked me whom I was coming to see, then pointed to a visitor parking area and said, "You need to have your car thoroughly washed before you leave. See that car wash area over there? You need to do this every time since the smoke particles are hard on the paint. Are you able to cover your convertible?"

"Yes," I said. "I can put the top up, and with the windows rolled up it will be quite watertight."

The vice president of the plant and two of his senior engineers were waiting for me. "Would you like to take a tour of the plant?" the vice president asked. "We are still running today, and you can see the stages of production and see firsthand what our problems are with the quality of what comes off the final machines. We think we have about 90 percent quality on each run, but we want to improve to at least 95 percent."

The stench of sulfur was not as strong inside the plant as in the parking lot and was barely noticeable in the internal conference room where we met to discuss the course and determine how many of their senior engineers and managers would be attending. I had spent time over the summer reviewing several statistics books and told them which one I was recommending for them. I then told them that with the help of our librarian at the university, I had found a special study published by a pulp and paper association in Canada on improving quality control, which I thought would be a helpful guide to my teaching and their concerns.

As my little car was going through a punishing car wash and heavy spray rinse, I thought about the weeks and months ahead, where I would be coming up here once a week for a two-hour class. In many ways, I would be learning along with these managers and engineers, but I could join them each week in assessing how the practical knowledge was helping to improve the quality of their production run. It would be grueling, and I would need to prepare thoroughly for each class.

When the last class ended just before the Christmas holidays, I was invited to stay for sandwiches and coffee and a discussion on what they thought they had achieved. The mood was pleasant, and I was almost exhilarated for having prevailed through the many doubts and concerns. But there was an evident sense of accomplishment from these engineers and plant supervisors, whose work responsibilities had required their attendance and also their full attention throughout the semester.

"We are pleased," the vice president told me with a friendly smile. "We were not sure all of this learning was going to help us, but it did. We can now get close to that 95 percent quality goal and your teaching and good case studies made this possible." Finally, he said, "We'll walk out with you now to be sure that your car is carefully washed and rinsed. We wouldn't want you to find pockmarks on it tomorrow morning."

That was not my only challenge that fall of 1961. The first day of the statistics class on campus, I was nervously taking roll call and being watched by expectant faces, when the door opened abruptly and in marched two military men, one wearing multiple medals and rows of colored braid, the other, a much larger man with stripes on the shoulders of his tunic. I must have looked shocked as well as surprised, so when the man with the medals asked, "Is this the Statistics 100 class?" I found my voice to say, "Yes, we are just taking roll."

"I am used to roll calls," he said to me and then laughed loudly. The larger man laughed loudly also. "And we are just in time. I am Colonel Able, and this is Staff Sergeant Baker. We have just signed up for this course."

The colonel told me later that semester that he had encouraged his staff sergeant to take the course with him, "So that I would have someone to study with." Whether this was a burden on the sergeant was never clear to me, but the aide-de-camp was there faithfully each week with his superior officer, both of them sitting in the front row, dressed in full khaki, as much an oddity to the regular students in the class as they were to me.

But the colonel was invariably courteous to me and the students, and he made a point of showing me and the rest of the class that he was doing his own work on the midterm and the final exam by sitting several seats away from his sergeant.

"Thank you, ma'am," he said in a loud and commanding voice on the last day of the semester. "This was a great pleasure," he said as he marched out of the class, followed by his faithful underling.

Learning to Make a Speech
(and Get Invited Back)

Early in the fall semester of my second year at the university, the department director sent a memo to our economics department informing us that he had received several requests from local organizations for faculty to speak at their luncheon or dinner meetings. Most of the topics were focused on questions about the state of the economy: Is this a strong recovery from the recession; what effect will the proposed tax changes have on the Virginia economy; what is the outlook for defense spending; and what should we know about the new Common Market in Europe?

In the coffee room the next morning, the older faculty members scoffed at the request, one saying, "Why should we do any of this? They are not paying us; they are just looking for free speakers." Another said, "I am not driving down to Newport News on my lunch hour to give a speech, even if they give me lunch. It will upset my day." Newport News was thirty miles east of Williamsburg, an easy half-hour drive, I thought.

I offered no opinion to the group, but when I returned to my office, I reread the dean's memo and realized this would be a good opportunity to get experience speaking before a group, not just my class, but adults and business or government leaders, and I would learn more about some of the topics than just casual reading of the newspaper or the weekly news magazines. The idea of the Common Market was particularly intriguing but speaking about it would take considerable preparation. I could easily make a speech on the U.S. economy — maybe not the tax cuts, since I did not yet know enough about the industrial structure in Virginia, or the tax rates on businesses — but a discussion of the economic business cycle would be good practice, to frame the topic with good data and take questions from the audience, certainly a more knowledgeable audience than my sophomores or juniors.

I walked down the hall to the director's office, carrying his memo, tapped on his door, and stepped in when I heard the friendly, "Do enter," in his Southern accent.

"I will do two of these speeches," I said to him. "The business cycle speech here in Williamsburg and the Common Market speech in Newport News." He set down his pipe on the ashtray and swung his chair around to face me directly. He smiled. "Well, that is just fine, young lady. I am real pleased, because it makes us look good if we are responsive to the local businesses. I was afraid that none of our faculty would agree. Now that you have stepped forward, perhaps others will."

The response of each luncheon group as I walked in the door and was introduced as the luncheon speaker was about what I expected. At first, all of the men (and they seemed to be all men) were startled, until their Southern manners took over to give me a welcome and perhaps a wary smile. My presentation to the local chamber of commerce went well, but without charts to use, I was dependent on my words and descriptions. Still, everyone seemed to listen and there were several good questions at the end, ones that I was able to answer. I was invited back a few months later to talk about our new Virginia Business Index.

The presentation on the European Common Market did take considerable preparation and I worried that someone might ask me a question that would give away the fact that I had never been to Europe. But I had read more than my audience and I think I was able to convince them that this was a topic they should all be following because of the trade that could develop between their great port of Hampton Roads and the great ports of Europe.

In my third year at William and Mary, I accepted every invitation to speak at lunch meetings that came my way. This was good practice, to do the careful preparation and to try to conquer the terror of being on my feet, sometimes without a lectern to cling to, and to get across some facts and ideas to an appreciative audience. But I turned down any invitations to be a dinner speaker. That sounded too risky, to be around groups who had begun their evening with cocktails and who could, like those fraternity men, forget that, after dinner, I was their speaker and not a potential date for after-dinner drinks.

Finding Sad Sam, the Beagle

We were out walking through the still-damp grass from an afternoon rainstorm in the large field behind Mrs. Wilbur's house on the outskirts of Williamsburg, Virginia. Mrs. Wilbur was the friendly and motherly office secretary for the three professors of economics, including me, whose offices were in a small suite in the business administration building on campus. She had invited me to come to dinner with her and her two daughters, who were both in their early teens. Suddenly we all stopped, all chatter and giggling silenced, for there on the patch of wet grass ahead of a was a small dog, lying on his side, panting.

"That dog is very ill, or he has been injured," Mrs. Wilbur said. One of the girls looked down at the dog, then at her mother, and asked, "Is he going to die?" We four knelt around this sad little creature and Mrs. Wilbur reached out to gently touch his stomach, then his head. The dog made no sound, but he looked at us with pleading eyes, still panting heavily. "There may be some hope for him, but we have to get him to a veterinarian right away," she said.

"I'll do it," I said. "I'll go back to my car and get my plastic raincoat. We can wrap him in that." So I ran back across the field to where my little sports car was parked in the yard, found the raincoat, and ran back to where the three women were still kneeling around the dog. I could hear one of the girls saying, "You will be all right, doggie; we're going to take care of you."

"It's a beagle, full-grown, and looks like he is a pure breed," Mrs. Wilbur said as she and I gingerly lifted the dog onto my raincoat. Mrs. Wilbur then said she knew where there was a veterinarian's office and that it would still be open since they frequently had to take the family cat there after work hours.

"Would you come with me to the car and help me settle him into the passenger seat? It is a bucket seat, so we will need to be careful placing him there," I said to Mrs. Wilbur.

"I will give you directions to his office," she said as we settled the dog into my car. He still made no sound, no whimpering, but was still panting heavily.

I pulled into the parking lot at the veterinarian's office, walked around my car to the passenger side, and, with shaking knees, bent over the low bucket seat to pick up the little dog, who was still wrapped in my raincoat.

What am I doing? I asked myself.

I knew nothing about dogs, but he needed help.

"Well, I can see some injuries. It looks like he's been beaten, but his spine is good, and none of his limbs are broken," the veterinarian said as he carefully felt around the dog's back and belly and his four limbs. "He sure is one frightened beagle. I'll keep him here for a few days, then you can call me, say, on Friday. If he's well enough, you can take him home."

"But he is not my dog," I said. "How do I find his owner?"

"You can leave a note on my bulletin board and maybe put a notice in the local paper," he said. I agreed to do that, then thought to add, "I will take responsibility for your fees, and I thank you."

So on Friday, I left work an hour early, drove to the vet's office, and in the waiting room the receptionist said, "I'll let the doctor know you are here." I looked at the notices on the bulletin board near her desk to see if there was any response to my note. The doctor appeared, holding the little dog in his arms.

"He is going to be okay," he said. "No serious injuries, but he will need lots of kindness and good care."

"What do you think happened to him?" I asked.

"Most likely he was being trained as part of a pack of dogs, beagles mostly. They hit the dogs with splayed bamboo rods to keep them in line, to follow commands. But some dogs just cannot take the training. They would prefer to pull out of the pack and just die."

I stood there, stunned at this revelation, and looked closely at the little dog, who was now looking directly at me. "Has anyone come to claim him? The owner of the pack or the trainers maybe?" I asked.

"No one," the vet said cheerfully. "He is all yours! You will need a collar and a leash, and he is required to have a dog tag. We can get all of that for you here in the office."

"But what do I feed him?" I asked. The vet suggested some brands of dry and canned dog food, saying, "Now don't overfeed him. He has had his supper already," and deposited the little dog in my arms.

The receptionist was getting the collar and the leash for me, and said, "What is his name? I have to put a name on this dog tag. I also need to put your phone number on this tag."

I looked down at this small, pitiful creature in my arms and said, "Well, this is a sad sack of a dog if I have ever seen one, so I will call him Sad Sam, Sam for the dog tag," I said. I set the little dog on the floor and we put on the dog collar with the jangling tag around his neck. I snapped on the leash, found my checkbook to pay for his bill, and with unsteady legs — my two and his four — we made our way through the parking lot to my little car. I lifted him into the passenger seat, came around to get into the driver's seat, buckled my seat belt, and reached over to pat the silky head and ears of this little dog, and said, "Sam, here we go."

And that is how Sam, the sad little beagle, came into my life, and for the next three years, became my constant, devoted little companion. I would rarely leave him home alone since he had been so traumatized and was so timid. I had my own small office in our suite at the college, so I took Sam with me every day. He curled up under my desk, his little head resting on my feet. In the apartment, he would sometimes rest on the dog pillow I had bought him, but at night, when I was getting into bed, little Sam would leave his pillow and sit on the floor by my bed, with longing looks. I would get up, lift him gently and place him at the foot of my bed, where he would curl up over my feet. Many mornings I would wake up to find his silky nose close to my ear, as during the night he had moved up to be closer to me.

We must have been an odd sight, the two of us driving together in my little red sports car. When the top was down, Sam would put his nose on the top of the windscreen, his front paws on the dashboard, long ears flying out behind him. When I became aware of Charles Schultz's *Peanuts* cartoons with Snoopy's ears flying out behind him in the panels of Snoopy as the Red Baron, I patted Sam, saying, "You were there first, little buddy."

Sam was to stay with me for the next three years, through my thyroid illnesses and hospitalizations, when my friend Glenda kept him at her apartment. When I moved to Norfolk, Virginia, to teach at Old Dominion University, Sam would clack along the terrazzo hallway beside me in our campus building while I shuffled along to my classroom wearing a form of bedroom slippers, since my feet, swollen after weeks of being confined to a hospital bed, would not fit into any of my shoes. Sam would curl up under the table, which I leaned against for support to deliver my lectures in economics. I learned to ask one of the students if they would please take Sam out for his walk, so each day, twice a day, Sam would have his perambulations around the campus and return to me in my office, panting happily, waiting for me to pat his silky head before curling up under the desk on my feet. No one ever objected to the dog being with me in the office, since he still never made a sound.

"He doesn't bay? All beagles bay," one of my colleagues said.

"No, he doesn't bay and he doesn't whimper and he doesn't growl," I said.

But if it is possible for a dog to be happy, I was sure that Sam was a happy dog with me, always staying close to my side, day and night, seemingly gratefully content with his food, never protesting over his occasional baths. And if it is possible for a dog to be deliriously happy, then I think he was as close to that state as possible when he could ride beside me in the Sunbeam Alpine convertible, his nose on the top of the windscreen, his long silky ears flying back in the wind.

When Michael and I married in April of 1965, the new apartment we had chosen did not permit dogs, so I asked my brother, Malcolm, and sister-in-law, Joan, who had come down from Nova Scotia for the wedding, if they would take Sam back with them in the car, thinking that this gentle dog would be a good companion for their two little girls. That arrangement did not last long, as Joan was pregnant and would be too busy with three little ones to take care of the dog, so Sam was brought down to Antigonish to live with my mother.

Mother knew little about dogs and was probably less than keen about this new arrival, but she took good care of Sam, fed him properly, and regularly let him out into her backyard for his twice- daily sniffs and visits around her plants and trees

"Oh, I have gotten used to him," she admitted on one of my phone calls. "I even talk to him sometimes, and I make sure that he does not wander into the front yard and then out on the street into traffic." But she learned about him, and said later, "I found that he was too smart to go into the street and I did not need to worry."

The day came when Mother noticed that little Sam seemed slow to move. She thought that the next day she should take him to the vet, and so called for an appointment. That evening there was a full moon. It had just risen and was shining brightly through the trees in her backyard as she opened the door to let Sam out onto the back deck. Sam, she told me later, slowly sat on the back deck, lifted his head, and bayed at the moon. A few minutes later, when she opened the door to let Sam back in, she found him stretched out on her deck, lifeless.

My normally stoic mother, she who had no time for dogs, told me that she wept as she wrapped him in an old blanket and carried him down to the basement until she could take his little body to the veterinarian the next morning.

Sometimes I think, now that I am retired, if I ever decide to move to the West Coast to be close to my grandchildren, I would need to have some sort of car, unlike here in New York City. And if I needed to have a car again, I would look for a small red convertible, with just enough room in the back seat for any of the two grandchildren from each family to climb in. But then I would have to find a small pure-bred beagle who could ride in front with me, his long ears flowing back in the winds of Oregon or California. And I would call him Sam.

The Cuban Missile Crisis

The week in October 1962 that the confrontation with Cuba began to become serious — and frightening — I was teaching a course in economics at the Christopher Newport Community College, a stepchild of the College of William and Mary. This community college was located in Newport News, about thirty miles east of Williamsburg, bordering the northern shores of Hampton Roads, the great enclosed harbor for Norfolk, Virginia, which housed the Fifth Fleet of aircraft carriers and destroyers as well as the Naval Air Station in Norfolk. Newport News was the location of the great shipyards, named after the small city, a place where giant aircraft carriers and sleek naval attack and supply ships were built, usually on a twenty-four-hour, seven-day-a-week work schedule.

My class in basic undergraduate economics was filled primarily with military personnel from the large bases in Norfolk or from the nearby airbase at Langley Field (which held not only the great bombers and reconnaissance planes but the fledgling space program, which, in those early days, sent a monkey into orbit).

In my classroom on those evenings there were one or two engineers from the shipyards who were beginning a graduate program in business administration and needed to know basic economics. And there was one air force officer who was preparing for his discharge during the following year and needed to have this course to get into graduate school at the Massachusetts Institute of Technology.

This officer was distinguished as much by his long and lanky frame as by his Boston accent and Harvard undergraduate hauteur, and he was my most nettlesome student, older than me by three or four years and intent on needling me throughout each two-hour lecture, trying to trip me up on facts as well as on theory.

But this Tuesday evening as I pulled out of the driveway of my apartment in Williamsburg in my small British sports car, I was not thinking about the Bostonian nor the two imperious naval officers in my class, for this was the evening that President John Kennedy was to address the nation with his ultimatum to Prime Minister Khrushchev of Russia, and, we thought, to order him to remove the nuclear missiles from Cuba under pain of attack. The rhetoric between the two world leaders had been ratcheting up the scale of serious confrontation for the past week, a most serious situation in that it could likely involve nuclear missiles being launched from both countries. The voices of the newscasters on radio and TV had become more somber with each passing day.

We were aware that the naval ships had left Norfolk recently and headed out to sea towards the Caribbean. My concern was heightened by the events of the night before, which had no ready explanation. All night long there had been a steady rumble, as of a looming thunderstorm that did not get closer or erupt into a full storm but rumbled on and sometimes gave the sense of rolling, almost like a small earthquake. This continued throughout the night. Certainly, it was close enough, and loud enough, to wake me and our entire household and we could be found brewing tea in the kitchen at half-past three in the morning, asking, "What is it? What is going on?"

Weeks later we learned that this steady rumble was from heavy armored vehicles and the armada of trucks and personnel carriers that left Ft. Eustis, the Army's transportation command center, located some fifteen miles east of Williamsburg. Their orders were to get to the Florida Keys under cover of darkness and in secrecy, so they were staying off U.S. 1 and stretches of new interstate highway, using instead the back roads where possible. These back roads put the convoys close to the outskirts of Williamsburg.

My British sports car had a portable radio that fitted into a rectangular slot under the dashboard. It was a good-quality radio, although it worked better when I brought it inside and set it down on a kitchen table, rather than trying to hear over the wind and the whoosh of passing cars while driving along the road with the top down.

This evening, President Kennedy's speech was due to be delivered just as I would be reaching the halfway point in my trip to Newport News. Since I was expected to be at the college and deliver my lecture, I left a few minutes early and just as the president's speech was announced from the White House, I pulled over to the shoulder of the road, away from the traffic, and reached over to pull the portable radio from its moorings to better hear the broadcast. There was static on the radio and noise from the passing cars, so I put the radio up to my ear, leaning down and away from the windows to catch the words of the president. There was increasing static, almost blocking out some of his words and phrases, but the sense was clear. This was possibly the great ultimatum, the threshold of everything we had learned to fear about the atomic bomb and then the hydrogen bomb, that everything we knew and loved about this world, this earth, about our families and best friends, could be gone in an instant.

I suddenly felt achingly lonely for my family back in Canada. Were they listening to this broadcast? Was my brother in his college dorm room with his engineering classmates glued to the radio or was he playing in a hockey game at some rink that had no radio or TV transmission? Were my sisters at home with my mother or possibly playing basketball in one of their tournaments? If so, that would mean that my mother was home alone. She would surely be watching TV, would know about this broadcast and the peril of the situation. The thought of my family in their respective pursuits, possibly alone or with their friends, or even together at home with our mother and supposedly doing their homework, brought me near to sobbing and also to such a sense of aloneness, of being alone in the universe. If the world were to end now, or in the next few hours, I would be facing it alone.

President Kennedy was now summing up his ultimatum, and through the static, he seemed to be giving Khrushchev one more chance, to allow his ships through the American blockade at sea to go into Cuba and dismantle and remove the nuclear missiles. There was some hope then.

I put the radio back into its slot under the dashboard, wiped away the tears, and started the car, resuming the trip down to the college. There was solace in a task ahead, in being able to carry on with some type of work, even if it was not a direct part of the military effort.

I walked into my classroom to find three people out of a class of eighteen sitting there. The annoying Harvard man was not there. All three facing me looked exhausted. When I asked them if they had been involved in the crisis, they responded, almost in unison. "We have been on twenty-four-hour alert," one man said. "I have not had any sleep for almost thirty-six hours." The other two chimed in with similar tales.

"So where is everyone else?" I asked, almost knowing the answer.

"They are either on active duty for the past twenty-four or thirty-six hours or they are trying to sleep until the next watch is called."

I did not ask them if they were worried. These were military people in front of me, either on active duty or on backup systems to the military. I would not embarrass them with this question. I sensed they were all worried, despite their military training; they had been taught to carry on and not show worry or fear.

"Then, we should cancel this class," I said. "There is no point in trying to carry on with the lecture. We four have too much on our minds and you have too much ahead to do, so please get some sleep and I will see you next week."

When I reached home, the news analysts on both radio and TV were reporting that the tone, as well as the content of President Kennedy's speech, was appearing to stay the Russian thrust with a time delay for action. But this was also a time-sensitive delay to give the Russian prime minister a chance to pull back his forces and dismantle the missiles without losing face.

Sometime later, we learned that the U.S. Navy, amid that set of tumultuous transactions, had jammed the signals along the Virginia Coast to cover the radio transmissions between the ships, the airplanes, the White House, and the Pentagon. The problems had not been with my portable radio, but on a larger scale in the airwaves. My class members had truly been on alert, on duty at an airbase or the shipyards or on the naval bases. And in the days to come, we learned just how close we had come to war, that we were saved by a president who had the belief that if he just waited for the next cable message from Moscow and not leap to action as his military commanders were urging, there could be a solution to this brinkmanship, to save the U.S. and likely the entire world, from nuclear annihilation. But that knowledge was days ahead, and after the several nights when the urge was to stay awake for whatever might come, that awful fear and those frightful nights were to haunt me for many years.

Harry

When I first saw Harry, he was dominating my classroom on this, the first night that I went down to teach the class in basic economics at Christopher Newport College. Harry was taller by a head than anyone else in the room, his long legs sprawled out on either side of the seat in front of him. With his pale coloring, he stood out from every other tanned face in the room, faces that had either spent time working outdoors all summer or playing on the sands at Virginia Beach. Harry was pale: he had ash-colored, almost whitish hair; pale skin, pale

311

blue eyes that looked at me in downright skepticism, and he wore his pale summer air force uniform in these last weeks of a still-hot September on the Tidewater Peninsula. Before I could finish going through the roll call that first night, he interrupted me to ask, "Can you guarantee that are we using Samuelson's textbook?"

Professor Paul Samuelson of MIT had written the pre-eminent textbook in basic economics, the famous Economics 101 textbook that almost every undergraduate student used and that I had studied from in my sophomore year. By now it was in a later edition, with more charts and graphs than in my first version. While its success around the world, not only in North American universities, had begun to attract competitor authors, in my judgment it was still the best and most authoritative text. "Yes," I said, "and why is this so important to you?"

"Because when I finish my service time a year from now, I am planning to go to MIT for a graduate degree in international finance and they insist that I take this course again, using Samuelson's book." He was laying down a gauntlet to me, more than conveying information.

"Did you say again? Does that mean that you have taken this course before?" I asked, aware now that there was a restless stir, that this dialogue was interrupting the class. I needed to continue the roll call of registrants, to focus on the other students.

"Oh yes. I took economics when I was at Harvard, but MIT doesn't like the fact that John Kenneth Galbraith was teaching the course and most likely working out the chapters of his next book, so MIT says I must be well-grounded."

"Thank you for this information," I said politely. But I was already annoyed and sensed that the rest of the class was annoyed as well.

We were all to stay annoyed for the next few weeks since at every class Harry persistently interrupted me to ask questions and to start a debate on whatever topic I was introducing. His combative stance was slowing down the class and it was becoming clear that I was not able to control him and focus enough on all the other members of the class. This was my third year teaching at William and Mary, but I was still only twenty-two years old, and I was once again conscious of my youth and inexperience.

But finally, on week five or thereabouts, when the inevitable questions started, I said as politely and firmly as I could, "Could you wait until after class? I will gladly try to answer your questions then, but we must move on through tonight's material." He agreed and stayed behind as the rest of the class filed out, then began peppering me with questions.

"Do you really want answers to these questions?" I asked him, "or are you trying to show me how much you know by asking them? Because if you genuinely want to know, I am going to help with answers. But you must also stop interrupting me during the class. You are taking time away from the other students."

He looked somewhat abashed, then smiled and said, "Of course, I understand."

"But you can always ask me questions after class; I will try my best to answer or at least try to find out the answer," I said.

Did I win this small victory? I wasn't too sure. But he did make good on his promise and sat through the remaining sessions in silence, obviously restraining himself. And most nights he stayed behind to ask another round of questions.

Did anyone else in that class earn an *A*+? I doubt it, but he certainly did. And no sooner was his corrected final exam paper placed in his waiting hand after class had ended that he looked around the room to be sure no one else was near enough to hear him and said, "There is a dance at the officer's club on Saturday night. Would you like to go with me? There will be great music."

This was a surprising departure. There was no sign of romantic interest in all of those weeks of being peppered with questions or being stared at with those pale blue eyes, just waiting, I always thought, to catch me fumbling over an answer or struggling to make a chart or theory clear. This was flustering to be sure, but it was not an ethical issue. He had taken his final exam. I had graded it along with the others. His *A*+ was genuinely earned, so there was no possibility that he was trying to improve his grade. I said, "Well, yes, I suppose I could go."

"Fine. I will pick you up in Williamsburg at 8:30. What is your street address? We can have something to eat at the club during the dance." This then was a "dance date" obviously, not a "dinner-and-dance date."

And so began a series of dates that remained mostly platonic throughout the next few months, less romantic than repeated dates might imply, but we were bound together with a discovered shared passion: We both loved jazz. Harry brought me by his suite of rooms that first night of the dance to play his piano for me. He was skilled on the great jazz songs of the past thirty years and deft at the more rapid bebop style. I even sang some of the songs with him, which later that summer he recorded on his eight-track tape deck.

I remember particularly one soft evening that summer, driving back up to Williamsburg in his great boat of a convertible. He was fiddling with the tuning dial on his car radio, and then suddenly said, "Here it is, the Chicago radio station. You must hear this music," he said as he suddenly pulled the car over to the shoulder of the road, stopped the engine, and said again, "Listen to this."

"This" was Antonio Carlos Jobim, Stan Getz, and Astrud Gilberto, and "The Girl From Ipanema."

"Bossa nova is from Brazil," Harry said, and then sat quietly so that I could concentrate on the song. This was the first time I'd heard of the bossa nova, and the first time hearing this amazing piece of music, coming through on this soft summer night in eastern Virginia from a radio station in Chicago.

My next vivid memory of Harry was to find him crumpling in a faint at the end of my hospital bed as I was coming out of anesthetic following surgery for removal of my thyroid gland. Did Harry know I was not feeling well that summer? Was he away on leave or reassignment for several weeks? We dated at least once a week, but I have no memory of talking to him during those last weeks of the summer when my health was going in strange directions.

Somehow, he knew about my surgery because he called me before I went into the hospital to wish me well and he promised to come and see me the day of the surgery to be sure that I was going to be all right. He said that the day of my surgery was also Yom Kippur and that while he was not an "observant Jew," he would fast as always on Yom Kippur.

I came out of the deep anesthetic coma sometime in midafternoon. My surgeon was leaning over me, smiling. "You are going to be just fine," he said. "You just can't move for two or three days. Those are sandbags near your head and your neck to keep you still and in place. Do you need anything? Would you like a sip of water?"

His face was swimming above me, and then off to the end to the bed, I saw my mother, who had come down from Nova Scotia to be with me for this major event in my life. She was looking tense and worried, but then smiled at me when she heard the doctor say to me, "Hello, dear. You will be just fine."

I watched the doctor leave the room, and then all at once, the door opened again, and in walked Harry, all six-foot-four inches of him, still lanky, still pale. He moved toward the foot of the bed, stared at me, and then turned even whiter, the white color of my sheets, and begin to sag at the knees. My mother, all five-foot-four of her, rushed to catch him before he hit the floor.

"I'm sorry," he said to her, his voice weak. "It is Yom Kippur and I have been fasting."

My no-nonsense mother, working hard to steady him, said, "Well no more of that. We must get you some fresh air and some coffee," she added, helping him out of the room.

I learned later that Mother steadied Harry as they left the room, both of her arms around his waist until the orderly rushed down the hall to help her. Together they got Harry out to the main entrance, where Mother had him sit down on the steps and put his head between his knees. She told the orderly to run and get him some cold water and some hot coffee with lots of cream and sugar. I do not think that at that time my mother had ever heard of Yom Kippur. She did know about fasting, since that was what we were supposed to do during the forty days of Lent, and certainly during the morning of Good Friday.

As Harry sipped the coffee, my mother sponged his forehead and back of the neck with the cool water. She introduced herself, telling him that she was my mother and had just come down from Nova Scotia to be with me for this surgery. She never did tell me how Harry introduced himself to her — did he say he was my boyfriend? Or friend? Boyfriend would have been a stretch, especially for Harry and certainly for me.

He did tell me later that he was shocked by my appearance and had never imagined that I would look so pale and be surrounded by sandbags. He was embarrassed that he had fainted and hoped that I would not think him a sissy because, after all, he had been fasting all day.

Harry left Virginia soon after his air force duty finished. He did go to Boston and enrolled, as he'd wanted to, in the international finance master's program at MIT, which he noted in a postcard from Boston sometime during that year. He then dropped out of my life for many years.

Somehow, some fifteen years later, he found me. How he found me is still a mystery since it would have taken some sleuthing to track me down in New York City, where I was working under my married name. He invited me to lunch at the best restaurant at the time, in the concourse of One World Trade Center.

We had a good lunch, typical of the prosperous years of the late 1970s, and Harry looked prosperous in his gray pinstriped suit and power-symbol red tie. He told me he was working for a boutique international finance company, although not a name I recognized, and that he was doing well in business and thought he might soon go out on his own. He was in his second marriage, with two stepchildren from this marriage but none of his own from either union. Since I was divorced also, there seemed little sense to talk about our personal lives, and he didn't seem much interested in the fact that I had two children. He was intrigued, at least mildly, that time and circumstance had brought me to New York City.

"Well, you were always a smart kid, even if you were from the sticks in Canada," he said with a mild twinkle in his eye. Humor was not one of Harry's more notable features, although he was never cruel to me or to anyone else that he ever mentioned, so I took this as his newfound attempt at New York City jesting.

Another ten or so years went by and, busy with my work and my growing children, I must say I rarely thought of Harry. But then I was asked to give a speech one afternoon to a finance group in Manhattan. It was not a group I was familiar with, and I was told there would be about thirty people in attendance. The man who'd invited me asked if I would be willing to discuss the recent developments in the economy and particularly of New York City and take questions. I agreed.

I entered the room and went directly to the podium to face the group and there, looming long and lean and pale in the middle of the room was Harry, smiling and nodding at me. Harry, of course, led the questioning, and later, when we were gathered over coffee and cookies at the side table, I asked Harry how he knew I would be speaking there. "I recommended you," he said. "I have been a member of this group for several years and the speakers' committee said they wanted someone who was an expert on the economy and particularly the New York economy, so I suggested you. Could we have lunch soon and catch up on our lives?"

The catch-up lunch took place the following week when Harry said he would next be in Manhattan. We met at a small restaurant, more of a luncheonette actually, on the West Side of Manhattan that he said was a favorite of his. "They make a great corned beef sandwich," he promised.

The luncheonette was crowded with a jovial lunchtime crowd. "These folks are regulars," Harry said as we squeezed into the remaining table for two near the back of the room. Harry flagged down a passing waiter, saying, "We are ready to order; we don't need menus." Harry announced he would have the split-pea soup and a corned beef sandwich on rye. "Bring two spoons," he said.

The waiter asked, "Is that all?"

"I'm sure that will be just fine for us," Harry said with a smile to the waiter that suggested he knew the drill around this place. I didn't think the waiter recognized Harry, even if this was his "favorite place."

When the soup came, Harry passed the extra soup spoon to me, saying, "Go ahead and share some, if you like." I thanked him but declined. "So how are you? What is your life like these days? Are you married?" he asked. I said I wasn't, not at this time.

"And you?" I asked.

"Well, my second marriage didn't work out, so I divorced and am married again. My new wife has two children from her previous marriage, so now I have four children from two of my marriages."

"And where are you working?" I asked. I was genuinely interested and wondering how and where he was pursuing his interest in international finance.

"I am doing my own investing these days and I have a few clients whom I advise on their international investment portfolios. I am living out on Long Island, and I can work from home. I don't need an office."

The sandwich came, an overstuffed layered assemblage. "Waiter," Harry called out to the retreating back of the man who had set the sandwich down, "we need an extra plate." When that arrived, Harry put one half of the sandwich on the extra plate and passed it over to me.

"I hope you are not fond of dill pickles since I really like these," he said, as he scooped up both halves of the pickle. Between mouthfuls, I tried to tell him of my current work and my recent trips to China. I was about to continue, eager to share with him what I had seen in that newly opened country and nascent economy, but he nodded and changed the subject, telling me about some of the "deals" he had done in Asian finance over the years.

The waiter came back to pick up the empty plates and brush the scattered breadcrumbs toward the floor. "Do you want dessert and coffee?" the waiter asked.

"No dessert. We don't need dessert, but coffee sounds like a good idea," Harry said. I rarely ate dessert at lunchtime and would have declined if asked, but a cup of hot coffee would be welcomed.

"Harry," I asked. "Could I have my own cup of coffee?"

Since that day I was invited to share his lunch, two decades have passed with no word from Harry. I wonder if he still plays jazz piano and if there is someone around who appreciates what he can do with the music, and to occasionally share his lunch.

Illness Again

In the summer of 1963, the sky seemed to hover heavy, dark, and low over Colonial Williamsburg, trapping the heat and humidity that seemed to settle on my shoulders. We were plagued by thunderstorms that arrived each day around four in the afternoon. The sky would darken further, then be pierced by zigzagging flashes of lightning followed instantly by crashing thunder. Those storms always seemed to be directly overhead. Then the rains came, in torrents so heavy that cars had to pull over to the side of the road to avoid the small rivers of water coursing everywhere. Visibility would be reduced to a few feet, then the storm would pass, leaving the heat and humidity as high as it had been before. My roommate, Millie from southern Georgia, might call the storms "gully washers," but she was away for the summer, and I was alone in the apartment and alone in the big colonial house since the owner was away visiting friends somewhere in the northeast. There was only little Sam, the beagle, for company.

So I plodded along in the heat and humidity, asking myself why I was here in this terrible subtropical climate when I could be in Nova Scotia, where the nights were cooler, the breezes came fresh off the sea, and the temperatures rarely climbed above ninety? My position at the university was a twelve-month appointment with a research assignment in addition to teaching economics. I was entitled to a two-week holiday in the summer season, but I had already taken that vacation time and traveled to Nova Scotia in early July. Not great planning, I told myself as Sam and I got into my little sports car to drive to the campus. Why didn't I plan to go in August instead of July, to be away from this oppressive heat and humidity? Little Sam waited patiently while I hoisted the soft top of the convertible into place, double-checking the metal clasps and making sure the windows were closed tightly to waterproof the car against the afternoon storms.

As the weeks of that summer dragged on, I felt increasingly like I was moving underwater. I was thinner than in the past winter, and I thought I must buy a scale to weigh myself to be sure if this was true. Also, I was having trouble falling asleep at night because my heart would race, and I would hear it pounding in my ears. I would read in bed for a while, sometimes up to an hour, to get sleepy enough to shut off the light, and then I would pull little Sam close to me so that his steadier breathing might help steady my own.

But it wasn't only my elevated heart rate that caused my sleeplessness. I was also being stalked every day by a young man who worked at some clerical position in the basement of my building. Afternoons, I would find him lurking in the long dark hall near my office in the economics department, so that when it was closing time, I would pick up Sam and hurry down the nearest stairway, clutching my purse and car keys and dashing for the car through the rain, telling little Sam that he could have his afternoon walk when we got back to our street.

I didn't think the young man was dangerous; our office secretary said that he was considered to be slow-witted when I told her about him loitering in the hallways every afternoon, watching me intently. Then one weekend, I noticed him walking around the cul-de-sac where our house was located. Terror-stricken, I stayed indoors for hours, but he would know I was at home since my distinctive little car was parked outside the house. I then phoned my friend Glenda, the only friend or close colleague who was around that month and told her what was happening.

"Come over to my place," she said. "We can make some supper and watch something on TV. Bring your dog, too, and you can stay overnight here." So Sam and I raced for the car and fled to the comfort of Glenda's small, rented house.

On Monday morning when I was back at work, I told our secretary about the man from the building being around my house on the weekend. "I'll keep checking the hallway this afternoon," she said, "and if I find him there, I will walk you to your car to be sure he is not following you. If he is there again tomorrow, we will contact the campus police. And Miss Mac?"

she asked, calling me by the nickname used by all of the economics faculty, easier for them, I thought, than trying to get their Southern tongues around all the *l*'s and *n*'s in my family name, MacLellan, "did you hurt your foot, because you have been limping these past few days."

I looked down at my right foot, which had begun to swell up some two weeks earlier; it was now swollen to where only sandals that had an expandable strap would fit.

"You should see a doctor about that, Miss Mac, especially if it isn't an injury," the secretary said.

Two days later, the doctor prodded the swollen foot, moving it around to test the ankle. He asked me several times if I could remember injuring it, then suggested I check myself into the hospital for the weekend, so that they could run some blood tests and prop my leg up in a sling. "If it is phlebitis or something similar," the doctor said, "elevating your leg should make the swelling go down."

I had planned to spend the weekend packing up my books and some of my clothes, as I would be moving to Norfolk in a week to begin my new position as an assistant professor at Old Dominion University. But being in the hospital would at least give me a good place to hide from the stalker. So I arranged with Glenda to take little Sam for the weekend and checked myself into the hospital. There I would remain for the next three weeks.

When the doctor stopped by on Sunday afternoon to check on my foot and noted that there had been no improvement in the swelling or in my pulse rate, I asked him, "Is it possible that my thyroid illness has come back?" I then proceeded to tell him about the weeks I'd spent in the hospital during my junior year in college. "I know that my pulse rate was very high then and I had lost a lot of weight, just like now."

The doctor said, "You should plan to stay here a few more days while we run some special tests." I decided to tell him how oppressed I felt as the heavy summer weather dragged on and about the stalker who was worrying me. "What if he finds me here in the hospital? I know I'm not paranoid because our departmental secretary also saw him lurking down the hall."

"You will be safe here," the doctor assured me. "We can check carefully on who asks to visit you."

The tests confirmed my self-diagnosis: I was in a state of severe hyperthyroidism and would have to stay confined to bed under special medication and eat a calorie-rich diet to see if the "metabolic mechanism," as the doctor called it, could be slowed to a normal rate.

"I am hoping this regimen will solve the problem; if not your situation will then require surgery," the doctor said.

How did I pass the time during those three weeks? I read through all of the books I had brought with me and then implored Glenda to bring me some more as well as books of crossword puzzles. My sometimes-boyfriend, shy George the engineer, who worked on nuclear submarines (my guess, since he had never said so explicitly, but he frequently worked at the Yorktown Naval Station, which we all knew was a nuclear submarine base), appeared one day carrying a baritone ukulele in a case. "I thought you could learn to play this since you play piano and I hear you are confined to bed," he said.

Millie, my roommate of the past two years, arrived the next afternoon with her small ukulele and a book of songs with ukulele chords and showed me the fingering for several basic chords. For the next weeks, I sat up in bed, entertaining the nurses and orderlies with "Ain't She Sweet" and "Don't Sit Under the Apple Tree."

Three weeks later and thirty pounds heavier, I was able to leave the hospital. I had given Glenda money to buy me a type of tank dress, since the clothes I wore into the hospital no longer fit. My shoes didn't fit, either so Glenda bought me bedroom slippers that were wide enough to accommodate my two fat, swollen feet.

"No wonder I gained so much weight," I told Glenda. "Every morning and afternoon, the nurse would bring me a chocolate milkshake with two scoops of ice cream in it. There was bread and muffins and dessert with every meal."

I also had to learn how to walk again. A few days before being discharged, the doctor said, "Now you must get up and practice walking to get back your strength and flexibility. I will want you back here for surgery in about four weeks. My office will schedule the date and let you know."

I could not walk the first time I tried. I clung to the bedpost, unable to move. The three weeks of bed confinement had made me stiff and helpless, so the next few mornings and afternoons the orderlies and nurses would take turns giving me "walking lessons," each one holding an arm and marching me up and down the hospital corridors.

I stayed with Glenda the weekend I was discharged, happy to be reunited with Sam, although the outside world seemed strange, like looking through a blurry glass, and a bit frightening. I had been coddled and nursed and protected in that long hospital stay, now I had to resume my schedule, somehow finish packing, and get down to Norfolk to the apartment I had found just before going into the hospital. I had to drive my car again. I had to begin my new job. Several of the professors had been covering my classes during these first two weeks of the new semester.

My movements were still slow and stiff, walking was still a challenge, and I was not used to carrying so much weight. I had only been this heavy once before: when I left the hospital in Nova Scotia six years before. I tried not to look at myself in the mirror for any longer than it took to put on lipstick and brush my hair. On campus and in our academic building, I shuffled along the corridor to my classroom, little Sam clacketing along beside me. Then he would curl up under the table that I leaned on to deliver my lectures. Several of my students took turns taking Sam out for his walks. That routine lasted less than four weeks, as I then reported back to the hospital in Williamsburg for thyroid surgery.

"I wanted you to gain some strength and movement," the doctor said as he briefly explained the surgical procedure, "because you will need to stay here for at least a week as you recuperate." But he hadn't warned me about the sandbags.

When I regained consciousness hours after the surgery, I became aware of being fixed rigidly in the hospital bed, with blocks of some kind around my head. "These are sandbags," the doctor said, as he bent over to fit one closer to my head.

"These are to keep you very still for the next two or three days. And how do you feel?" he asked. He was a kind man.

"I want a cigarette," I said.

"Well, maybe just a puff or two," he said as he pulled a pack of cigarettes and a lighter out of his breast pocket, lit the cigarette, then placed it between my lips. I took a few puffs. "That's enough for now," he said. "You can have your own cigarette in a couple of days."

The next year, we were all to read the surgeon general's report on the dangerous effects of smoking, but in the fall of 1963, most adults were smokers, even my kindly surgeon, right there in the hospital room.

My mother came into the room then, looking worriedly at me and the doctor. She asked him how the surgery had gone and if I was going to be all right. My sweet mother had left her teaching duties to substitutes to fly down from Nova Scotia to Williamsburg, Virginia, to be with me for this major event. She was staying with Glenda and driving my little sports car.

"She did well throughout the surgery, and she will be just fine in the future," he told Mother. And those were his words again to me the day I was being discharged.

"You will be fine. You will find that you will be calmer, and you won't be kept awake at night with a pounding heartbeat." He smiled, then added, "But if you marry and become pregnant, you must tell your doctor because you may need a thyroid supplement for the baby's growth. And after ten years, you will need to watch for signs of change in your system. I left a small section of your thyroid in place, but it may no longer work after ten years." And time proved him to be correct, on both counts.

A New Apartment, A Roommate with a Boat-Car and a Cat, and a Momentous Meeting

The summer before beginning my second year on the faculty of Old Dominion College, I went in search of a new apartment, as the one-year lease on the apartment I had rented for the first year was ending. That apartment was dark and drab with no distinguishing features, so I did not want to renew, thinking there must be something better in this town. So, with a map of downtown Norfolk and a folded newspaper with circled "Apts. to Rent" listings on my lap, I drove down Hampton Boulevard in my Sunbeam Alpine convertible. Sam, the beagle, was sitting happily on the other bucket seat, his paws on the dashboard, his beagle ears flowing in the breezes off the windscreen.

I had looked at two vacant apartments, both also in the nondescript category and was in search of a new development along the renovated canal district of the old downtown. The building was being called the Yum Yum Apartments, after a recent film with Jack Lemmon called *Under the Yum Yum Tree*.

This sounds pretty daring, I thought, *but at least it might be more attractive than nondescript.*

I found the street and the address, parked the car, put Sam on his leash, and stepped over some rough pavement and construction remnants as I approached the new building. There appeared to be four apartments, two on each level. A young man was standing on the doorstep of the nearest apartment, talking to a very tall woman.

"Is this the apartment that is available to rent?" I asked the man. "But I am also here to look at this apartment," the tall woman said to him and then turned to me.

"Well," he said, "come in, both of you, I may as well give you both the tour of the apartment at the same time."

Everything was gleaming new — the floors, the freshly painted walls, the kitchen with all new appliances, fridge, stove, even a dishwasher. There were ample cupboards with good lighting and a counter bar with stools separating the kitchen from a large rectangular living room that had a fireplace on the outside wall.

"And it works," said the man, who by now had introduced himself as Gary, the owner and developer of this new complex.

"Come see the bedrooms — there are two, and they are both good-sized, lots of closets, and there are even two bathrooms."

"Would my dog be welcome?" I asked. "He is quiet; he doesn't bark at all."

"And would my cat be welcome?" asked the woman.

"Yes, either one," the man said, then added, "this is the only apartment left. I just rented the other three."

"And what is the monthly rent? I asked, "And would there be a one-year lease?"

When he told us the rent, the woman became quiet and said nothing as we three walked back to the front door.

"Could we discuss this by ourselves outside? We'll let you know right away," I said as he smiled and closed the door behind us.

I stood beside the tall woman for a minute or so, then said: "You were here first. Do you plan to take the apartment?"

"I just can't afford it," she said. "My heart fell when he told us the monthly rent; I really like it, and I have good furniture for that living room."

"I don't need a two-bedroom apartment," I said then, impulsively, "Would you like to share it, as roommates? I know we do not know each other.

I don't even know your name, but…."

The woman broke into a great wide smile, put out her hand to shake mine, and said, "My name is Delores, but everyone calls me Dee Dee. I am recently divorced, and I have a job, and sharing this apartment would be great. I don't want to be alone in this town."

So that is how I met Dee Dee, both of us laughing at our impulse to take this big leap and share the apartment.

We knocked on the door and told the mildly surprised man, our new landlord, that we would jointly take the apartment, that we would be roommates, and did he have the paperwork for us to sign?

As we walked out together, Dee Dee asked, pointing to her car, "Do you need a ride?" That car was the biggest car I had ever stood beside: a blue-and-white Cadillac with silver accents gleaming in the sun and two huge tail fins that looked as if they would help the car take flight as it accelerated.

"Thanks, but I have a car," I said, "the little red one down the block."

We both laughed at the size difference between the two cars.

"Let's hope your dog and my cat get along," Dee Dee said, still laughing.

"I'll be ready to move in on September 1, as we agreed with the landlord," I said.

"And I'll get here early that morning with my furniture. There's even an extra bed that you can have."

So, that began my pleasant months with Dee Dee. We settled in that first day in September. I had bought some extra sheets, towels, and dishes, and we worked side by side to set up the kitchen and arrange the living room. Dee Dee's shy little cat hid in her bedroom for days on end until discovering that Sam, the beagle, was only there in the evenings, always staying close by my feet. Sam still spent the days on campus with me.

Then one afternoon I came home early after going food shopping and I left the main door ajar while going back to my car to bring in another bag of groceries. I was in the kitchen, putting the food items away in the fridge and the pantry when there was a loud knock on the door.

"Who's there?" I called out before opening the door.

"Your upstairs neighbor."

I opened the door to find a young man wrapped in a blanket holding Dee Dee's cat.

"Is this your cat?" he asked. "He was crying outside our door and woke me up."

And that is how I met the man I was to marry, some seven months later.

I had this photo taken in October 1961 after my first year
of teaching at The College of William & Mary.

My first car was a Sunbeam Alpine from the
Rootes Group of the UK. I purchased it in 1961.

My wedding day, April 24, 1965. The ceremony and reception was held at the Officers' Club on the Norfolk Naval Base in Norfolk, Virginia.

Actor-Officer Marries Professor

Miss Rosemary MacLellan, assistant professor of economics at Old Dominion College, and Michael Scanlon, Naval officer known for his contributions to Tidewater theater, were married Saturday at 4 p.m. in Our Lady of Victory Chapel on the Naval Station.

The bride's uncle, the Rev. Alex MacLellan of the Redemptionist Order of Montreal, Que., celebrated the nuptial mass. Lt. Cmdr. Senieur Jude, Ch.C., performed the ceremony.

Scanlon, a lieutenant (j.g.) in the USNR, is a New Yorker known here as a talented actor through his work with little theater groups. His most recent appearances were in the Norfolk Little Theatre's Experimental Wing production of "Under Milk Wood" and the Little Theatre's "Little Mary" in which he played a starring role as Corporal Billy. He is a graduate of St. John's University, Brooklyn, N.Y.

His bride, a Canadian, was graduated from St. Francis Xavier College in Antigonish, Nova Scotia, and holds an M.A. in economics from the University of New Brunswick in Nova Scotia. She is the daughter of Mrs. Agnes MacLellan of Antigonish and the late Donald MacLellan.

Scanlon's parents, Mr. and Mrs. Augustine Scanlon, live in New York City. His brother,

John, also of New York, was his best man. Ushers were Lt. Edwin Urie, USA, Harrisburg, Pa., and Dr. Gordon Schaye, New York City.

The bride's brother, Malcolm MacLellan of Antigonish, gave her in marriage. Her sister, Miss Donalda MacLellan of Antigonish, was her maid of honor.

After a reception in the Chesapeake Room of the Naval Station Officers' Club the Scanlons left on a wedding trip. On their return they will live in Pelham Place.

Photos by Gordon Mitchell

No Stage Kiss This

Scanlons at Their Wedding Reception

A newspaper clipping from the *Norfolk Ledger-Star* that ran on or about April 26, 1965.

CHAPTER 4

Discovering America's Cities
(and Toronto!)

Hollywood to Houston 1965-68

When I was first married, I had the opportunity to visit twenty-two North American cities in ten months, accompanying my new husband in his first professional acting job as understudy to the young male lead in that year's Pulitzer Prize–winning play. This was an experience that not only changed my life by being in the center of those cities, but it also changed the focus of my career as an economist.

I had been living in Norfolk, Virginia, for two years, teaching at the local university, Old Dominion, which had just moved out on its own from being the "Norfolk William and Mary." This was following my three years as a young faculty member at the College of William and Mary in Williamsburg, Virginia.

Unlike Williamsburg, which was a small town (but not my small town, I would tell myself, thinking of my hometown back in Nova Scotia), Norfolk was a significant small city, famous for its proximity to the great shoreline at Virginia Beach, but known primarily for its huge naval base and naval air station. I began to think that I was becoming an extension of the military since many of my students in my advanced economics classes were military officers who were finishing their undergraduate degree or polishing up courses in advance of attending graduate school when their twenty-year commitment to the military was finished.

I met and married my husband, Michael Scanlon, in that second year in Norfolk. He was nearing the completion of his three-year commitment as a junior officer in the U.S. Navy, and we happened to move into the same apartment complex in Norfolk's reviving canal district. Our marriage and wedding reception was held at the officer's club at the naval base on April 24, 1965, and was attended by my family from Nova Scotia and Michael's family from New York City as well as several of my colleagues from the university and his actor friends from the local little theater group.

Michael received his formal separation papers from the U.S. Navy on May 9, and when my academic year was completed in late May, we moved to Washington, D.C., where Michael was to act in Shakespeare in the Park during the summer months. Then he would begin his formal acting career in September as an intern at the Arena Stage Theatre in Washington, D.C.

While Washington was beautiful and stately in the main government sections, it was rundown and dangerous if one ventured too far from the spine of the Jefferson Memorial to the Capitol, or from the few safe picturesque blocks in Georgetown. We found an apartment in the only new building, except for the Arena Stage Theatre, in the southwestern part of the city. All else was rubble. Summer is never Washington's best season: it is hot and humid, steaming on many days and nights, and the atmosphere seemed particularly oppressive that summer as President Lyndon Johnson began calling up a million troops for the escalation of the war in Vietnam.

One summer morning, we noticed a casting call audition in the New York Herald Tribune for the national tour of *The Subject Was Roses*. We had seen that play during a visit to New York City in late spring, and both of us had been particularly moved by its setting in the Bronx, where Michael grew up, as well as the snappy dialogue. That morning I urged Michael to take the Eastern Airlines shuttle to New York to audition. This would turn out to be a successful audition and Michael was chosen to understudy the young male lead in the bus-and-truck company that would tour smaller American cities. But shortly afterward, when rehearsals began in New York City, Michael became part of the national touring company, where he would act as understudy to Martin Sheen, who was playing the son of Jack Albertson and Martha Scott. This three-person play had just won the Pulitzer Prize for Best Play of the Year.

Since this would be Michael's first professional acting assignment, it meant immediate acceptance into Actor's Equity, the all-important union that guaranteed good salaries and benefits. This also offered us a way to escape Washington, and this national tour was the "big time." We both would have the chance to see many of the great American cities — Chicago, Los Angeles, San Francisco, Boston, and intriguing-sounding places in between, including Cincinnati, Omaha, Minneapolis-St. Paul, St. Louis, and Denver. We would even spend several days in Toronto, which would be my first visit to that major city in my native Canada.

On Labor Day 1965, with the three-person cast, two other understudies, a tour/stage manager and small stage crew, and me, we were off to Los Angeles, our first stop on the tour. Of the twenty-two cities we were to visit in ten months, some stays would last as long as three or four weeks, as in Los Angeles, San Francisco, Detroit or Chicago, while in others such as Toronto, Philadelphia, Washington, D.C. or Boston, we were

341

booked for a week's stay. There were shorter stays of three- or four-day stopovers in such cities as Omaha, Minneapolis-St Paul, St. Louis, or Columbus, Ohio.

The cast and tour manager traveled by plane on the long-distance moves, but frequently by train on the more moderate distances since Martha Scott had little fondness for air travel. This did provide several scenic and memorable trips, particularly through the Imperial Valley between Los Angeles and San Francisco, through the Feather River Canyon and the Rockies into Denver, and down along the Mississippi from Minneapolis-St. Paul to Des Moines and on to St. Louis.

I had few functions in this touring life — packing and unpacking the wardrobe trunk in time for it to be picked up by the stage truck, and on Wednesday mornings, I offered to "hold book" for the three understudies as the tour manager took them through a reading rehearsal of the play to keep their memorization of the lines and stage directions fresh in case they had to step into the role some night if one of the leads took ill. As a result, I used my free time during the days to go out with my new 35 mm camera and explore the downtown of the host city, including visits to museums, art galleries, and public libraries.

The tour opened in a sun-washed Los Angeles, with its early mornings of light fog and cool air before the strength of the midmorning sun left the sky a bright blue. The air was a thrilling change from the stifling humidity of Washington, and the quality of light in the city — bright and direct, then mellow and gently shadowed — was totally unlike anything I had ever seen or experienced on the East Coast. I do not recall that we had many days of severe smog, although that topic featured regularly in the *Los Angeles Times*, and there was no sign in those three weeks of our stay in the city of the fabled Santa Ana winds, which I was to experience a year later when we moved to L.A. and our son was born.

The opening night of the play was filled with excitement. Our tour manager said there was ample advance publicity and that we should see many celebrities. Those of us associated with, but not in, the production, were to dress up in formal wear; the after-party was to be at the famous Chasen's restaurant. The art deco black-and-silver lobby of the theater was lined with theatergoers as I entered. I peeked around to see if there was anyone famous, but it wasn't until after the final curtain call and the crowd milling around in the lobby that I spotted one well-known face, the dancer/singer Ann Miller.

"There'll be more. Just wait till we get to the restaurant," said the tour manager, who had joined me in the lobby. We went ahead of the cast, who were still removing their makeup and getting into dress clothes. But Ann Miller was the only celebrity of the evening, a disappointment matched next by the menu for the after-party, which consisted of large stainless-steel pans over Sterno flame pots containing, first, Canadian bacon, then scrambled eggs, then hash brown potatoes. "I could have made this late-night dish in Nova Scotia," I whispered to my husband when he made his appearance.

But while I scoffed at Ann Miller that night, standing there in her vivid red ball gown with lipstick to match and looking around in anticipation (as I was) to see who else was there, years later I watched her tap dancing in the movie *Kiss Me Kate*, and still later on a Broadway stage in *Sugar Babies* with

343

Mickey Rooney, dancing superbly at a time when she must have been in her mid-sixties. I quite changed my early disappointment to total admiration for her talent and showmanship.

We took the train to San Francisco from Union Station in Los Angeles. The old station, designed in Mission style with white stucco walls and a red-tile roof, was surprisingly charming in an otherwise dilapidated and quite small downtown. "Old Town" might have been a more accurate description since there was no discernible downtown to be seen in Los Angeles in the fall of 1965. "Seventy-two communities in search of a city," as one taxi driver told us. But then Hollywood Boulevard was rather tacky also, enlivened mostly by Grauman's Chinese, fronted by the marble pavement with its celebrity stars, and several blocks further east, by the then-radical circular "pancake" structure of the Capitol Records building.

The train ride out of Los Angeles took us through the San Fernando Valley and to the Pacific Coast through beautiful Santa Barbara, then inland for the long ride through the Imperial Valley. I had a window seat with a clear view of the vast tracts of vegetable farms that went on for many miles. Here was America's mighty fruit and vegetable basket, irrigated by giant rotating arms of water pipes.

San Francisco

San Francisco was breathtaking on that first day of our arrival, gleaming under an early-October sun and deep blue sky, its white and pastel buildings shimmering above the sparkling waters of San Francisco Bay. We saw too little of the city during that first week since we were invited to stay with New York friends of Michael's who had recently relocated to the area and were renting a modern single-family house in Palo Alto.

"This sure isn't New York and it sure isn't the Bronx," our host told us that first evening as he showed us around the grounds, which overlooked a steep chasm. I noticed that the back part of the house was propped up on long poles. I said nothing but remembered what I learned about the San Andreas Fault from my geography books: this house and many others like it that we saw silhouetted on the skyline south of San Francisco must be located right on the fault line. This type of construction, propped up by poles, seemed to be perilous, even in a moderate-strength earthquake.

There was much to discover in the city, as I found while accompanying my husband each day. I became enthralled with this extended honeymoon. San Francisco was an ongoing series of delightful discoveries, scenic vistas, fresh seafood, crisp salads, Napa Valley wines, and Ghirardelli chocolates. While Michael went to the theater, I rode the cable cars, found the museums, walked through Chinatown, and became so enamored that I convinced my husband that we should move to the city for our final two weeks of the schedule. This way we could find some interesting restaurants and piano bars for music after the theater, maybe even meet other young people our age, since the theatergoers in San Francisco were older, middle-aged people who arrived at the theater in near-formal attire, the women wearing gloves and sometimes pill-box hats with half veils; the men in hats and wearing dark suits with white shirts, formal, and, we thought, rather stiff and maybe even "uppity," a trait that we had not expected to see in this city that we had thought of as filled with youth and vigor.

Denver

We boarded the Western Pacific Zephyr train to Denver, already pining for San Francisco, with all the cast and crew vowing to come back one day. Our train route was through the Feather River Canyon, and we could walk back to the observation car with its glass dome and elevated seats to watch dusk fall over the river as the mountains loomed higher and the train hugged the tree-lined walls of the canyon.

We crossed Nevada during the night, enjoying the relative luxury of the dining car and the sleeper car in what was considered the "last great train left in the United States." I woke at dawn to watch our arrival into Salt Lake City, and then throughout the day, we crossed the Bonneville Salt Flats of Utah. By late afternoon, we were beginning the long slow climb up the foothills of the Rockies. At a high elevation we entered a tunnel underneath the Continental Divide that seemed to go on for hours, then suddenly the train broke out of the tunnel to expose the night sky, and far below our level, the lights of Denver sparkling like jewels. Since Denver is a mile high in altitude, we must have been at least at 8,000 feet to have that breathtaking view. The train moved as slowly on the descent to the city as during the climb up the Rockies during the late afternoon.

At the Brown Derby Hotel in Denver, with its fourteen-story atrium, I hugged the walls from the elevator to our room on the top floor to avoid the terror of looking down at the lobby far below. But I managed through the thin altitude, although we were told that there was an oxygen tank in every dressing room in case the actors felt lightheaded or dizzy.

Most of the theaters we played in during this national tour were Shubert theaters and they were all located in the downtowns of American's cities. Most had been built during the 1920s, when theater, whether vaudeville, musicals, or dramatic plays, flourished in the U.S. That was also a time when America's cities were flourishing, many growing rapidly from the infusion of new immigrants following the end of the WW I. And despite the Great Depression, theater continued to thrive during the 1930s.

Except for Los Angeles, San Francisco, Denver, Chicago, and Boston, most of the American cities I visited during those ten months were rundown, losing major industries and population, and particularly their white population and their young people. The flight to the suburbs with nearby shopping malls and neighboring industrial parks, was by now full-blown, with access assured by the national highway system. The effect on the formerly proud and vital cities was a trail of tired buildings and tired people, with older stores and diners in the better situations or instances of nearly deserted department stores, empty lots, and potholed streets — and, especially in Detroit, dangerous streets. These were situations of dilapidation and despair. And now, in the mid-1960s, the theaters were left behind, often on dreary streets, functioning like small islands of activity with a nearby restaurant that served only theatergoers.

Cincinnati

Cincinnati that year was an exception to the otherwise bleak scenery, with a small downtown clustered around the theater consisting of a department store and crowded Germanic pubs filled with cheerful patrons. It had the feel of a mini New York City, with lively pedestrian traffic. I was to return to Cincinnati some twenty years later to attend a conference and was shocked to find that those few sections of the old downtown had disappeared, only to be replaced by ugly concrete slab structures of no apparent design merit and featuring one-story-high walkways between the buildings, leaving few pedestrians walking at street level.

While Cincinnati had seemed prosperous enough twenty years earlier, and largely because its main company, Proctor and Gamble, was still doing well, any new investments were made in the surrounding suburbs, slowing draining away the vibrancy of the old city until it was replaced by urban renewal and this sterile rebuilding.

Omaha

Omaha, by contrast, had no apparent downtown, just a long main street with some drab blocky buildings. It smelled of cow, as did the strangely narrow hotel with steep staircases where we were booked. In a street laid down on the wide-open plains and in a city with large boxy buildings, we could not understand why anyone would build a hotel so narrow and so seemingly steep without being particularly tall. Nor were we happy to find out that Omaha was a dry city on a Sunday. "Not a chance," said the hotel clerk as we checked in and asked where we could find dinner and cocktails. "This is Omaha. This is Sunday. There is no liquor served."

A drink seemed called for by all the cast and crew because of the nightmarish landing we had experienced flying into the Omaha airport. The Boeing 727 with its high-pitched tail and whining jet engines placed high up on that tail was new that year, and as we were told later by a travel agent, was still being introduced around the various airlines. Pilots were being trained, we were told, but not all and not all right away.

We were flying at about 25,000 feet, when I looked out the window to see an airport almost directly below us. I thought that this might be another airport, not Omaha's, since why would we still be at such a high altitude? At that point, the plane took a steep bank, did a wide half-circle, and then aimed, nose down, toward the airport, just like the photos and movies of dive bombers in World War II that we grew up with. My head almost burst with pain, and then I had a massive nosebleed, a burst of blood that sprayed over the back of the seat ahead of us, causing my husband to begin yelling and the flight attendant to come running to find me covered in blood, then rushing to bring a wet towel from the galley. The nosebleed stopped by the time the plane had taxied up to the gate, but my clothes were drenched in blood, and I was weak from the loss. The flight attendant brought me a glass of water, and my husband found my trench coat to cover up the splattered dress. While mine was the most visible reaction to the dive-bombing approach, it was soon evident that our entire group was frightened by the experience.

Everyone wanted a drink — a scotch, any strong drink, at least a beer. The tour manager tried to reassure us. "Everyone check into your rooms and freshen up. Meet me here in a half-hour, and let's see what I can find." He did find a place for us, calling back to the theatrical booking agent in New York to ask what we could do on a Sunday in Omaha if we wanted a drink. He was told that by paying a $20 initiation fee at such and such private club with our Broadway connections, we could have drinks and a good dinner, which we did, giddy and chattering loudly about our hair-raising plane ride. The city still smelled of cow as we made our way back to the steep, narrow hotel.

Des Moines

We arrived in Des Moines, Iowa, for three days beginning November 9, 1965. On our first evening, I decided to stay in the hotel to write letters to my family back in Canada rather than go to the theater. I turned on the TV to watch the news and was startled to see Walter Cronkite, the famous anchor of the CBS Evening News, sitting behind a candle with a dark background. It was instantly evident from his tone of voice that something was wrong, seriously wrong.

"There appears to be no power anywhere in the northeast," Cronkite said, and then he read a news bulletin: "The power has gone out in Toronto and all of southern Ontario." Then he began to list the areas in the northeast that were blacked out: Boston to Rochester and Buffalo, parts of Ohio and Pennsylvania, all of New York City, and south toward Washington, DC. "Fifty million people are without electricity," he said.

Was this some major accident, I wondered, or perhaps sabotage? I called the hotel operator to phone my in-laws in New York City, my mother in Nova Scotia, and my sister, Louise, in Montreal.

"It will be hours, I think, before that call can go through," the hotel operator told me. "We can't get any calls through to the East Coast."

I set the phone down on the cradle and watched again to see if Walter Cronkite had further news or theories as to the cause of this major blackout. The only new piece of information was that the trouble appeared to have begun at Niagara Falls. Two days later I was to learn that the blackout had not reached Nova Scotia but did cause power outages in Montreal. It would be years before a final report was released with details of the cause: it had started at Niagara Falls, the location of the great power plant, before cascading along the various grids in the northeast. There was no evidence of sabotage.

Chicago

In Chicago, we checked into a comfortable apartment hotel on the near North Side called 14 West Elm for our two-month stay. The hotel's piano bar and skilled jazz pianist became a favorite hangout for Martin Sheen, Michael, and me after the theater, until Martin's wife, Janet, and their three young children, Emilio, Ramón, and baby Carlos, joined him and our group at the hotel. Carlos had been born just before the tour began, and while Janet and the children and the baby had been with us in Los Angeles, accompanied by a nurse, Janet had returned to New York City for the next two months when our stops were briefer.

Chicago was cold and windy, but the snow held off until early January, so it was easy to navigate around the art museums and libraries, as well as to the department stores on the Magnificent Mile. We enjoyed the great food in the city's restaurants, although one evening I hung the strap of my 35mm camera on the notch of the chair and absentmindedly walked out. The next day when I discovered its loss, I went back to the restaurant. "No," the maître d' said, "no one reported they found a camera last night." I had lost my new camera and all of the photos taken since the start of the tour in Los Angeles.

One night during a performance in Chicago, Martin developed severe laryngitis and could barely make it through the first act. Michael, backstage, was rushed into makeup as the tour manager anxiously asked if he remembered his lines and if he was up to performing. Then, as the second act was about to begin, the tour manager stood in front of the curtain and told the audience about Martin's condition and that his understudy, Michael Scanlon, would step in to finish the play. A drama reporter from one of the Chicago newspapers was in the audience and wrote a highly favorable review of Michael's performance and the seamless transition of the role of Timmy between the two actors. And Michael was terrific in the role, especially under those circumstances.

Martha Scott invited us to celebrate New Year's Eve in her hotel suite. The bellman wheeled in a crate of iced champagne and trays of hors d'oeuvres for the cast, the understudies, and the crew. All of us dressed in formal clothes, grateful for the opportunity to be together, and most of us giddily drank too much champagne, including me.

When we left the great Chicago Union Station for the train ride to Milwaukee, Michael and Martin raced along the marble floors to recapture the two little runaways, Emilio and Ramón, who had stripped off their diapers and were running free in the great space. I was holding baby Carlos so Janet could have a few quiet minutes over coffee in the nearby cafe. Several times during that train ride, and on the old Penn Central line into Philadelphia, Michael and I offered to watch the little ones, with sturdy baby Carlos in my arms, so Martin and Janet could have a quiet dinner by themselves in the dining car. It was startling, two decades later, to watch the movie *Platoon* and realize that young Charlie Sheen was baby Carlos, all grown up.

Milwaukee

We arrived in Milwaukee to face minus 25-degree temperatures with wind chill yet were lured out on our day off to tour the famous Pabst Brewery. I occasionally drank a beer, especially on a summer's evening, but just as we walked through the large, solid doors of the main brewery building, I was overpowered with the heady smell of hops and mash. My stomach heaved in a sudden wave of nausea, and I had to return to the hotel.

That afternoon when the first cigarette of the day resulted in the same instant nausea, I asked my husband, "Is it possible I am pregnant? Now, what are we to do?"

"We'll call Gordon," Michael said. Gordon was a doctor in the Public Health Service when he shared an apartment with Michael and Ed at the complex in Norfolk where Michael and I met.

"Didn't Gordon go to medical school in St. Louis?" Michael asked. "And isn't the tour going to St. Louis in another week?"

Gordon, when we reached him by phone in New York City, asked us for the exact dates we would be in St. Louis, saying he would contact his gynecology professor.

"But don't be alarmed if you see odd names on the door of his office; he and his top researcher are doing some new-fangled research on sexual behavior."

And that is how I came to meet Dr. William H. Masters. The words printed on the door of his office suite read Reproductive Biology Research Foundation. "Weird. Just as Gordon said," Michael muttered as we were ushered in by the receptionist to the doctor's office, which looked more like an academic's study than a medical office.

"Sit down, young lady." Dr. Master's voice was pleasant and warm as he sat down opposite me and looked deeply into my eyes.

"I would say you are seven weeks pregnant."

"How can you tell?" Michael burst out.

Dr. Masters smiled at Michael, then looked back at me: 'Because of the dilation of your pupils," he said to me. "But we will do the usual tests just to be sure."

We waited outside for perhaps a half-hour, and I suspected that the woman wearing a white lab coat we saw entering an adjoining office and glancing back at us was Virginia E. Johnson, Dr. Master's research partner.

"Well, right on target," Dr. Masters said warmly as we went back into his office. "You are seven weeks pregnant. Now I want you to go to a maternity store and buy a maternity bra and maternity girdle and begin wearing them right away and throughout your pregnancy. This will help reduce stretch marks."

I had never heard of stretch marks, but then suddenly remembered parting advice from the surgeon who had performed the thyroidectomy on me in 1963. He said he had left a small portion of my thyroid intact and said to be sure to be alert to changes in my system and to be sure to tell my doctor about this if I ever became pregnant because I would need to take a thyroid supplement.

When I told this to Dr. Masters, he reached over to his desk for his prescription pad and said while scribbling quickly, "You certainly will need this. Take as prescribed throughout your pregnancy. Best wishes now and give my regards to Gordon."

We went to visit the famous St. Louis Arch during that visit, but meeting Dr. Masters was the highlight. A few years later, when his first book was published, Michael and I took turns reading the book review and said, almost in unison, "So that was what that office was all about!"

Columbus

In Columbus, Ohio, winter had returned with new snow and slushy streets when we arrived for a four-day stay in the downtown hotel next to the old Shubert Theatre. The city, with its wide streets — "We call them boulevards," the hotel concierge said — and Greco-Roman buildings looked abandoned, no one was walking along those "boulevards" just snow-covered cars that were inching along in the traffic. Where were all the young people, we wondered. My husband, Martin Sheen, and I seemed to be the only people under thirty to be seen. "Perhaps everyone goes to Ohio State," Martin said. We knew that the university was very large by East Coast standards and that it was located outside of Columbus.

"They certainly can't be in St. Paul," I said, remembering how that city had been similarly bereft of young people when our tour had stopped there a few weeks ago.

The dining scene was as dreary as the cityscape. I was craving seafood at this stage of my pregnancy. There was none to be had in the restaurants, just tuna casseroles or a sandwich of canned tuna. At night I would lay awake dreaming up recipes for shrimp or crab dishes, or poached salmon, or broiled red snapper, all dishes that were standard restaurant fare in Williamsburg, Virginia, with the great bounty available from the nearby Chesapeake Bay. "Except for the salmon," I thought as I was drifting off to sleep, hungry, trying to stifle the cravings. "The salmon is from Nova Scotia or maybe Alaska."

Boston

Our taxi drew up in front of a charming old hotel in downtown Boston. "This is as close as I can get with the piles of snow. I can't park right by the curb," said our friendly driver with his broad Boston accent so that car became "cah" and curb was "kurrb."

Boston must have gotten the same snowfall as they'd had in Columbus, but here, there were even higher piles by the side-walks. We threaded our way through a narrow path that had been shoveled in front of the hotel, leaving a snowbank of at least three feet in height. Then, just to the left of the hotel en-trance, was a stand with fresh flowers: daffodils, tulips, carna-tions, and roses. We set our suitcases down on the snowy side-walk and stared. Flowers! We had not seen fresh flowers since leaving San Francisco some months ago. Here was a blaze of color against the snowfall and the charming old hotel building, whose brown tones now seemed to glow.

"And where is the nearest seafood restaurant?" my hus-band asked the desk clerk as we were checking in.

"Next door, and it's a great place. Lots of fresh fish," he said.

So I had my seafood — plates of oysters and clams on the half shell, martini-style glasses of shrimp cocktail, and poached salmon with a creamy sauce made with chopped hard-boiled eggs, served with mashed potatoes and peas. And a dessert called Boston cream pie. I was in heaven.

The next afternoon we went to a French movie called *The Umbrellas of Cherbourg*, filmed mostly in the rain, it appeared, but awash with colorful umbrellas, with the heroine and her sis-ter dressed in raincoats and rain boots of vivid red or brilliant blue. Michael and I walked down the street to the movie theater — our first movie in many months, since there was never a movie theater near us in any of the midwestern cities, and our shorter stay in those cities did not leave free time for movie-going — sharing the sidewalk with hordes of young people, probably college students, maybe graduate students, since they were about our age, in their mid-twenties. There seemed to be music everywhere, young, bearded troubadours standing by a lamppost singing and strumming their guitars, trios entertaining in restaurants or folk singers in late-evening bars.

There could have been ten feet of snow on the streets of Boston that year, with spring nowhere in sight, but this was a city alive with young people, unafraid to display fresh flowers on a snowy sidewalk, and filled, it seemed, with music. And like the French movie, it was awash in color, which stood out against the piles of snow and the great old brown buildings of Boston.

The Roosevelt Hotel, Washington, D.C. April 7, 1966

Dear Mom: Just a note to say we're fine and glad to be leaving Washington since, despite our efforts, we seem to react negatively to everything this place stands for. The weather has proved a bit of a disappointment; outside of two misleading days, it has been cold, windy, and cloudy. However, the play is doing superbly here. We grossed $43,000 last week, a record for this play, and this week should be even higher. Tonight we're expecting Don Grant from New York City for the weekend. He's such a great guy and a good friend, and next to me, he must be one of your most successful products (such egotism!). We'll do some sightseeing tomorrow, and then Don and I plan to go to Arlington to see President Kennedy's grave. After

Washington, the tour goes to Wilmington, Delaware, New Haven, then Detroit, maybe Toronto, and then Philadelphia, where we hope you will be able to visit us when your school term is finished.

Detroit

Detroit was not welcoming. We were told by the tour manager during the flight to Detroit that, because the city was dangerous, we were not to go out of our hotel alone, day or night. An approved car service was hired to transport the actors to and from the Fisher Theatre. Our hotel was midway between the theater district, which seemed to be two or so miles up the street, and at least a mile from the Old Downtown, as it was called. There seemed to be almost nothing in between these destinations except empty lots, rubble, and vast stretches of vacant land.

There was a restaurant in the hotel, which served breakfast, lunch, and dinner, and that was to be our "cafeteria" for most of the time since we were warned not to leave the building. One evening there was a reception for the cast and crew at a restaurant connected to the Fisher Theatre, but all of our other meals were in this hotel.

Detroit, May 23, 1966

Dear Mom: Spring finally arrived in this ridiculous city this past week after the first two weeks when the weather has been awful. We're looking forward to Toronto — anything to get out of Detroit. We've had a nice apartment in this hotel, bright and sunny, and it's been great to be able to cook at home, but this is an awful city... dark, dingy, dirty, rundown, and grubby. We can't find a single thing to do, so most of the days we stay home and read. I'd sure like to be heading back to L.A., to The Montecito Hotel, and that swimming pool surrounded by palm trees.

I didn't mention anything in the letter to mother about how dangerous Detroit was and that we were warned not to go out by ourselves. But one day I needed to get out, wanting some fresh air and somewhere to walk. By this time I was five and a half months pregnant, so I asked the hotel manager to call for the car service, telling him I needed to go downtown to make some purchases and that the car should wait for me there and bring me back to the hotel. What I really wanted to do was see the Old Downtown and what had been built by all of the money made in this famous city over the past century. My destination was the main department store, Dayton-Hudson, famous, we were told, throughout the Midwest.

The driver left me off in front of the store, a tall, gray, sad-looking building. When I walked through the revolving doors to the main floor, the scene was one of despondency. There were few shoppers, just rows of tired-looking older women, gray and graying, standing behind the cosmetic counters. They looked at me anxiously, waiting for me to approach one of the counters and purchase something. I noticed also that the few shoppers were African American women, while all the staff was white. I took the elevator up to the floor selling women's dresses and suits, thinking that the retail would be livelier here, but again, the mix was the same — a few African American women leaning over sweaters or scarves, the staff all older white women.

I found the elevator, went back down to the main floor and went out through the revolving doors. My car service was not in view, so I decided to walk across the street and into a small park that occupied the center of a square, surrounded by other gray buildings in this dismal downtown. It was the end of May, but spring was late. The grass was brown, and while there was no sign of anything flowering, there was some warmth from the sun. I found a bench, sat down, and looked around at the dreary little park, more a patch than a park, I thought, strewn with pieces of paper and crumpled brown paper bags.

The gray or brown buildings surrounding the square looked mostly empty and sad, just like the people in the department store, staff and shoppers alike. It was hard to believe that so much money had been made here in Detroit, the automobile capital of the world, whose many factories were also the powerhouses of the tanks and trucks used to win the war. Where did the money go? Why hadn't anything been built down here since the war ended? Americans had gone back to buying cars, all Detroit-made, and driving extensively on the new interstate highways. I burst into tears, and was digging through my purse for a Kleenex to wipe them away when a booming male voice said: "What's wrong, lady? Are you all right? Are you injured? What are you doing here by yourself?"

I looked up to see a tall man in a police officer's uniform, holding a baton in both hands. What was I to say to him? How could I tell him that I was crying for his poor city? He would think I was mentally ill.

"Excuse me, Officer," I said, snuffling and wiping my nose. "I came down to the department store, but I am pregnant and needed to sit down."

"Where do you live?" he asked. I explained about the hotel and that we were visiting Detroit with a Broadway play. I also explained about the car service, which I could not see at the edges of the little park.

"Well, lady, we will take you back to your hotel, unless you want us to take you to a doctor or the hospital." I did not want to investigate Detroit's hospitals, so I told him politely that I just needed to rest, have a cup of tea perhaps, and that I would be fine.

So I was transported back to the hotel refuge in a police cruiser, grateful for the safety. I had my walk by going down the hall of the hotel to the restaurant for tea.

A year later, living in Hollywood and up early one morning to give my little son his bottle, I turned on the television for the morning news to see the screen ablaze with fire. The announcer's voice said that the Fisher Theatre and all of the buildings on that block in Detroit were on fire and that many buildings in the downtown were burning, as riots had broken out overnight and fires had been set throughout the city. So sad and shocking, the announcer intoned, because some people had been killed. Sad yes, but not, I thought, so shocking.

Toronto

We were next in my native land, although this was my first visit to Toronto. There we were, staying at the historic Royal York Hotel, the play highlighted at the Royal Alexandra Theatre, and my youngest sister, Louise, who was now beginning her fashion career in this city, meeting us for dinner and on our free day, walking us through the newly hip neighborhood of Yorkville. We found the city to be beautiful, clean, and well organized. The people we met were pleasant and civil, and above all, there was a pervading sense of safety.

Hotel Sylvania, Philadelphia, late June 1966

Dear Mom: My heart is heavy, seeing you go this morning; I'm still fighting tears. You looked so pretty, like a little girl, and I could only think of the many times you and I have said farewell like this, these last eleven years; and it gets harder every time. But the week was wonderful, and I appreciate your coming more than I can ever say. As lonesome as I feel now, I would be far more so if we were starting our indefinite stay in California without seeing you. Thank you for what you put in that envelope! I will put it away to buy things for the baby. I'll write from Denver and let you know how Mike does. Again, it was such a pleasure having you with us.

Our play, *The Subject Was Roses*, was invited back to Denver for another week. Martin had other commitments for that week, so Michael was to play the part of Timmy in the cast, with Jack Albertson and Martha Scott.

The Continental Denver, June 28, 1966

Dear Mom: Greetings from beautiful Denver. The sky is clear, the temp is in the high eighties; our motel is outside the city, and we have a beautiful pool plus a fountain and gaily blooming rose bushes. The play opened last night to a very responsive audience. Mike did beautifully and the reviews this afternoon are so good as to be almost heady. I'm sending along a copy, and we bought about twenty newspapers so there will be plenty of copies for his agent, etc. in Hollywood. Jack Albertson was especially pleased with Mike's reviews. Jack's wife is here, a lovely woman; we went into town today to try and find me a bathing suit, but all three maternity shops were completely sold out. I had to settle for shorts and a cutaway top for now until I can find one in L.A. We have tickets for L.A. for next Sunday morning.

Hollywood, The Montecito, and Meeting Alice Ghostley

Michael and I arrived in Los Angeles from the week in Denver in time for the three-day July 4th weekend. At the suggestion of our road manager, we booked a room at The Montecito Hotel on Fountain Avenue in Hollywood. This was an apartment hotel favored by New York actors in town looking for work in movies or TV or to finish dubbing or sound details from an out-of-town acting assignment.

Shortly after we settled in, Alice Ghostley arrived from on-location shooting for *To Kill a Mockingbird*. Robert Duvall, who played Boo in that movie, arrived a few days later. Alice's husband, the actor Felice Orlandi, later arrived from his location shoot in San Francisco for the movie *Bullitt,* which starred Steve McQueen. Felice had an important role at the beginning of that movie as the government witness brought in from Chicago under protection and lodged in a seedy hotel in south San Francisco. His protection failed, and the government witness was shot and killed in that motel room by Chicago mobsters.

The Montecito was a comfortable, pleasant hotel of some ten to twelve stories, with an old-fashioned "birdcage" elevator that had bronze accordion doors. The hotel had opened during the 1930s and was considered quite fashionable in those days. In our time, it was clean and nicely appointed. There was no longer a restaurant or coffee shop, but each hotel room, or "suite" as they were called, had a serviceable kitchen with a stove, a small refrigerator, and a small dining area with a table and four chairs. The double bed was housed on a wall, to be pulled down at night, which meant that during the day there was ample sitting space, a desk, and a black-and-white TV. A walk-in closet and dressing room led to a large, pleasant bathroom.

We could walk down the block to a Ralph's Supermarket, which was open twenty-four hours and sold liquor, wine, and beer as well as groceries. These features were astonishing to us, coming from the East Coast where there were no such amenities at supermarkets, much less stores that stayed open for twenty-four hours. We could buy breakfast and lunch food, and I soon learned that we could buy the meat, fresh fish and vegetables, rice, and potatoes that I could cook for dinner to save on restaurant outings since Mike's last paycheck for the foreseeable future had ended in Denver. Mike and I would stop at the fruit and vegetable counters, marveling at the fresh produce, the crisp lettuces, the giant-sized strawberries. Over the months that we lived there, I learned to make a good spaghetti sauce for pasta or large pans of lasagna. We frequently invited some of the other actors, particularly one very large man who I suspected was hungry, as he was also doing the rounds looking for acting jobs. He later was hired as a sidekick for a popular western show that ran for years in first run, then in reruns. He no longer needed my lasagna or garlic bread.

The greatest feature of The Montecito was its outdoor swimming pool, with lounge chairs and tables, and, critically for the actors, a phone that sat on a tall table in full view of the poolside crowd. Everyone would jump when the hotel operator put a call through for one of the actors, most of whom had hired a telephone service, where a staff of young women handled calls from agents or casting companies. That telephone call at the pool could mean a casting call or an audition.

That early July, I had eight or nine weeks to go on my pregnancy. I was healthy, I even acquired my first-ever tan as I sat by the pool in the afternoon, growing larger and heavier during those summer months. I found a shop that sold maternity bathing suits, so I would take my book of the week to the pool, settle into a lounge chair, and eventually venture into the shallow end of the pool and try what passed for swimming for me — a modified dog paddle with a sidestroke across the short side of the rectangular pool.

Alice Ghostley rarely came down to join the poolside group, but Felice was a regular and lively presence, often leading an in-pool volleyball game, sometimes a rubber football game, with much jousting and splashing. One of the older character actors, Phil Coolidge, who sat quietly watching the afternoon's events, said to me one day, "Felice Orlandi has the face of a Roman coin," noting his dark close-cropped hair and chiseled features.

Alice would frequently join me for lunch in our hotel suite, especially if Michael or Felice were out on meetings. I knew little of her work since she had primarily been on Broadway in musicals, or as I later learned, in the award-winning Lorraine Hansberry play *A Raisin in the Sun*. These were years before Michael and I were in New York City and became familiar with Broadway shows. Some of the older actors told me of Alice's early success in *New Faces of '52* and its repeats in subsequent years, tales told with much admiration for her comedic timing and hilarious vocals.

Alice was modest, talked little of her career, but regaled me with tales of her earliest days in New York City after she arrived with her sister, Gladys, from Oklahoma, both taking whatever part-time jobs they could find to pay the rent on their fifth-floor walkup in Greenwich Village. Alice enjoyed being an usher in theaters, where she could watch plays or movies for free. "We barely scraped by in those days," she said. They ate simply, surviving the hot New York City summer nights by putting their sheets in the icebox to get cold, then sitting on the fire escape, hoping for a breeze.

Michael and I found a doctor who would guide me through these last stages of pregnancy and who recommended which hospital to use. His nurse gave me typewritten lists of suggested items to buy in advance for the new baby, which led to leisurely morning shopping trips. I thought I should be knitting something for this baby, so after scouring the Yellow Pages, I found a small shop where I could buy yarn in colors of pastel green, yellow, and white, since we did not know the gender of the baby; knitting needles and several patterns for infant sweaters, socks, caps, and a blanket. I had not knitted anything since growing up in the country, where each autumn we busily knitted socks and mittens, and when we were skilled enough, cable sweaters and scarves in preparation for the long winters in Nova Scotia.

The nurse also gave me the name and number of a diaper service. "They will be a big help to you if you do not have your own washing machine and dryer," she said. We did not have a washer or dryer in our tiny kitchen, so Michael called the number when we got back to the hotel and set up a weekly diaper delivery starting the week of my due date.

Except for Yaphet Kotto, who had a four-year-old girl and a baby boy, none of the actors staying at the hotel had children or at least none who were traveling with them. Yaphet was a genial six-foot-five giant with ebony skin and a great wide smile of perfect teeth. He lived on his army severance pay and was doing "the rounds" of agents, as it was called, hoping for a breakthrough. While playing with his little children during our afternoons at the pool, he would often set up a betting game with the other actors "on which lap would Rosemary sink?" as I ventured into the pool, heavily pregnant in those final weeks. By this time I could only manage one lap.

I didn't sink, but a few days later, I got stuck in the elevator and had to be hoisted out, to the great concern (and then merriment) of all who were around the lobby or the pool that day. Yaphet, on the scene when I emerged up the step ladder, laughed heartily and said to all around, "We should have taken bets on this one, too. What if Rosemary had given birth in the elevator?"

The elevator was an early model, designed like an elegant cage with its brass door, a diamond-shaped accordion that one pulled, or pushed, sideways. I was riding the elevator alone when the cab suddenly stopped between floors. I pressed the button marked DOOR OPEN and DOOR CLOSE several times and the accordion door finally opened, but the cab was at least five feet below the lower edge of the doorway above, and that door was closed. I pushed the red ALERT button and heard bells clamoring on some floor I hoped was the lobby. Someone shouted up through the shaft, asking me where I was. "I think between the sixth and seventh floor," I yelled back, "but maybe it's the fifth and sixth floor."

"Press the elevator button again," the voice shouted. I tried several more times, then rang the alarm bell again. I could hear voices and then the door to the floor above me opened and the manager dropped to his knees to see me. "Are you all right?" he asked. "Can you climb up?" He held out his hand. Only then, peering down into the cab, did he realize that I was the very pregnant guest in his hotel. "Wait a moment," he said, and then I could hear him on the house phone, which was on a table across from the elevators on each floor. "Get up here at once," he barked into the phone, "and bring a step ladder!" Peering over the edge he said to me, "Now don't worry, Mrs. Scanlon. Just be calm. We will get you out without any problem." I could hear footsteps pounding up the stairs and there were the faces of my husband and Yaphet and Felice Orlandi, peering down, all asking at once, "Are you okay?"

"Make way! Here is the ladder," the manager shouted, and I stepped to the side of the elevator car while two of the handymen from the hotel positioned and then lowered the step ladder into the car. I looked at the vertical ascent on these steps, then called up to Michael, "I think I will need some help to get up and maybe a push," so Michael scrambled down the ladder, helped me position first one, then the other foot on the ladder while Yaphet leaned over with his long arms and reached down to catch my shoulders. Michael may have been giving me a gentle push, but Yaphet carefully hoisted me out of the elevator cab to cheers and clapping from the crowd that had gathered.

First-Time Parents, on Our Own

The second week in September I awoke feeling something different, that some change had occurred. The hotel maid asked me how I was feeling as she came in for her morning rounds of our room. "It will not be long now, I think," she said. "Will your mother be coming to help you?"

"Oh no, my mother lives thousands of miles away in Canada and my mother-in-law lives in New York City."

"Well, you can ask me some questions if you like," she said. "I have four children.

That night, when the time had come to leave for the hospital, Michael went to the lobby to order a taxi, and Yaphet, passing by, decided he would come along. "After all, I am the only one around here with little children. I am the only one who knows what to do." But Felice then appeared and announced that he would drive us to the hospital and told us to cancel the taxi. So off we went, Michael in the back seat with me and Yaphet riding up front with Felice. Michael was not permitted in the delivery room. This was the mid-1960s — before the revolution in child birthing and rearing — so I was on my own.

Two days later we arrived back at The Montecito Hotel carrying a blond, fuzzy-headed infant boy who looked exactly like his sixty-four-year-old grandfather, Gus, in the Bronx. Michael had picked up a copy of the Hollywood Reporter, one of the daily trade papers, to discover that our baby's birth at Hollywood Presbyterian was mentioned just below the notice of the arrival of Tim Conway's son, born the same night. The notice read: "Son, Sean Donald Scanlon, born to the actor Michael Scanlon. Mother non-pro."

Yaphet, his wife, and two little children were waiting in the hotel lobby for us with a gift package of Johnson's baby products — baby oil and lotion, Q-tips, soft washcloths. There were lots of smiles and goo-goos as they peered at the wrapped bundle of baby boy, lots of assurances that they would help, here's our phone extension call any time, even in the middle of the night. We thanked them, gratefully accepted the gift, and headed upstairs.

I was exhausted and needed a nap and thought that the baby should need a long sleep as well. But the baby had other needs and started to wail as soon as we entered our room. "What could be wrong with him?" Michael asked.

"Perhaps he is wet and needs his diaper changed," I said. Michael phoned down to the desk to see if the diapers service had arrived.

"It's there. I'll be right back," he said, heading out the door and for the elevator.

When Michael returned with the diapers, we laid the wailing baby down on the double bed, which Michael had had the foresight to leave down before taking me to the hospital. I carefully unwrapped the bundling blankets, looked again in amazement at this tiny creature, and set about opening the pins of the hospital diaper. The nurses at the hospital had shown me how to put the pins in carefully, reminding me to slide my fingers under the diaper, shielding the baby's skin, when putting them in and taking them out. "See this, Michael?" I asked as I showed him how to safely fasten the pins.

Michael handed me one of the diapers that had been delivered and, between the two of us, we maneuvered the wet diaper off and fumbled with the dry replacement. It didn't look right. "Oh, yes. I forgot. We have to fold the sides in," I said, adjusting the diaper the way I had been shown. I wrapped the baby in his blankets and held him up to my chest. He started to wail again.

"Maybe he is hungry," Michael said.

This meant I would have to try to nurse him. I wanted to sleep, but this would take work. I had decided to nurse the baby even though I knew of no one in my family or my age group except for Janet Sheen, wife of Martin and mother of their three little sons, who nursed the youngest, Carlos, during the months she joined us on tour with the play. One of the nurses at the maternity ward had given me some brief instructions: "If this is what you really want to do," she'd said, not sounding at all convinced that this was a good idea. "You could always give him formula; most of the mothers do," she added. But she found a leaflet with some drawings of a woman nursing an infant and put it in my take-home bag.

I propped up against the pillow on the bed, opened my blouse and bra, and brought the baby up to the nipple. He was still crying. I pushed and fumbled, then tried the other side. The baby was crying too hard to "latch on," as the leaflet described.

"Maybe we better call Yaphet's wife to see if she has any suggestions," said Michael, reaching for the phone. I watched as he placed the call twice to be sure he had asked for the correct room. "They have gone out," Michael said, hanging up. "The desk clerk saw the whole family heading out to the park."

"The nurses gave us two small bottles of formula," I said. "Why don't we give one of those to him?" I thought this might be merciful if the baby couldn't nurse just yet. "He must be hungry. We can't wait for this nursing process to work. But you must warm up the bottle, just a little bit, so please put a saucepan half-filled with warm water on the stove and warm up the bottle. But be careful."

Michael did as I requested and brought the warm bottle back to me. I cradled the baby and put the nipple of the bottle in his tiny mouth. He seemed to reach for it and began to swallow rapidly. He was hungry. "Now we are supposed to burp him," I said when the baby had finished. So Michael got another diaper out of the large bag and put it on his shoulder. He lifted the little bundle up and held him close on his shoulder, then began walking around the room, humming first, then singing softly, "He's my bonnie, bonnie wee," repeating the refrain over and over. I fell asleep, perhaps before the baby.

The Montecito Hotel September 17, 1966

Dearest Mom: It is quiet and peaceful here and I've been thinking so much about you so if you don't mind my shaky hand, just a few thoughts. I'm propped up comfortable in bed, listening to the Dodger-Pirate game on the radio, wee Sean Donald is sound asleep in his bassinette, and my beloved Mike is sterilizing bottles and mixing formula in the kitchen, no doubt cooking himself in the process since it's 95 degrees out today, for the second day in a row. Somehow, for a couple of greenhorns, we've survived the last three days, armed with no more help than Dr. Spock's book and daily calls to the pediatrician. Mike is incredible. He is chief cook and bottle washer, does all the shopping, and with the help of Dr. Spock's book, prepares the formula for extra feedings; is chief burp-er, my nurse, brings me the baby for feedings and for diaper changes, at which he assists. If I scoured the four hemispheres with a fine-tooth comb, Mom, I couldn't have found a better man — he is simply fantastic. By day four of being home from the hospital with our infant son, I was still exhausted — but also exhilarated — by this major event in my life, our lives. Most of the exhaustion was due to lack of sleep, for even though Michael eagerly leaped up in the night when the baby cried, I still needed to be awake to help oversee the diaper change and more importantly to try once more to breastfeed this hungry creature. Then, I needed to take my turn trying to soothe the little cries of anguish that characterized his waking moments. Michael would put another cloth diaper on his shoulder, hold the baby close, and pace the room on a diagonal march, once again singing softly, "He's my bonnie, bonnie wee." Sometimes the baby would fall asleep. I always fell asleep.

The next morning as we both began the diaper changing, Michael reached into the long plastic bag containing the supply of cloth diapers, pulled one out, and said, "This is the last diaper. What are we supposed to do? They said the delivery was for every eight days."

All I could think of to say was, "We'll just have to call the diaper service and ask for another large bag." I could hear Michael on the phone a few minutes later, as I held the baby close. Michael kept repeating, "No, there are no more left. We used them all up." I heard him hang up in frustration.

"What is wrong?" I asked, worried now, for what would we do?

"The man at the diaper service kept saying over and over, 'That is not possible. You had an eight-day supply. How could they all be used up after only four days?' But he is going to send another bag over in the next two hours," Michael said. He sounded as relieved as I was. We realized then that we were using the diapers as burp rags, for pads to use when changing diapers, and for drying the baby since the fiber in the diapers was much softer than in the hotel towels.

The Montecito Hotel, September 20, 1966

Dearest Mom: Your letter just arrived and pleased us so very much. We love your letters, eagerly devour them over and over. Now while Sean Donald has settled down to sleep and I'm back in bed for a rest, just a note to keep you informed on proceedings. It is a week today since the baby and I came home and believe me, I think it has been the happiest week of my life. I've never felt so complete and utterly satisfied in just being — every minute of the day seems to be what I always wanted. Mike feels the same way. We have managed to get the baby on a pretty good schedule; yesterday he slept a full four hours between each feeding and well over five during the night, giving us a chance for a good rest. I've finally managed to get him nursing. He is really beautiful, Mom, and cute besides. I wish you could see him. His eyes focus extremely well; he stares right at me when I talk to him. For the first few days, we were afraid he might be colicky but now I think he was just hungry. He's a lusty eater and a prodigious pee-er.

I feel extremely well. Mike is becoming a whiz in the kitchen; yesterday was grumbling about having "dishpan hands." But he cheerfully and lovingly has taken over all my chores, plus his own, and it is a joy to see him with the baby.

We've had cool weather the last three days, and even had a few showers of rain, the first we've seen here. It cleared away the smog and made everything so fresh and clean but I notice this morning that the smog is building up again. This air pollution is tragic, and something will have to be done soon before there is no fit air left to breathe. It's not as bad here in the Hollywood Hills as further downtown, but some days I can feel my throat dry and my eyes burn.

Noon that day brought not only the merciful replenishment of diaper bags but also an invitation to a dinner that was being prepared by Felice Orlandi and would be brought up to our room. "He and Alice are making chili and salad and garlic bread and will bring it up around 6 tonight," Michael announced, hanging up the phone. This was a relief because I was too tired to think of how we were supposed to find time for preparing food with this new schedule.

"That is very thoughtful; actually, it is wonderful," I said.

The diaper service man came, smiling oddly at us — what did he think we were doing with those diapers? The baby and I managed to take a simultaneous nap and then it was time for another attempt at the breast, a moment or two to tidy up, comb my hair and find my lipstick before the doorbell rang with Alice and Felice and the promised dinner. Felice was gripping the large pot of chili; Alice was holding a bowl of salad and the garlic bread and had a bottle of Italian Chianti tucked under her arm. Michael cheerfully led them to the small kitchen and dinette. I climbed out of bed and brought Alice and Felice over to the sleeping baby for their inspection and received the hoped-for oohs and ahs. They did not have children, so I kept this part brief.

We four adults settled in around the dinette table while Michael found forks, knives, and spoons; plates for the salad and bowls for the chili; and water glasses for the Chianti. Felice served with a flourish of arm movement and sang some Italian boat songs. The garlic bread was delicious, quite unusual for my northeastern taste, but bread, and delicious bread, I thought, reaching for a second slice.

"I can only have a few sips of the wine since I am trying to feed the baby myself," I said to our guests, reluctant to use the word "breastfeed" or even "nursing," lest they think I had adopted a radical Sixties hippie movement thing to do. But I ate the delicious chili and the garlic bread like a starving orphan might, thanked Alice and Felice for this thoughtful gift as they were leaving, and settled down in the Murphy bed to nurse the baby, who had just awakened.

Michael changed the baby and placed him gently back in the crib and we sighed with relief at an early night and maybe a full night's sleep. This was not to be, as, within two hours, we came bolting out of bed to anguished howls from the baby. "These are not whimpers or cries," Michael said as he reached into the crib to pick up the baby. "This baby is in anguish."

And he was: the howls from this tiny infant were painful for us. "He is in pain," I said, not knowing what else to say, as I took my turn holding him close to my body, hoping that my warmth would help his digestion. Then Michael took over while I pulled the bedclothes over my head.

At six in the morning, we called the elderly pediatrician, Dr. Van Ornum, who had been assigned to us by the hospital. "It's too early," I groaned, thinking of how gentle if firm he was when we first met. The doctor was patient on the phone, asking if the baby had a fever or was having trouble breathing. "No," we said. "It seems to be his tummy. It looks like he's in severe pain — anguish, actually," I added.

"Is he still nursing? Did the mother have any spicy foods?" the doctor asked.

The chili! I'd had the chili.

"The baby is suffering from the spices in the chili," the doctor said, and again kindly. "For the next twenty-four hours give the baby formula from the little bottles you were given at the hospital. And Mother, you should eat only plain foods for the next while."

Months later we told this story to Oliver and Betsy Hailey when we were invited to their rented house in Malibu. Oliver was working on a screenplay of his successful Broadway play and Betsy could frequently be found scribbling at the kitchen counter when making coffee or heating up the bottle for her baby girl, born about the same time as our son. Years later I bought a copy of Betsy's second book, *Joanna's Husband and David's Wife*, and was startled to see our chili story written intact as having happened to the couple in the title of the book.

When our little son was four weeks old, the actors and actresses who were staying at The Montecito gave us a baby shower with gifts that included tiny blue socks to match a blue sweater and cap, rattles, and a mobile for the crib. Phil Coolidge, the actor who played many character roles over the years, gave us Charles Kingsley's book *The Water-Babies*. One afternoon by the pool, shortly before I was to leave for the hospital, Phil had said, "What are you going to call the baby? Will his name be Sean Donald?" We were shocked to hear this. Only the night before, Michael and I were going through a list of names for a boy — we did not know that we were having a boy, but we had not discussed any names for girls — when I said, I wanted his middle name to be Donald, after my father, but what was the first name to be? James, or John? Suddenly, we both said at once, "Sean." We had recently watched the John Wayne-Maureen O'Hara movie *The Quiet Man* as a rerun on our small black-and-white TV set. John Wayne's name in the movie was Sean Thornton. Sean was Irish for John. Yes, we agreed, if a boy, the baby would be Sean Donald, but we told no one. Yet that afternoon, here was this shy, quiet older man saying the name we had chosen.

The book *The Water-Babies* looked yellowed and weathered; Phil must have found it in a special secondhand bookstore. I kept that book throughout our subsequent travels, and today it is on my son's bookshelf, looking yet more weathered and still special to me, and Sean, now that he knows the back story.

So we three were surviving, and for some hours of every day, even flourishing, finding good (non-spicy) food, taking walks with the new baby carriage on sunny afternoons in Hollywood. We still missed our respective mothers and family members back East who would have been helpful to us in our pathetic ignorance of becoming parents. I missed my sisters, knowing their delight in this first child of the family and perhaps even offering some advice from their babysitting days. Our fellow actors at the hotel were warm and friendly, but since most did not have children, they could not offer much guidance. But we had the hotel maid who asked questions about the baby each day, and, for our frequent phone calls, the support of kindly Dr. Van Ornum. We three would be just fine.

Living Through My Husband's Struggles
Hollywood – 1966-68

Hollywood, in those two years, was a major disappointment for Michael, a frustration of the dream he had to become a successful actor in movies and TV. Michael was the one to live with the frustration, the disappointment, finding his dreams slowly dashed against the bitter reality of this strange business. But it was also painful for me, living through those days when he would be excited about a call from his agent, gearing up for the promised audition, almost always followed by the crushing news that he had not gotten the part. Somehow, I had to help him accept each rejection, and encourage him to keep trying.

Young aspiring actors in Hollywood spend endless days waiting for something to happen. How to fill the time? How can you polish your craft? Should you take a few more classes in film technique? That assumes that you are not working at a job to pay the rent and could afford the cost of such classes. An unemployed actor has little recourse to improve. A writer, or painter, a singer or even a dancer, can keep writing, painting, or rehearsing, even if hungry and discouraged. An actor needs to be hired into a project in order to learn and perfect his craft.

A good week in Hollywood was being sent on one casting call, but that could mean a rejection each week. A young aspiring actor trying to break in with few or no film credits looked anxiously for that first film job, which could mean building on that credit and getting recommendations from the director or casting agent. So, each casting call was critical. Without that successful casting call, an unemployed actor sits and frets. In

Michael's case, that meant sitting and fretting and chewing his fingernails. I learned to tell the extent of his worry and frustration by the ferocity of that nail-biting. One month this even resulted in some type of fungus that caused swelling and discoloration in his thumbnail. We had to find scarce dollars for a visit to the doctor who proscribed a special ointment. That cured the fungus, but it didn't cure the nail-biting.

I don't recall that the first turndown was devastating. Disappointing, no doubt, as Michael had been sent by the agent he had acquired when we first arrived in Hollywood, to audition for the young male lead in a George C. Scott movie. Despite the agent's optimism and that he had been called back twice by the casting director, Michael was not chosen. "At least the agent is working for you, and sending you out for major projects," I probably said as a form of support even though I had no knowledge whatsoever of how this industry operated.

The Montecito Hotel, early November 1966

Dearest Mom: How we relish your letters! Your second one just arrived and it made me lonesome. Our big dream all fall has been to get back to both homes for Christmas, but we'll probably have to keep dreaming about it for a while longer. You know how it is when there is something you want to do and insist on giving yourself a chance, which is the way it is with Mike. I knew this was what he wanted when I married him and I want it too for him. Anything I can do to help I will. It gets discouraging at times, Mike gets restless and worries about me and the baby, and I need to keep his spirits up. This is a tough business. The performing arts are especially difficult because one must be hired to do what you do.... Until that happens, you sit around and chew your nails. We'll stick it out for a few more months; we're still all right financially — our savings pay the rent, and Mike is collecting unemployment insurance, which allows us to live simply but comfortably. Last year when on the road tour we lived royally, with money to burn, so this year we tighten our belts. And we're very happy and our baby is a constant joy.

My journal: January 1, 1967

And so another year begins. I hadn't quite adjusted to '66 at all. Last night Mike and I spent a quiet evening — sipped some white wine, reminisced over our meeting and engagement two years ago; perhaps things were too quiet — I had very real moments of fear, downright cold, clammy fear, remembering how grimly the last half of '66 treated us and thinking of how few defenses we have with which to face 1967. Mike was edgy and restless, so I suspect he may have felt the same way. But Sean came to our rescue again and provided the necessary diversion to get us through those dark moments.

Later, when we went to bed, we lay awake, talking occasionally, listening to the radio (in these modern times! — really!) while some tipsy DJ played some surprisingly good music. At midnight the DJ "counted down" the last few seconds, and from somewhere in the vicinity of Hollywood Blvd., car horns were blowing. So that was our salute to 1967. I hope it is not too prophetic. Certainly, I have never started a year

*with fewer resources, both material and spiritual (not that I'm
not happy — I am blissfully so with Mike and Sean, but it is
just that there are so many demands on me that the ledger is
becoming increasingly unbalanced, and one of these days I
simply won't have the wherewithal to cope with the next cri-
ses), and fewer prospects. How Mike and I ever got this low,
I'll never fully understand. We're now so completely and utterly broke. Poverty-stricken, as a matter of fact. I suppose I'll
always blame him at least a little for allowing this to happen
— for sitting around unemployed for six months, hoping something would happen, living in whimsy and rationalization, and
allowing himself to be easily led by all the wrong examples,
meanwhile, watching our savings dwindle to nothing and still
not doing a damn thing toward providing some support for us.
And never again will I sit back, trying to be the sweet, loyal
wife, and watch that happen. However, I still love the bum,
very, very much.*

My journal: January 9, 1967
*Surely this must be the most endless evening I have ever
spent. Mike has been gone now since 2:30 this afternoon and
won't get home until at least 12:30 a.m. I can hardly bear being
without him. We both resolved to start this week off differently
and to really try and do something about our lowly position, so
Mike got up at 6:30 a.m. and went down to the Casual Labor
office to see if he could pick up something there, but altho' he
waited until almost 11 a.m., there was nothing for him. Then
this afternoon, he went down to Brown's temporary agency and
they sent him right out on some filing job at $1.70 per hour —*

it's almost too ghastly to think of — Mike down there, doing some miserable menial job at miserly wages, and probably hungry since I doubt if he had a chance to get anything to eat. Our unemployment check came today, but I didn't get out to shop, so I have nothing to give him but soup and eggs. Oh, if we only had a guaranteed income of about $400-$500 per month and Mike could concentrate on the acting and we could be together most of the time.

Sean, celebrating his 16th week, seemed to realize that we were alone, and as if to keep me company, decided not to go to sleep before 11 p.m. Finally, I plopped him in his crib, said goodnight as firmly as Dr. Spock cautions, and left the room, only to sit in the living room and feel guilty while Sean sobbed away, so I went in and rocked him, gently, and very soon, with a contented sigh, he fell asleep. Now to wait for my love.

1837 N. Gramercy Place, January 18, 1967

Dear Mom: Your most welcome letter just arrived, I have a lull in the storm, which means Sean is temporarily amused with a rattle. I'm such a slowpoke, all the more so it seems these days than ever, but a 4-month old baby does take up an enormous amount of time. I start on some project, when I hear "mum-mum-mum" and the little arms are outstretched to be picked up and cuddled, or he's lost his rattle (for the 14,000th time), or his diaper is wet (for the 61st time). But he is adorable and such a constant joy that I can never really complain.... Things are starting to improve a tiny bit for us — we've had so many bad breaks, and for the past month we've also been quite desperately "poor," where scraping together money for bus fare has been a major effort. The typical starving artist and family, I guess, but luckily our courage and sense of humor have held out. Last week Mike finally found a part-time job, which is surprisingly difficult in this town since no one will employ an actor. To get this job, Mike had to say he is a graduate student. It is a good job, with IBM, the money is good, and he'll still have time free for interviews. At least we've got some financial security now and will try and get ourselves an old car this month. Mike spends so much time and effort trying to get around by bus — their public transport isn't much better, relatively, than in Antigonish. We've been living so simply and quietly — no TV, no car, just a transistor radio and free books from the library. Mike and I have been out once since Sean was born; one night, Felice and Alice took us out to dinner.

My journal: Sunday, January 21, 1967

Several of our old friends in Norfolk would be more than amused, I am sure, to hear that Mike is now working for IBM and in his spare moments is reading a biography of John Maynard Keynes, while I am reading a biography of James Joyce and contemplating the writing of a television script. Ah, the supreme irony of it all. To add further insult, here we are, we two liberal-arts types, spending a rainy Sunday afternoon trying to figure out math problems on a sample aptitude test in preparation for a test the IBM people are planning to give Mike later on this week. Even the most elementary of fractions or series problems elude us.

My journal: January 26, 1967

Gordon has pulled a coup of another sort, for Michael. (The director) Mike Nichols has been advertising for a young lead in his new movie, The Graduate, so Gordon wrote a glowing letter and sent a picture of Michael, telling of having worked with M. in summer stock and what a great young actor he was. Somehow, the letter arrived at Lynn Stalmaster's office and Milt Hammerman called Mike in for a reading. M. is not quite the type they are looking for, but apparently, he gave such a good reading that Hammerman called Paul Wilkins to comment and promised to keep Mike in mind for other projects. Well, we'll get excited about that if and when something concrete happens. But good old Gordon! His letter did more than Mike's agent was able to do in six months. Mike also started a TV workshop with Curt Conway last night and so far, is most excited about it. This, at least, is something concrete to do.

It was this big turndown that was so disheartening. Michael was called back for a second reading for the Mike Nichols movie. After that second reading, we waited, anxiously, and for what seemed days, for the call to come in. When it finally came, the agent said, as Michael later relayed to me, "You were very good; they liked you but decided you were too good-looking for the role. They don't want the audience to think that the older woman in the story might be falling in love with this young man." That sounded puzzling, but many months later, when we could finally find a babysitter for baby Sean and go to see The Graduate, *we understood the reasoning. Dustin Hoffman was terrific in the role, but we could see throughout the movie that Mrs. Robinson was using him, not falling in love with him.*

As wonderful little bundles of joy as they are, babies are not complete compensation either, altho' I find that Sean fills my spirit (as well as my day) on most occasions. Babies are time-consuming —no question of that — also very attention-demanding when they are awake, and in Sean's case that amounts to a good part of the day, as his naps get briefer all the time. He is a joy — to feed, even the endless diaper changes, the soothing of little pains and miseries, the winding up of mobiles — all accented by little eyes following me around the kitchen and occasional wide, companionable grins and chuckles. But since he is not talking yet, I find myself repeating the same little phrases over and over again, and they begin to sound pretty ludicrous echoing back from the empty apartment.

So I leave the radio on and become glutted on newscasts, weather reports, "sig alerts" and all the other paraphernalia they use to clutter up the airwaves between record-playing. (At least I'm not becoming addicted to daily soap operas on TV, although I can well understand now how easily that can happen.)

Well, the night is here, Sean has finally been soothed to sleep; I got a few shirts washed and ironed, the formula made, some dishes washed. Sounds like very little, and yet, except for feeding the baby, this is the first time I've sat down all day. I look over and see a few more dishes in the sink — where they come from is perplexing, because I don't believe I've eaten anything of consequence all day. Now to wait for Mike. This is the really miserable part, because the night makes it worse —

emptier, much more alone. James Joyce was certainly right on this point — that there are two different worlds, the day world, and the night world. Perhaps he was on the right track, trying to use two different languages to distinguish the two worlds.

If I can just fall asleep now, until M. gets home, I'll be all right. Then he can soothe me to sleep, as I did to Sean. Then it will be the morning world, and if it is sunny, I love the morning world. And tomorrow morning, I get to go out, to the bank, the post office, the market — my weekly, and usually only, contact with the outside world. So, while waiting, I worked on our budget from Jan. 30 to Feb. 7, 1967, and projected budget for the next few weeks, to March 6, 1967.

1837 N. Gramercy Place, February 6, 1967

Dear Mom: Your most welcome letter arrived the other day — how surprised I was to find the money order! Honestly, dear, we're beginning to feel like charity cases. However, I am deeply appreciative and put it to immediate use.

Michael did get some film work in that year, but in two industrial films: one shot in San Diego where he played a young naval officer (easy casting; Michael had been a young naval officer). Little Sean and I could tag along and enjoy the luxury of a hotel room and pool and meals in the restaurant.

The other industrial film was shot in Marin County, with views looking back at the Golden Gate Bridge and the white gleaming city of San Francisco. Michael was excited about this job since it meant a full week of camera work as well as a well-paid week for our small family. My mother was visiting us from Nova Scotia, eager to meet her little grandson, and so traveled with us to San Francisco to spend adventurous days touring the city and riding cable cars with Sean and me. Sean was then about one year old, snuggled in his little stroller, chomping on his pacifier, taking it out to grin his wonderful wide, crooked grin with perfect new baby teeth at nearby travelers or waiters. We rode the cable car down to Fisherman's Wharf, enjoyed an Irish coffee, and watched the fog roll in over the Presidio and the Golden Gate Bridge.

On one of the days, the friend we were staying with, Peter, drove us over the Golden Gate Bridge and to the edge of the film set. We sensed immediately that something was wrong, and Peter said quickly, "Get back in the car; lock the doors," as some forty, maybe fifty, Hell's Angels roared around the set on their huge motorcycles. Michael told us later that the director yelled at him and the young blonde actress playing the female lead to, "Get in the van; push her to the floor," so the wild bikers would not catch sight of her. Michael said he was truly nervous until the last of the motorcycles had roared away, heading toward Sausalito.

The following months were heartbreaking, with repeated rejections on casting calls, even on calls for commercials. Being cast in a commercial was always welcomed by the actors we knew, especially if this would be for a nationwide brand and campaign. One actor we had met was also "doing the rounds of commercials," and not successfully. I had Mike invite him to dinner at least twice because we thought he was struggling and possibly hungry. Some months later, Michael met him at

Ralph's supermarket and learned that the actor had indeed filmed a nationwide commercial and described to Michael that residuals were pouring in "like kicking a fire hydrant and drinking the gushing water." He never did invite us to dinner.

Being with little Sean was a godsend, watching him grow from infant to bouncing baby boy to first words and steps. He was a constantly entertaining presence for us and a great distraction for Mike especially, this little tyke with his bright and bubbly personality and his great crooked grin at whatever the day offered him — watching the neighbor's cat, bouncing on Michael's knees to an Irish jig. Michael would go "diddle-dee-diddle-diddle- dee-dee" and Sean's peals of laughter would get us both laughing along. The ongoing childcare tasks kept me busy and focused each day.

How Did I Spend My Time in Hollywood?

Certainly, my days were filled with the care of our son, first as an infant, then as an active toddler who kept me running after him as he romped around our apartment. Despite my vigilance, one day as he was running into the living room, he tripped and knocked his chin against the wooden coffee table. I ran after him but I did not reach him in time and watched in horror as the blood gushed from his chin. I picked him up and rushed to the sink for a washcloth and cold water. After some frantic calls, we took him to the pediatrician, who put in several stitches. Many decades later, Sean still carries faint traces of that scar on his chin. But all other days — with this delightful baby and then as a special little toddler — were filled with joy as we watched him learn to crawl, learn his first words (Mum-Mum, then kee-koo for cookies), take his first steps. He kept my heart light each day with his laughter and giggles. But there was a daily challenge to keep my mind active. I would read or write letters while Sean napped in the afternoon or after he had been tucked into bed for the night.

The *Los Angeles Times* and TV news kept us occupied each day with the ongoing street battles by hippies against the Vietnam War and the LAPD in both 1967 and 1968, and with the two terrible assassinations in 1968. It seemed that those tensions were almost palpable on the streets of West Hollywood, and one Sunday afternoon, it came close to our little family. Michael and I had planned to take Sean in his stroller to join an anti-war protest organized by young professionals, many of whom were also parents with small children, being held on the great lawns of Century City. But late that morning, Michael got a call from his computer company asking him to come in at once since several of the staff had not shown up for work. Since Michael needed to take our car to get to downtown Los Angeles, I could not get to Century City and instead decided to take Sean for a stroll around our neighborhood. When we returned to the apartment, I turned on the TV news to find the screen filled with video of screaming parents fleeing across those lawns at Century City with their babies in strollers amid clouds of tear gas and being chased by police on motorcycles. We could have been there, in that melee, injured and tear-gassed, as many young parents were that afternoon.

Our next close encounter occurred on a sunny Saturday morning. I was giving Sean his breakfast in our small dining room, he happily spooning cereal or maybe scrambled eggs, when the doorbell rang. Michael was asleep, having worked the night shift. I picked Sean up from his highchair and set him on my hip to walk to the door. When I opened it, my heart stopped: standing there were two young men dressed in dark suits, white shirts, and narrow ties. No young people in L.A. dressed like this.

"Does Michael Scanlon live here? Is he home? We want to speak with him. We are from the federal government," they said and each took a badge out of their breast pocket. I was too shaken to try to read the badges.

I moved to close the door, telling them that Michael was sleeping and that I would wake him. I didn't want them walking into our apartment. Michael, too, was worried as he scrambled into jeans and a t-shirt. "Why are they here? Why do they want to speak to me?" he asked me. I followed Michael through the living room and watched as he opened the door and stepped outside to speak to the two men.

They can't be after Mike, I thought.

He had been formally discharged in May of 1965 after serving three years as a naval officer. We were both careful not to sign the many petitions pushed at us on the streets each day by anti-war protesters — Michael because of his naval background ("I respect that status," he would say), and me because I lived in the U.S. with a Green Card and did not yet have citizenship, so dared not risk deportation with a young son to raise. Rumors were floating around that President Lyndon Johnson was planning to round up all the hippies and protesters and put them in the old desert camps that housed Japanese Americans during WWII.

Michael came back into the apartment, looking upset, but relieved.

"They are from the FBI," he said. "They are looking for one of the staff on my night shift. I told them that this guy hadn't come to work last night. They said he had been given his third and final draft notice to appear yesterday at the army recruiting office and he must have gone into hiding. He is now subject to a criminal procedure," Michael said. "I suspect he went to Canada because I overhear some of the young guys who work with me saying they will go to Canada rather than be drafted."

Both Michael and I enjoyed, perhaps even sought refuge in books, and read what we could find in the local library or in dusty secondhand bookshops. I read some novels but also read copies of *The Economist* while in the library. Living in California with the potential for earthquakes — the *LA Times* seemed to carry a major article at least one Sunday a month, warning residents that Southern California was overdue for a major quake — kept me fascinated to learn more about seismic activity and the San Andreas Fault. We did experience three moderate earthquakes during those two years. One quake, about 5.1 on the Richter scale, struck right under Hollywood late one evening. We were later to learn that it was a shallow quake, but it hit so sharply and noisily that I first thought a truck had hit our apartment building.

Michael's mother, Mamie, was visiting us from New York City. She burst out of her bedroom in her nightgown shouting, "What was that?"

"An earthquake," I said, running to get eight-month-old Sean out of his crib with his blankets, shouting to Mamie, "get your robe and slippers, we will go out into the courtyard."

I ran into the kitchen and to the fridge to get a bottle of milk for the baby and then back to his bedroom to grab some diapers and his pacifier. Our building was rocking back and forth. Our neighbors from the apartment complex were also pouring into the courtyard, talking excitedly. Mamie said she would be relieved to get back to New York City. "We have lots of problems there, of course, but no earthquakes," she said.

One day as I was wheeling Sean in his stroller around the physical geography stacks of our library I noticed an older book in a rusted brown cover with the title *The Origin of Continents and Oceans* by Alfred Wegener, published in English in 1924. Dr. Wegener was a German scientist of meteorology and polar research. In this book, he wrote that once in ancient geologic history there had been a supercontinent that he named Pangaea, but since, there was "continental drift," the spreading apart of the ocean floor. He had analyzed both sides of the Atlantic Ocean and found similar types of rocks, geologic structures, and particularly, similar fossils of plants. He wrote that if one measured from the continental shelves, it was possible to see that North and South America would have fit into part of that supercontinent along the west coast of Africa. He also posited that there was a separation in the underwater Mid-Atlantic Ridge of mountains, where those mountains were spreading apart, spewing out magma from the earth's core.

This is fascinating, *I thought, as I remembered my textbook on economic geography, with its maps of the continental shelves.*

I went back to the library in search of a similar geography book with perhaps more recent maps of those shelves. Then, a few months later, perhaps in 1968, came the stories of how scientists at Columbia University's Lamont-Doherty Earth Observatory had completed a detailed mapping of the ocean floor. One of the scientists, Marie Tharp, who eventually became known as "the woman who mapped the ocean floor," was initially given no credit for her work. In fact, her observation that the Mid-Atlantic Ridge was indeed spreading along a rift in the ridge, spewing out magma, and that the continents were in motion through "plate tectonics," was scoffed at by her research director.

Alfred Wegener, who had also been severely criticized by scientists of his time, was right after all. Plate tectonics made seismic faults all the more understandable, and there we were living on the San Andreas Fault and its offshoots in sunny Southern California. Michael thought I was becoming somewhat obsessed and suggested that I go back to worrying about the economy. There can be fault lines there, too, I said to myself, thinking of President Johnson's assertion that we could have "both guns and butter" in financing the Vietnam War. There was always plenty to worry about in economic policy, or lack of good economic policy, I told Michael.

But I also had a new slice of knowledge, however unlettered I might be in science, to keep me worried about earthquakes: I learned to keep an extra bottle of formula, two or three jars of baby food, a couple of diapers and an extra pacifier in a pouch at the corner of the fridge — just in case.

We also had good times with our several good friends, particularly Alice and her husband, Felice. Whether we'd go on a picnic in Griffith Park, where Alice and I would stroll around with little Sean and sip cold Gallo rosé while Sean feasted on his Gerber's and then napped in his stroller, while the men — Michael, Felice, Yaphet Kotto, perhaps Robert Duvall when he was in town — would toss around a football, yelling and triumphing as if they were catching a touchdown pass in the NFL; or over to Alice and Felice's suite at The Montecito Hotel where Felice would make one of his famous pots of chili, served with garlic bread, and both he and Alice would regale us with tales from their years on Broadway. These times, life for us could seem enriching and exciting. And I could eat Felice's chili without worry since little Sean now drank regular milk in his bottle.

Then, Michael did get a break: a theater audition for the West Coast premiere of Brian Friel's play *Philadelphia Here I Come*. We had seen the play in New York and liked the two characters, the "Public Garth" and the "Private Garth." The latter voiced his inner feelings and reactions in run-on dialogue that veered from poignant to side-splittingly funny. Michael was chosen at the audition and he settled happily into rehearsals and the eagerly awaited opening night.

Michael was excellent in the Brian Friel play and he and the production were well-reviewed.

Our financial situation had improved somewhat: and since our lease on the apartment was up, we went looking for a new apartment, closer to the heart of Hollywood, near Sunset Boulevard. Our first visits were total discouragement — no landlord wanted to rent to a couple with a child, or children. Finally, one Sunday afternoon we decided to try one more listing, this one on Fountain Avenue, and we were waiting in the walkway while another couple ahead of us was being interviewed. That couple walked quickly out of the door and down the path with what seemed to me a painful expression on their faces. We were then summoned into the living room and the landlord looked us over, ignored Sean who was in Michael's arms, and said, "Well, we don't want to rent to those other people, but we will be glad to rent to you."

We stood there stunned as we realized those "other people" were a young African American couple, whose status was considered even lower than ours.

My Brief Hollywood Career and
My First — and Last — Minidress

While I was living in Hollywood, Twiggy galvanized the modeling and fashion world with her dramatically short minidresses and knee-high plastic boots. By this time, I had a part-time, off-the-books job in "the business" to help ease the financial strains on our small family. For a few hours each day, I worked with a personal manager of actors and singers.

One of the clients of this personal manager was a young, long-haired rock group hoping to get a record contract to give them a boost from their late-night gigs in small, out-of-the-way clubs around Los Angeles. "You take them," the personal manager, Ellis, said as he headed out the door. "I'm busy Thursday."

By "them" he meant the long-haired rock group. "Take them" meant going to the A&R office of the recording company, facts I knew because I had helped to arrange the meeting over several days of repeated phone calls. "But I have never done this before. I have never been in an A&R office," I said to Ellis as he started down the outside steps.

"It's just like any other office," he said with a wave of his hand. "You'll do fine. Just be sure to get their names and titles," he said, referring to the A&R reps at the meeting.

I was not hired to help him in this way. He hired me while we all stood in line at a dry cleaner on Santa Monica Boulevard where I was picking up a shirt that Michael needed for an audition. This man, who was standing behind me, apparently listening to me ask if the shirt was ready, said, with no introduction, "Are you working? I mean, do you have a job?"

"Why do you ask?" I said, flustered.

"Because I like your accent and I need someone in my office a few hours a day to answer the phone and help me schedule appointments."

He told me later that British accents were "in" that year in Hollywood, and while I am not British, my Canadian accent with my mother's clear diction apparently would do. I took the job, as Michael worked nights at the computing consulting company and could take care of our little boy while I worked afternoons.

The man who hired me, Ellis, was a personal manager. This, I found out after asking some of our acting friends, was different from an agent whose focus was finding scripts and possible acting roles for his stable of clients. A personal manager did just as it sounded: he helped a songstress, as he was doing with one of Stan Kenton's ex-wives, find good song material, arrangements, classy outfits, and musicians to fit her style as well as get her bookings in some small clubs around Los Angeles. However, Ellis's main income appeared to come from handling the career of an actor on *The Big Valley*, a long-running TV series that starred Barbara Stanwyck.

Then there was Gaye "Mama" Spiegelman, the "Topless Mother of Eight" who had appeared in San Francisco's South Beach in the new wave of topless strip clubs headlined by Carol Doda. The Topless Mother of Eight had now moved to LA.

"I want you to help me find her some gigs in Santa Monica and also make some calls to Las Vegas," Ellis said. "Maybe we can book her as the thirty-eighth act or something. We have to do something. She left her husband and there are all those kids to feed. But under no circumstances are you to open any of those file cabinets in the annex behind my office," he warned. (One day I did, and to my horror, saw endless photographs of breasts fitted with silicone implants.)

I did spend many hours trying to get Gaye booked in Las Vegas, but this assignment — to take a baby-faced, long-haired rock group to an unfamiliar office called A&R had never been part of my job, which, of course, had no description of duties anyway. I knew almost nothing, and cared even less, about rock 'n' roll, still preferring the world of jazz and classic pop songs. What is more, I could easily be described as a "square" by those youngsters. Here I was, an economics professor for the previous five years before marrying and moving to Hollywood. It wasn't that I was so much older in years, no more than nine to ten years older than this group, but I felt more like two generations removed from them.

Besides, I had nothing to wear. My meager wardrobe consisted of a few items cobbled together from earlier years.

Wednesday afternoon found me on Santa Monica Boulevard, peering at window displays in the fashionable new boutiques. Two stores later, there it was in the window: a bright-yellow, shrink-wrapped minidress, straight from Carnaby Street, and the mannequin was wearing tall, shiny, white plastic boots, which matched the style of the dress perfectly. I brushed off the slyly scornful looks of the pert salesgirl who seemed surprised that the dress fit me so well, in contrast to the loose outfit I had on, and that I could also pull on those boots while standing. I had just enough cash for the two items, although buying them would require some careful budgeting for the next two weeks, and went home, excited by my purchases. I might just look the part of the trendy agent at the A&R office, despite my ignorance of what else might be required.

The memory of that actual encounter with the rock group and the A&R staff has long faded away, perhaps because it all happened in a blur of miscommunications and forgotten names or perhaps because the event was less eventful than the preparation of my wardrobe. But the minidress and boots had a second act, which remains seared in my memory.

A few months later, my husband, little boy, and I traveled back to New York City, his hometown, where he had several auditions for Broadway plays and regional theater. We stayed with his parents in the Bronx, both of whom were delighted by the antics of their eighteen-month-old grandson.

One evening while Michael was downtown doing the rounds of theatrical agents, my mother-in-law invited some of her friends in for cocktails to meet me. I looked over the items in my suitcase, rejected most as being too drab for "the daughter-in-law who was living in Hollywood," and spotted the yellow minidress and boots that I had brought along in case Michael and I were invited out to an event in Manhattan.

I sat perfectly upright in a hard-backed chair in the living room in my bright-yellow, shrink-wrapped minidress with the shiny white boots, pleased to meet these women, all Irish-born immigrants like my mother-in-law, and glad that I had a trendy outfit to wear for this occasion. But there was a stiffness in the room and the women were looking intently at me.

I thought, *Is there something wrong with my makeup? Is it too heavy for New York or at least the Bronx? Was I warm enough in saying hello to each one or too tense in trying to remember their first names?*

Suddenly, in a swift, almost furtive, move, Mamie, my mother-in-law, reached over and tried to tug my dress down towards my knees.

"My goodness," was all I could think to say. "these are the latest style in Hollywood," and then added, "I will excuse myself for a few minutes," as I fled to the bedroom to find a sensible skirt and blouse.

What happened to that dress and those boots? I never wore them again. I do hope they found a customer of about eighteen years of age who would have retrieved them with delight from the Salvation Army bin I tossed them into on our return to Hollywood.

1263 N. Flores, Los Angeles, Friday morning, April 5/68

Dear Mom: This is such a sad morning; we are sick over the assassination of Martin Luther King. He was truly a modern saint and in the past few years has stood more for the conscience of a country than any of the established churches. He was such a brave man, so often the center of controversy, especially in recent months. when he took a strong stand on the war and was still planning marches.

My job is just about finished. It has been interesting, but his business is in financial straits, and he simply cannot afford to keep me. I will probably go in one day next week to do letters for him. Mike will be off next week, so I'll have a chance to look for another job and a good babysitter. Until now, we didn't need a babysitter; I kept Sean in the morning while Mike slept, then, before leaving for work, I would put Sean down for his nap; he and Mike would wake up around 2:30 and go to the park. This time I'll concentrate on making more money (although my $60 a week off-the-books salary has been vital for us).

Well, Mom, Sean is running out of patience with me, and I'd better start on my chores. He "helps" — bounces on the bed as I make it, pulls his highchair over to the sink, climbs up on it, and helps with the dishes: This consists of taking the rinsed dishes out of the rack and putting them back in the sink as fast as I can wash them. But his attitude is one of such serious dedication that I just let him keep helping me.

Meeting Doris Day

Alice Ghostley invited me to have coffee on a Saturday morning with Doris Day. Alice and Miss Day had just finished filming the movie *With Six You Get Eggroll*, starring Doris Day and Brian Keith. Coffee was to be in Beverly Hills. Of course, I said yes!

Doris Day was a legend both as a singer and as an actress. She was an icon in my family when we were growing up in the 1950s. My younger sister, Donnie, adored her and surrounded her bed with pictures of Doris Day cut out from *Photoplay* or any other magazines she could find. Donnie loved the movie *Calamity Jane* and talked the local barber into cutting her hair in a Doris Day-like ducktail (or D.A., standing for "duck's ass," as we called it when our mother was not listening), as Doris Day wore in that movie. Donnie bought the LP with the featured song "Secret Love," and played the album so often that we all knew all the words of every song. We would break into a chorus of "The Deadwood Stage is a-headin' on over the hills..." while clearing up the kitchen after dinner.

My affinity for Doris Day was less strong, although certainly bolstered by seeing the movie she made with James Cagney, *Love Me or Leave Me, The Ruth Etting Story*, which showcased her acting as well as singing talent, as did the poignant movie she made with Frank Sinatra, *Young at Heart*. But by the early 1960s, my views were diminished by the movies she made with Rock Hudson in which she played the reluctant virgin, albeit with a glamorous wardrobe and snappy short haircut. We read that she always insisted on special gel lenses for the cameras used in shooting her films to hide her many freckles. Certainly, one never saw freckles on those Technicolor close-ups, just a soft aura, highlighting great makeup, her blue eyes, and winning smile.

So on a Saturday morning in the spring of 1968, on yet another sunny day in Los Angeles, I dressed my eighteen-month-old son in his smartest outfit, did up my hair, put on some makeup, and joined Alice Ghostley for coffee with Doris Day. I couldn't imagine what we would talk about, since I was only tagging along in this acting world and I was feeling a surge of guilt for all the critical comments I probably made to friends about her movies with Rock Hudson.

Suddenly, there she was, Doris Day, cheerful and bubbly, greeting Alice, polite and warm to me when I was introduced, and thrilled to meet my handsome little boy, who smiled cheer-fully at her with his new teeth and crooked grin.

I was struck dumb; tongue-tied. Here I was, sitting across a table from Doris Day. She had freckles, thousands of them, glowing beneath beautiful translucent skin. Her voice had the same timbre, like a bell, which I remembered from her mov-ies. I listened closely to her friendly conversation with Alice Ghostley — they clearly liked and admired each other and ob-viously had a good working relationship on this last movie. But I had nothing to say. I could not think of a thing to say as I sat there transfixed, doing my best to hide behind my beau-tiful little boy who was standing beside me on the restaurant bench, enjoying his new friend with her winning smile and warm words.

Santa Monica Boulevard: Where Wardrobe Choices Ceased to Matter

It was 8 a.m. on yet another sunny morning in West Los Angeles. I was up early with my little son, who was then about fourteen months old, and the cupboard for breakfast was alarmingly bare. So I dressed him in a pullover shirt and short pants, found a skirt and blouse and sandals for myself. Sean needed no shoes as he would ride in the runabout stroller with the little plastic safety belt strapped over his toddler's tummy.

This was a great excuse for an early-morning walk, I announced loudly to the street and got the expected giggles from the stroller as we headed down Fountain Avenue to the twenty-four-hour Ralph's market on the corner of Santa Monica Boulevard. I recited our shopping list to a continuing set of giggles from the stroller: "Milk," I said. "Cookies," I added for effect to hear kee-koos come back from a suddenly jubilant tyke. This was his second word (after Mum-Mum), and he knew exactly what this word meant. "Eggs," I continued, "bagels and cream cheese," since this was Sunday morning, "the newspaper, and some orange juice!"

"NEggs," my little son shouted, so he now had his third word, his little blond head bobbing in satisfaction. "Eggs," I echoed, as we navigated through the door and said good morning to the young clerk who was restocking the soft drink shelves.

I still was amazed by this twenty-four-hour store that carried not only food, dairy, and packaged products, but wine and liquors, which were prominently displayed along two aisles of the store. That certainly did not exist back East.

My toddler and I headed first for the dairy department for the milk, eggs, cream cheese, and orange juice, then on to the bakery department for "New York–style bagels" and the promised cookies. The morning newspaper could be found just before the checkout counter, and as we turned the corner to get in the checkout line, we stepped aside so as not to collide with a woman carrying a small dog.

I think I gasped slightly, then struggled not to stare: the woman was dressed in lilac Jax slacks, shimmering tight-fitting cropped pants. She wore a matching halter top, and the skin on her arms and shoulders and midriff was deeply tanned and vastly wrinkled, probably from too much sunbathing. Her short hair, worn Lana Turner style, was dyed lilac to match her outfit, and the small poodle dog she was holding in one arm as she balanced a bottle of vodka in the other hand until setting it down on the checkout counter, was also dyed a matching color of lilac.

The clerk was polite to her, but after she finished paying for the vodka and moved away towards the automatic exit doors, he chortled a bit and gave his colleague from the soft drink aisle a did-you-see-that look. I was surprised by their reaction since the woman in lilac must have shopped there at other times, but then, this was Hollywood, where locals tended to go somewhat gaga over celebrities. My husband always remarked on this, saying that New Yorkers — he was a New Yorker — were always more sophisticated and would let Broadway stars, even baseball players, walk down the avenues without mobbing them or standing around gazing at them slack-jawed.

Maybe so, but at this time of my life I had never lived in New York and the few celebrities we had encountered in Hollywood had been in safe company in someone's living room or in a reception area or sitting beside the pool and I had learned not to stare, and if possible, not to stammer. But this was different, I thought, as I watched the woman and her dog pass by the supermarket window.

I found money for our purchases, paid the cashier, looped the grocery bag over the handles of the stroller and said to Sean, my fourteen-month-old as we wheeled out through the automatic door, "You know, it just doesn't matter what one wears. Whatever is okay. We have now seen it all, little boy. It just doesn't matter."

Meeting Isobel Lennart

Brian Friel's play led to more theater rather than any film or TV work, as Michael was next cast in a two-act play about Dylan Thomas, the Welsh poet, where one act was part of the Kingsley Amis play about the older Dylan and the other act was about the young Dylan, written by Isobel Lennart. It was a dramatization of Dylan's poems, particularly Fern Hill, which began, "When I was young and easy under the apple bough." We were to learn that Miss Lennart had won a BAFTA for the screenplay of Inn of the Sixth Happiness.

Michael was to play the young Dylan, with an actor named John Harding playing the older Dylan. John Harding had been married to Isobel Lennart. They had a son and a daughter who were both in their twenties. John Harding had been an actor all his life, but seemingly not in the top tier of successful Hollywood actors. I thought he looked quite like James Mason and perhaps that had held him back. He certainly performed well as the older Dylan.

I went to several performances when it was possible to find a sitter for Sean, but that was helped by the arrival of Louise from Montreal to spend New Year's with us. She was delighted to stay with her little nephew as well as to take her turn seeing Michael in the play.

On New Year's Eve, Isobel Lennart invited the cast and crew and their families to her house in Malibu, which meant that Louise and I could go with Sean. I packed his pajamas and blankets and bottles of milk and jars of his favorite Gerber's food, knowing that he would likely be asleep well before midnight.

We were greeted at the door by a slender Japanese man, perhaps the butler of the house, followed by Isobel Lennart herself, wearing a colorful full-length caftan and wielding a foot-long spatula. "I'm cooking tonight," she told us. "We are having hamburgers on the grill." She pointed to the fireplace that seemed to take up half the back wall of her large living room and to an insert on the upper right side that turned out to be the grill. "Come in. We have chilled champagne for you all and some juices for the little ones."

The large room could easily sit the twelve or fifteen of us there — this was a small cast and the play required only a few crew members. The fireplace crackled, the hamburgers sizzled, and we could hear the ocean hitting the rocks below the house on the beach.

Little Sean was asleep on the divan, under his blanket, cuddled between Louise and me. He had howled at being left alone in a nearby bedroom, so I told Michael to leave him with us where he'd be happier and would soon fall asleep.

Just before midnight, John Harding arrived, saying he had been in San Francisco to visit their son and daughter. He accepted a glass of champagne from the silent Japanese butler, then settled in to talk with Michael and the other people from the play. He and Isobel Lennart appeared to be comfortable with each other and exchanged pleasant words as she put more hamburgers on the grill for him.

A few years later, after we had moved to New York City, I bought a copy of *Variety*, the main weekly for Hollywood and Broadway, to find the notice of the death of Isobel Lennart, killed in an automobile accident as she was driving from Palm Springs to Los Angeles. What could have happened? The *Variety* notice gave no details of the accident, although the obituary we found later in *The New York Times* reported that the accident had occurred in dense fog, which had led to a collision with a large truck. John Harding, who was with her, was injured but survived the accident.

When the year lease on our apartment on Fountain Avenue was coming to an end and there was no acting work in sight, I called our friend Peter in San Francisco to ask if he could use his contacts to get Michael an audition at a regional theater company, thinking that the steady work and regular paychecks would give him solid acting experience and our family some financial security.

Michael did get an audition and was accepted by the Alley Theatre in Houston, where he would play a "spear-carrier" in the first two repertory plays, then have the lead in the third play to be staged in February.

We decided to go to Nova Scotia to visit my family in the five weeks before leaving for Houston. I sold the life insurance policy I had taken out during my first year teaching at William and Mary to buy the airplane tickets to Halifax and then to New York City to visit Michael's family. This gave us much-needed time to recuperate in the warmth of families and both mothers' good cooking, spend warm sunny afternoons at Cribbons Beach in Nova Scotia or dancing around the living room with my youngest sister, Louise, to songs by The Mamas and the Papas.

Only watching the turmoil of the Democratic National Convention in Chicago on television marred that idyllic interim, prompting me to ask Michael one evening as we were putting Sean to bed, "Are we sure that we want to go back to the United States?"

"We have a contract in Houston," Michael said. "Things should be much better then for me, and for us."

Houston

2207 Mimosa Street, #7, Sept 27/68

Dear Mom: Here we are, as Sean calls it, in "Nouston, Dexas." It is amazingly hot, (85-90° F) but, we are told, cool compared to the summer. Everything is air-conditioned, including, luckily, our apartment, found for us by an agent hired by the theater group. He took us to a furniture rental store called Finger Furniture. We literally pointed our finger at furniture and it was delivered later that day. Meanwhile, I went to a store to buy sheets, blankets, towels. The rent is $125 per month, including utilities and that AC. At first glance, this city reminds us of a cross between Norfolk and L.A. We are two blocks from a bus stop but we'll need some kind of car. We enjoyed our last week in New York City, stayed out at John and Laura's new brownstone in Park Slope. I helped babysit and did the cooking while Mike painted their new terrace and washed windows. It is a madhouse there, with people coming and going, but we were thrilled to have Malcolm arrive and glad there was enough room for him to stay. All love, Rosemary.

Sept. 28, 1968

Dear Mom: Greetings from the roving tinkers! We are settled in a nice little apartment after our extra week in New York but were able to see Malcolm, who saw a lot of the city and a Broadway play. He and I went to a Yankees game. We'll keep in touch. As ever, Michael.

Sunday, Oct. 6/68

Dear Mom: It is a very quiet, muggy, and warm Sunday afternoon here; Sean and I have been entertaining each other through breakfast and tidying up as Mike had to be at rehearsal at 10:30 a.m.; He should be home by 4 and perhaps that will be all for today. He has a good schedule, really, about 3 hr. each afternoon, another 4 hr. at night, and gets home in between for dinner. Getting to and from the theater is a little tedious on the buses. We're getting slowly settled; our few things should arrive from L.A. in a week or so, which will give Sean toys to play with and me some "Great Books" to read. I'm ever so grateful for all that lovely silverware you gave me, plus the jam, which brought a touch of Nova Scotia to our lives this past week and made us a little bit homesick. Yesterday we bought Sean his birthday gift from Louise, a little red tricycle or "bi-go-joo-joo" as Sean calls it. We haven't been out at all yet; tomorrow is Mike's day off so we'll go downtown and join the library, find the post office, etc. A week from today the theater is having their first social, a dinner, and I look forward to that. Now to find us a babysitter. We'll probably get a phone in next week, but they demand a $25 deposit. Penury has its interesting aspects. Well, Mom, this is really a dull letter, but it's been a dull week. I am finding the time long and empty, so now that Mike is settled, I must find something for me to do. I think I would like to go back to school and study oceanography. On that optimistic note, I'll say goodnight. We miss you very much. All our love, Rosemary, Mike, and Sean.

Several days later, I became quite ill with a fever, a cough, and chest congestion. Sean also fell ill, with a sore throat and a nasty cough, perhaps with the same illness as I seemed to have. His four molars were coming in all at once, so that might have added to the problem. At my fever's peak, alone in the apartment at night, I held Sean on my chest to see if my body warmth would help him, although he was running a fever as well. I hoped he was not sensing my fear and worry that we two would not survive. The next day I told Mike we had to find a doctor right away who could treat both of us.

The kindly doctor examined Sean and me together, listening in turn to our chests with his stethoscope, asking questions about our life and where we were living. "You both have bronchitis," he said. "I will give you each a dose of antibiotics that you must take over the next ten days." Then he asked to speak to Michael alone. Later I asked Michael what the doctor said. Michael hesitated, fumbled for some words, then finally said, "He wanted to be sure that I was taking good care of you and the baby."

My journal: November 4, 1968
Sean and I are finally better. We were so healthy leaving Nova Scotia, but the weather was hot here when we arrived and the air-conditioning in every place is much too cold, so I blame those extremes for our illness. Today was Mike's day off and we ventured out in our "new" car, a 1960 Fiat that we bought for $150, to the zoo. It was a lovely late-autumn day, sunny, crisp, and invigorating, and we had the zoo almost to ourselves. Later we went to Sears and bought new slippers for Sean.

My journal: November 19, 1968
Yesterday was Monday, Mike's day off, and it was a quiet, peaceful day. We sent to L.A. for our few possessions in storage, then took Sean down to see the new Children's Zoo and finally opened an account at a local bank. I cooked a big turkey

for dinner; we picked up the Sunday New York Times *and settled in for a long evening of reading, but "peace comes dropping slow," (per Dylan Thomas) and goes all too quickly. Mike came home from the theater very upset this evening. He has been having considerable trouble with his role of the Little Monk in* Galileo. *Mike said that the director and artistic director of the Alley Theatre have been giving him a hard time, one saying, "You're not right for this role anyway." They have now dropped him to a most minor role in the next production,* Saint Joan. *I think Mike is afraid that they're not going to use him for* Billy Liar, *the third production, and where he is to have the lead. I am removed from whatever is going on down at the theater, as Mike doesn't tell me much detail.*

My journal: November 20, 1968
And so fearful, all-encompassing depression sets in again. Today has been rather grim, just like those endless, grinding days in Hollywood... despite a fairly good weekly salary, we're still flat broke and haven't even bought dishes yet; each paycheck has been completely earmarked for rent, the car, our stuff in L.A., the doctor, etc. My life with Mike involves tremendous demands — the insecurity of acting per se, Mike's insecurity as an actor, our constant lack of money and material possessions, our separation from friends, our lack of any social life or outside intellectual stimulation

My journal: November 29, 1968
Galileo *opened Tuesday night (in the new Alley Theatre) amid much local splendor, with a few national and*

415

international notables to give it a real lift. I was very tense all day, heaven only knows how Mike must have felt. I wore that faithful black evening gown and coat, had on my old patent leather shoes, fixed for $2.50, bought bargain gloves, a new bra (for extra lift!), but my earrings didn't arrive from Nova Scotia on time. Mike left early, and I went later by myself in our little Fiat. I couldn't help being impressed by the glittering sky-line of downtown Houston, was even excited to see a Klieg light arcing the sky in the vicinity of the theater. Managed to walk in by myself amid all the TV cameras and handsomely dressed women with their escorts, found my seat and settled in for the real loneliness aspect of being an actor's wife. But Mike was excellent in his role of the Little Monk! Can't imagine why the theater director gave him such a hard time — he was just as good as he ever was before in any of his plays that I have seen. Perhaps it was a case of an old amateur encountering a young professional. Bless his heart, and all the pains she caused him, and then me. At the buffet supper later we met and talked with Alan Shepherd, the astronaut (several were there, all easily dis-tinguishable because they were the only men with crew cuts). Alan Shepherd is quite charming, very approachable, rather boy scout and navy. I also talked for some time with Maggie Smith (mostly about Alice and Felice) and with her husband, Robert Stephens. So it was a nice evening; Mike and I were very close, really communicating.

But something else, something truly special, happened to me that evening, which changed the music I listened to in sub-sequent years. As I was entering the main lobby of the theater and descending the stairway to the first level (this theater is

built upside down!), there was a quintet playing on the small
plateau between landings. They were playing a soft jazz version
of "Fool on the Hill." I stood there, stunned by the beauty of
the music even more than by the majesty of the setting, and
vowed that from here on I would listen to every Beatles song
with new awareness. Certainly, I would never again scorn any
songs by the Beatles.

Inspired by Juanita Kreps:
A Special Remembrance

July 7, 2010: *The New York Times* reported that Juanita Kreps,
the economist, and former secretary of commerce under President Jimmy Carter, has died at the age of 89.

I went immediately to this story, bypassing headlines, business, or arts, even the baseball news. I had never personally met
Juanita Kreps, but I attended a conference in Houston, Texas,
where she was the featured speaker, and her words that day,
about her commitment to her profession as an economist and to
the role that women should play in the workforce, helped me
make an important decision at a turning point in my life. In fact,
she was pivotal to that turning point in my life.

I, too, was trained as an economist, and for five years after
I finished graduate school, I taught economics at a university
just across the line in Virginia from Duke University, which
was Juanita Kreps's location. But for those three years before
arriving in Houston in September of 1968, I was out of the
workforce, accompanying my husband as he was starting out
on his acting career in Hollywood, and becoming the mother of

a beautiful baby boy. Now we were in Houston, beginning an eight-month assignment in regional theater. I spent my days in a dark, damp apartment with my two-year-old son, my work experience fading to a hazy memory and with no return to my professional life in view.

Then, one Sunday that October, I noticed a full-page announcement in the *Houston Sunday Chronicle* of a daylong program to be held at the University of Houston directed toward women who wanted to go back to work, after leaving their job to raise children or to look after aging parents.

I read and reread the program. It seemed to have been designed for me, at home with my little boy in a strange city, worrying about our future with my husband's precarious relationship to the acting world, and constantly worrying about sufficient money to keep our family afloat. I noticed that attendance was free and studied the list of speakers, suddenly realizing that I knew of one of the speakers, an economist from Duke University named Juanita Kreps, who had co-written an economics textbook that was introduced at the university where I was a faculty member. The new Ferguson and Kreps economics textbook received considerable attention that year.

I reread the program for the conference titled "Women Who Want to Go Back to Work" a third time to make sure there were no hidden costs, even if registration fees had been waived. Our budget that fall would not allow for anything as substantial as registration fees for a conference or even fees to cover morning coffee and lunch. Then, if I went, who would look after my little boy? My husband had rehearsals each day and we had few friends, except for one or two actors who worked in the regional theater with Mike but who probably knew nothing about children even if they did happen to have the day off.

I thought of the young woman, Janice, who lived down the hall with her baby boy and was not working. I had helped her by looking after her baby for an hour or two the previous month, and while she seemed to be constantly flustered and worried, as well as notably overweight, she was kind and appeared to be a good mother. Would she look after little Sean for the entire day? I would offer to pay her at least a small amount: We could afford $20, and she no doubt could use the money. So I went down the hall, rang her bell, and asked my big favor. She was excited by the request and said, "Of course."

The next challenge was finding something reasonably suitable to wear. My wardrobe was meager and dilapidated from two years as a stay-at-home mother on a severely limited budget and further depleted by jettisoning items during several moves. Somewhere, lost in a warehouse in Washington, D.C., was the accumulation of beautiful sheath dresses, jackets, and high-heeled pumps with matching purses built up during my five years of teaching at the universities in Virginia, my previous life.

During our lean days in Hollywood, we could no longer pay that storage bill, so all those clothes were lost along with my sizeable library of economics books and novels, and all of my photographs. I combed through the few items in the dank closet of our down-market Houston apartment, settled on the one decent black skirt, a white blouse, and black cardigan. The cardigan was splattered with dried baby food and needed a wash, which I had time to do, along with the blouse; and the skirt could be aired on the back of a chair on our second-floor open walkway. Dry cleaning was out of the question.

My outfit set, I announced my plans to my husband, who was annoyed. "Why bother with this? You can't go back to work right now anyway," he said.

"Yes, I know," I answered, "but soon you will need me to go back to work, to help out. Our boy will be safe with Janice. I have watched her with her little fellow, and she is very loving with him."

Juanita Kreps was the only speaker of the day that I remember. She was a major professor by that time and a successful author with her economics textbook. I sat, frozen, agonized, and shamed because I had walked away from my education and my profession, but I heard her every word, and some are fixed in my mind after these many decades. She told us her story about finishing her degrees, wanting very much to utilize them, and needing to not only secure a teaching position at the university to help out her family situation, but to convince her husband that she could do this; that she could find a housekeeper who would look after their school-age children and run the house in her daily absence, and then, importantly, to convince her children. None of the other mommies they knew worked. "'Why can't you stay home and bake cookies for us?'" she reported her children had asked her, and then, she told us her reply: "You don't like my cookies all that much and the housekeeper makes great cookies."

She then spoke about the importance of women using their education and using their minds and interests to the fullest. There was a hush in the room, as the audience of women listened intently. I realized that many of them must have been experiencing the same crisis as I was: how to regain their confidence and find their way back into the workforce.

I was still sitting mesmerized, numb, as the conference broke for lunch. Then, a voice at my elbow, an English voice, almost cockney, said, "Aren't you going for lunch? They have a free box lunch ready for us." I looked up at this open, smiling face, and said, "Okay!" Then I scrambled to my feet and introduced myself. She said her name was Ann, that her husband worked at NASA, and that her son was in high school. Ann's husband didn't want her to work but, she said, "I am just going nuts at home and have to break out somehow. This conference seemed like a good place to start."

Ann and I found our box lunches and sat together, trading life stories. We became friends for the rest of my stay in Houston, and, thanks to her invitation, spent one of the warmest-ever New Year's celebrations with the Irish and Scottish Club of Houston. There were Celtic songs and plenty of laughs and even a bagpiper. We could tuck Sean to sleep in his stroller beside us for the evening without having to worry about leaving him with a babysitter.

I do not know how Ann's life and work were ultimately shaped by this conference, but mine certainly was. Late that afternoon, I came back to our apartment and my little boy, determined to get back to my profession and a job. I needed to study again, to refresh my knowledge, to reactivate my brain doing something besides crossword puzzles or double acrostics. I had no economics books with me, but I could go to the Houston Public Library and see what was available, read at night when Sean was asleep and Michael was at the theater, and revisit the basic tools of my profession. I had no idea of how or where to look for a position or a housekeeper since we still had several months left in the theater contract and had no idea of where we would be next.

My opportunity came much sooner than expected, because less than two months later, Michael was abruptly dismissed from the repertory company. He would not get the lead in their third production. They gave him plane tickets to the city of his choice. He chose New York City, his hometown, and within days we were on a plane to Kennedy Airport.

En route, I said to Michael: "You can continue to act or whatever you want to do next, but I am going to look for a job and go back to work full time. We will find a nanny for our son and manage our schedule somehow. But I am going back to work."

I looked out the plane window and said a silent thank you to Juanita Kreps. My child would have to do without my homemade cookies also, but I would have time in the evening to make dinner for the family and read him bedtime stories. As Juanita Kreps said, someone else could bake the cookies.

In all those intervening years, I never wrote to Juanita Kreps to tell her the important impact she had on my life. Of how she helped steer me out of those doldrum days in Houston and back to life as a functioning working adult, even progressing in a career.

New York City, Mid-January, 1969

I was standing by a curb on some Midtown Manhattan street. I was going to an interview for a job. A real, full-time job in my profession of economics, a job in economic research. The street was wet, the part of the street near the curb was filled with slush — wet, cold, wintery, icy slush.

I was not used to this. I had just arrived here, in New York City, after living five years in coastal Virginia, two and a half years in Los Angeles, and the last five months in Houston, Texas. There was no weather like this in any of those places. I did not have the right clothes. I knew how to dress for this kind of weather, but that was years ago when I was growing up in Nova Scotia or going to graduate school in Fredericton, New Brunswick. I had only a light jacket on, courtesy of one of my two sisters-in-law, both of whom were four inches shorter than me, so the jacket was scrunched on my shoulders. It was too short on the arms and the wrist, and much too short in the rear. That nether region was now about frigid. I was wearing ankle-high rain boots that were much too short for my size 9 feet, so my toes were crunched and cold. No wonder — the rain boots were not lined, even should they be my size. They, too, were on loan to me from a sister-in-law.

I was about ready to step off the curb when a yellow cab came around the corner, almost knocking me over. The driver rolled down his window and yelled, "Lady, are you crazy? Get back on the curb!"

I looked at him, stamped my cold, wet left foot and yelled back, "Don't you yell at me!"

I had arrived in New York City.

423

Felice Orlandi holding baby Sean with proud daddy, Michael Scanlon in Hollywood, September 1966.

Out for a stroll with baby Sean in Hollywood, Spring 1967.

Alice Ghostley (above) and my mother, Agnes (below),
with baby Sean in Hollywood, Summer 1967.

My mother-in-law, Mamie Scanlon (left), with me and Alice Ghostley in Hollywood, Summer 1967.

Michael with little Sean in Hollywood, December 1967.

(Above) Michael, little Sean, and me in Hollywood, December 1967, and (below) with Louise and little Sean, New Year's Eve 1967-68, Hollywood.

Two photos of me in Hollywood, Spring 1968.

www.ingramcontent.com/pod-product-compliance
Lightning Source LLC
Chambersburg PA
CBHW020915140626
46545CB00015B/49